Helping College Students Write

Although many educators want to help their students overcome their writing challenges, most higher education instructors do not have formal training in teaching writing. This book provides a detailed roadmap for college educators to help students make substantial improvements in their writing, particularly in courses where writing is a component, but not the primary focus.

This accessible guide offers conceptual tools and practical strategies, including lesson plans, stock comments instructors can use to explain frequently occurring writing problems, and writing prompts to help struggling students address writer's block. Covering topics such as managing grading time, reducing students' anxiety about writing, giving clear and formative feedback, troubleshooting, and providing practical tips for helping ESL students, this book is a one-stop shop for assisting students across academic disciplines.

By implementing the guidance offered in this manual, college and university faculty and instructors can guide students effectively and efficiently in improving their writing.

Laura M. Harrison is a Professor in the Department of Counseling and Higher Education at Ohio University, USA.

Becky Challenger is Professor of Instruction, Academic Coordinator, and Assistant Director for the Ohio Program of Intensive English (OPIE) at Ohio University, USA.

Erin Morgenstern is Assistant to the Vice President for Priority Projects and teaches in the higher education and student affairs graduate programs at Ohio University, USA.

Oumarou Abdoulaye Balarabe is a graduate assistant and teaching assistant in the Department of Counseling and Higher Education at Ohio University, where he is a doctoral candidate in higher education and student affairs.

"This is a very special and important book, told from a perfect blend of professional and personal perspectives. Instructor and student voices offer the reader very practical and sympathetic paths towards fostering quality writing experiences. Writing is approached as a mindset and a means of connection-making. Anyone whose teaching involves academic writing will benefit from this one-of-a-kind resource."

Bob Klein, *Professor and Chair of Teaching, Learning, and Foundations, Eastern Illinois University*

"Chock full of effective writing strategies and teaching approaches for college students across disciplines, this book offers a journey of self-reflection, composition literacy, and growth mindset to discover the writer within our students, as well as ourselves. As an instructor of first-year writing for over 25 years, I highly recommend this book for helping students develop confidence in writing and reading. Writing in prose that is personal and engaging, the author gives language to the roadblocks and breakthroughs all writers experience."

Robyn Lyons-Robinson, *Professor and Chair, English Department, Columbus State Community College*

"This is a book that should be read by all faculty regardless of discipline. We have all encountered the challenges in student writing, with the proclivity to assign fault to a lack of college preparedness, covid or other issues, rather than view students through the lens of the new majority. Harrison and colleagues seamlessly combine proven and constructive practical advice with well researched pedagogy, making it a comprehensive and engaging resource to assist all students to become better writers. Indeed, I would make this book required reading for all new faculty to help them start their careers in academia on the right foot."

Donal C. Skinner, *Dean of Hobson Wildenthal Honors College, The University of Texas at Dallas*

Helping College Students Write

A Guide for Educators

Laura M. Harrison,
Becky Challenger,
Erin Morgenstern, and
Oumarou Abdoulaye Balarabe

NEW YORK AND LONDON

First published 2025
by Routledge
605 Third Avenue, New York, NY 10158

and by Routledge
4 Park Square, Milton Park, Abingdon, Oxon, OX14 4RN

Routledge is an imprint of the Taylor & Francis Group, an informa business

© 2025 Laura M. Harrison, Becky Challenger, Erin Morgenstern, and Oumarou Abdoulaye Balarabe

The right of Laura M. Harrison, Becky Challenger, Erin Morgenstern, and Oumarou Abdoulaye Balarabe to be identified as authors of this work has been asserted in accordance with sections 77 and 78 of the Copyright, Designs and Patents Act 1988.

All rights reserved. No part of this book may be reprinted or reproduced or utilised in any form or by any electronic, mechanical, or other means, now known or hereafter invented, including photocopying and recording, or in any information storage or retrieval system, without permission in writing from the publishers.

Trademark notice: Product or corporate names may be trademarks or registered trademarks, and are used only for identification and explanation without intent to infringe.

ISBN: 978-1-032-51434-5 (hbk)
ISBN: 978-1-032-50503-9 (pbk)
ISBN: 978-1-003-40220-6 (ebk)

DOI: 10.4324/9781003402206

Typeset in Perpetua
by SPi Technologies India Pvt Ltd (Straive)

Contents

Foreword *vi*
Preface *ix*
Acknowledgements *xiii*

PART 1
Helping Students with Academic Writing   **1**

1   Setting Students Up for Success   3

2   Giving Solid Feedback   26

3   Troubleshooting   50

4   Developing a Writing Course   72

PART 2
Helping Specific Populations with Writing   **93**

5   Helping ESL Students with Academic Writing   95

6   Accessible Writing Pedagogy   128

7   Professional Writing Matters   152

    Conclusion   *178*

    Index   *181*

Foreword

Coming to the United States as a graduate student presented me with a fair share of challenges. I had the proverbial fish-out-of-water experience. Adjusting to the social, academic, and technological cultures in the United States, coupled with fast-paced and rigorous graduate school coursework, was overwhelming. While the Kenyan education system uses English almost exclusively as a language of instruction, the academic culture in the United States posed a real challenge. The student-centered classrooms and academic writing conventions in particular almost threw me off balance. The horror of earning participation grades when coming from a culture where that is not the norm, learning to identify and craft strong thesis statements, and mastering the APA citation haunted me for some time. What was more frustrating, though, was the assumption by some faculty that every graduate student knew what thesis statements and APA styles entailed. Coming out of my shell to earn the participation grade was entirely on me, but I needed guidance on the other two issues.

Reflecting on these experiences makes me feel deeply honored to write the foreword for *Helping College Students Write*. I am a product of Laura's inspiring, enlightening, insightful, and empowering mentorship. I met Laura at the 2012 Ohio University's Department of Higher Education Administration and Student Affairs Ph.D. program admission interview. The first impression I got of Laura, which I witnessed up close for the five years that followed, was her unique way of building rapport. That rapport left an indelible impression on the learners, leading to a conducive environment for learning and meaningful interactions. Her approach to that interview so profoundly impacted me that by the time it was over I had already decided to join the program. As luck would have it, I was assigned Laura as my academic advisor upon admission into the program. Laura later became my dissertation chair and mentored me throughout the job search process after my Ph.D. program at Ohio University. I am currently an assistant professor in the Program of African Studies at Northwestern University, where I teach Swahili. My research interest has revolved around the role of foreign

FOREWORD

languages in enhancing college students' intercultural competence for the 21st-century realities with which they will grapple after college. The 21st-century realities expect them to be able to communicate effectively with a global audience, preferably in multiple languages, which can be in written, spoken, or sign formats.

Laura's Scholarly Writing course, which forms the foundation of this book, was truly transformative for my cohort and me as first-year doctoral students. She dispelled many novice writers' fears by demystifying and dissecting the academic writing process into sizable chunks. Through the writing phases that she has so eloquently and coherently addressed in this book, ranging from prewriting to writing and revising, she guided us to navigate the writing project for that course; this transformation reverberated in all other courses we took. I started the course receiving feedback about not burying my thesis statement and ended the course with an award for the same paper at an academic conference. Laura clearly understands that her Scholarly Writing class students are products of their sociocultural, political, and technological milieu. Furthermore, their writing styles and approaches are as diverse as the lenses through which they view their realities. Since the goal is to transform students' assorted writing styles and citations to succeed in a U.S. graduate school, her ability to ignite, nurture, and hone their interest in academic writing is exemplary. The book shines a light on empowering students to achieve all these accomplishments.

Laura is well positioned to address, advocate, and offer insights into academic writing in higher education. She has taught a scholarly writing course to doctoral students at Ohio University for over a decade. During this time, Laura has amassed immense experience working with diverse groups of graduate students whom she has empowered to become scholarly writers. In *Helping College Students Write*, Laura coherently crystallizes the issues she has identified as impediments to students' scholarly writing and how to navigate them. Aware of how neglected this area is, Laura makes a compelling case for faculty to be deliberate in guiding their students through the all-imperative academic writing metamorphosis. Crucially, the book provides practical techniques to overcome faculty biases in order to offer constructive feedback.

Laura captures the transformative power of constructive feedback in igniting and nurturing the learners' motivation to write intelligibly and coherently. At the same time, she alerts faculty of the obstinacy that might arise from some students contesting the feedback and highlights potential root causes and remedies. Laura walks her audience through a step-by-step gradual release of responsibilities and approaches that she has successfully used in her scholarly writing classes. Students move from writing thesis statements to providing peer review/feedback to their classmates. This approach was most impactful when I took Laura's Scholarly Writing course. The long-term benefit of taking this course at the beginning of my doctoral program was that it infused confidence

FOREWORD

and equipped me with the academic writing tools I needed for my other doctoral courses and dissertation writing.

Laura's co-authors' chapters on supporting students writing in English as their second language, promoting accessibility in writing instruction, and teaching professional writing skills are equally insightful. The experiences and observations resonated with me perfectly and evoked memories of my academic writing journey. I grappled with the American academic writing culture, ranging from thesis statements to citations. Additionally, as a multilingual from Kenya, interference and transfer from my other two languages often sneaked into my writing, creating comic relief for my dissertation chair and me during our one-on-one conferences. Moreover, there are many grammatical elements in English, such as the elusive articles, which are not present in the other two languages I speak. For this reason, I tended to decorate my writings with enough of them, resulting in confusion and frustration. The authors call for empathy from faculty dealing with students grappling with various issues from their diverse backgrounds. Aware of the limited time faculty might have to help their learners perfect their writeups, the book contains invaluable tips on addressing identified issues.

Writing skills are essential in any foreign language class, such as the Swahili program I run at Northwestern. In fact, my students have presented their spring quarter papers at international Swahili conferences. Since the apple does not fall far from its tree, I have been implementing Laura's approach to teaching writing. However, *Helping College Students Write* clarifies many techniques that Laura employed in her Scholarly Writing class and those I have relied on to teach academic writing in Swahili. Thus, *Helping College Students Write* applies to any college course that involves academic writing.

Dr. Peter Mwangi
Assistant Professor of Instruction, Swahili
Northwestern University

Preface

"I have never received feedback on my writing until your course." Students say and write variations on this sentence to me (Laura) with remarkable frequency. At first, I suspected they weren't remembering the times they did get feedback. This may be true to some extent, but students tell me about the lack of writing feedback so frequently that I eventually came to believe there must be something going on. I started talking to my colleagues across academic disciplines about my students' claims; most of their responses resembled something like a confession.

"I'd love to help students more, but it takes so long." "I do give them feedback, but they don't incorporate it into their work." "The writing is so bad that I don't know what to say to them." Most of the comments faculty make to me are variations on one of these themes: time, patience, and skill. This makes sense because professors receive little to no pedagogical training generally, much less education about how to teach writing specifically. Coupled with all the other challenges facing college faculty (for example, "efficiency" measures like increased enrollments, increased teaching loads, and increased student mental health challenges), it's not surprising that faculty assign less writing now than they did in the past (Berrett, 2012). Although writing has been identified as a high impact practice (Kuh, 2008), there is a paucity of recent research about how much writing is prioritized in K-16 education.

Assigning less writing is an unfortunate trend for many reasons, not the least of which is that employers assign a high priority to writing as an essential skill (National Commission on Writing, 2016). At a time when higher education is under multiple pressures due to automation, "the enrollment cliff," declining public funding, and a host of other challenges, we cannot afford to produce graduates who lack the skills employers value. More importantly (to me, anyway!), writing is an essential part of intellectual development. Writing is thinking, the heart of what a quality higher education should enhance in its students.

In his aptly titled book, *Why Write?* Mark Edmundson answers his title question with a short treatise on what he calls "the habitual self" (p. 141). He defines the

PREFACE

habitual self as the part of us that goes through the motions of life or what some might consider to be "the grind." To be sure, the habitual self is important for things like remembering to get an oil change or pick up groceries for dinner. The habitual self is also the boring part of us, the setting to which we default unless we make an intentional effort to challenge it. Edmundson (2018) advocates writing as a way to "get loose from the habitual self. If you're going to tap into what's most creative inside you, you've got to find a way to outwit the pressures of the ordinary" (p.141). If higher education is still about developing human beings to reach their potential, we must help students push back against the habitual self, and writing is a highly effective way to achieve that goal.

Edmundson's (2018) assertion works on the practical level as well. The habitual self is good at tasks that are vulnerable to automation. Much as students may think they want only academic skills that lead directly to a specific career, this knowledge won't do them much good if that particular job is not robot-proof. As Epstein (2021) points out, "The more constrained and repetitive a challenge, the more likely it will be automated, while great rewards will accrue to those who can take conceptual knowledge from one problem or domain and apply it in an entirely new one" (p.53). The competency Epstein identifies here requires analytic skills, creativity, and depth of thought, none of which come from work that reifies the habitual self, but all of which can be developed through writing.

Ten years ago, I developed and started teaching the writing course in our Higher Education and Student Affairs program at Ohio University. In my years of refining this course, I think and talk about helping students with writing quite a bit. It occurred to me that I might be able to take what I've learned and turn it into something useful for other educators who want to help students with writing but may find the task daunting due to the time, patience, and skill challenges mentioned previously. While there are many resources for those who teach writing, there are few addressed to educators who teach something else but want to incorporate writing assignments into their course. Similarly, there are many books about writing theses and dissertations, but few to help those who guide students writing these works. If you are in either or both of these groups, this book is for you!

Many authors include some sort of a caveat along the lines of, "This book is not a recipe/roadmap/formula, but a way of thinking about X/Y/Z." We are aiming for the recipe/roadmap/formula in this work, which we hope will serve as a useful guide for educators who do not have a lot of extra time to learn everything there is to know about writing pedagogy. That said, not everything will transfer perfectly so we encourage readers to adapt our advice the way chefs improve upon recipes depending on their own unique tastes and talents.

You probably noticed the shift from "I" to "we" in the previous paragraph. I realized early on that this book would be smarter, richer, and more useful if it included student perspectives on the process of teaching and learning writing. I invited three highly talented doctoral students in our program, Oumarou Abdoulaye Balarabe, Becky Challenger, and Erin Morgenstern, to join me as they each have unique knowledge and experience that add value to this work. You will occasionally see designations like "I (Laura)" throughout the book when author clarity is needed. I (Laura) wrote the chapters included in Part 1 of this work, so most of these designations will occur in Part 2.

The Part 1 chapters focus on concepts and strategies for helping students write. In the first chapter, I provide an overview of concepts like the expert blind spot, growth mindset, and deep work as key topics for diagnosing and treating students' writing challenges. Chapter 1 also contains concrete strategies for how to manage your own time, reduce students' anxiety about writing, inculcate focus and concentration, and teach students how to develop a writing practice based on separating the work into prewriting, writing, and revising stages.

Chapter 2 offers approaches to giving feedback that are clear and formative without being too time-consuming. I present a list of "stock comments" that can be plagiarized (help yourself!) and/or modified to address what I like to call the "frequent flyer" problems in student writing. Chapter 3 continues this theme of troubleshooting, diving deeply into issues like procrastination and perfectionism and presenting tips for fixing them (or, even better, launching a preemptive strike on them). Chapter 4 closes Part 1 with elements to help the reader develop a writing course. My goal in this chapter is to provide a "Writing Course in a Box" with lessons and assignments the reader can adapt to their own context.

The Part 2 chapters focus on specific kinds of writing and/or considerations for working with different student populations. In Chapter 5, we discuss strategies for helping students with professional writing generally as well as across different cultural and linguistic traditions in employment contexts. In Chapter 6, we introduce relevant terminology, writing conventions, the effect of personal perceptions, and practical tips for helping English as a Second Language (ESL) students with academic writing. In Chapter 7, the focus shifts to assisting students with disabilities using strengths-based approaches to writing. Our goal was to provide a book that could be read either sequentially or as stand-alone chapters based on the reader's priorities. If you're reading sequentially, we now welcome you to turn the page or click the screen and consider how you set yourself and your students up for success in courses where writing plays a role.

REFERENCES

Berrett, D. (2012, October 15). An Old School notion: Writing required. *Chronicle of Higher Education.* https://www.chronicle.com/article/an-old-school-notion-writing-required/

PREFACE

Edmundson, M. (2018). *The heart of the humanities: Reading, writing, teaching*. Bloomsbury Publishing USA. https://www.bloomsbury.com/us/heart-of-the-humanities-9781632863096/

Epstein, D. (2021). *Range: Why generalists triumph in a specialized world*. Penguin. https://doi.org/10.22454/fammed.2020.358948

Kuh, G. D. (2008). Excerpt from high-impact educational practices: What they are, who has access to them, and why they matter. *Association of American Colleges and Universities*, 14(3), 28–29.

National Commission on Writing. (2016). New York, NY: The College Board. https://archive.nwp.org/cs/public/download/nwp_file/21479/writing-a-ticket-to-work-or-a-ticket-out.pdf?x-r=pcfile_d

Acknowledgements

LAURA'S ACKNOWLEDGEMENTS

I turned 50 while writing this book. There is a remarkably consistent theme in the literature about late middle age; namely, that success at this stage of life depends on the ability to let go of the self. The idea is that a person necessarily spends the first half of life focused on achievement, but that fulfillment in the second half of life requires losing one's ego attachments and focusing more on serving others.

All of this was on my mind when I invited the three student co-authors to join me in writing this book. They were already strong writers, so they did not need much guidance in that area. The gift I could offer was shepherding them through the book conceiving, pitching, revising, and promoting processes. It was an honor to be part of what I know is just their first book; they will keep adding value to the educational enterprise through their thoughtful writing and incredible work ethics. Hence, I first want to express my heartfelt gratitude to Becky Challenger, Erin Morgenstern, and Oumarou Abdoulaye Balarabe for giving me this truly fulfilling experience of creating something meaningful together. Extra kudos to Oumarou for accomplishing something I have never achieved: writing a book in one's fifth language.

I also want to thank my student, Frank Osei, for introducing me to Carol Kuhlthau's work on the information search process. This concept has informed my thinking and writing; I appreciate Frank sharing his knowledge of this work with both me and our colleagues. Additionally, I express gratitude to my colleague and friend, Dr. Dianne Gut-Zippert for consulting with us on the material concerning accessibility in writing pedagogy. I also thank all my students and colleagues in the Department of Counseling and Higher Education at Ohio University for being such a remarkable community of scholars. There were many nights in which Becky, Erin, Oumarou, and I toiled away in our office suite cheered on by this community of people generously expressing interest in our work. Thanks for keeping us motivated and inspired.

ACKNOWLEDGEMENTS

Writing a book has many moving parts that could not be handled with more grace and professionalism than provided by our colleagues at Routledge, Heather Jarrow, Sofia Cohen, Pakhi Pande, and Andrea Harris. Thank you for communicating with us so clearly and helpfully at every stage of this process.

Finally, I thank my wife, Christy Zempter, who lucky for me, has a very high threshold for discussing student writing. I'm grateful to spend my life with someone who shares the love of both writing and teaching.

BECKY'S ACKNOWLEDGMENTS

To this incredibly talented team of authors, Laura, Erin, and Oumar, I couldn't have dreamed of a more supportive, smart, and thoughtful group of people with whom to navigate this journey! I am forever grateful for your generosity of care, encouragement, guidance, and wisdom.

To my family and friends for their relentless encouragement and support of all of the new adventures I take on.

To my colleagues, near and far, for their collegiality, support, and inspiration. And to my current supervisor and colleague, Gerry Krzic, specifically for always being willing to share the wealth of his wisdom on intercultural communication.

To my former supervisor, colleagues, and all of the students who have taught me so much throughout my career so far, I am deeply grateful.

ERIN'S ACKNOWLEDGEMENTS

Thank you to Laura, Becky, and Oumar, my wonderfully supportive and dedicated co-authors. Your guidance, encouragement, and unwavering empathy as we were all going through this process together was incredible. I would write with you a million times over.

Thank you to my husband, Justin, and son, Rowan, for your unconditional support and love. I know I missed some evenings and weekends playing because Mommy needed quiet time to write, but I promise to make it up to you.

Finally, to all the students that had such a profound impact on my life. I am who I am because of my relationship with you and the knowledge I gained from being in your presence every day.

OUMAROU'S ACKNOWLEDGEMENTS

Embarking on this writing journey has been a transformative experience, one that wouldn't have been possible without the unwavering support and guidance of remarkable individuals.

First and foremost, I extend my deepest gratitude to Laura, Becky, and Erin for the invaluable opportunity to contribute to this collaborative effort. Laura's

ACKNOWLEDGEMENTS

mentorship and belief in our capabilities provided the foundation upon which this book stands. Becky's commitment and insight enriched every step of this endeavor, while Erin's dedication and vision were truly inspiring. This collaborative effort has been a testament to the power of teamwork and shared passion. Thank you for the privilege of working alongside you on this meaningful endeavor. I am humbled to have been a part of this exceptional team.

As a first-generation college student, this journey holds profound significance to me. It's a testament to the transformative power of education and the unyielding support of my family, in Benin, Nigeria, and those who have become my family here in academia. To my parents and extended family, your sacrifices and belief in my dreams have been the guiding force behind my pursuit of knowledge.

To my beloved wife, Fatou Drammeh, I am grateful for your love, patience, and encouragement throughout this journey. Your support has been a constant source of strength, and your belief in me has been a guiding light. Thank you for standing by me, for understanding the demands of this endeavor, and for being my source of inspiration.

Also, I owe a debt of gratitude to my friends and mentors, both past and present; your encouragement and wisdom have been invaluable throughout this process.

Lastly, to the readers and educators who will engage with this book, my hope is that it serves as a guiding light in supporting students' writing endeavors, fostering growth and confidence.

Part 1
Helping Students with Academic Writing

Chapter 1

Setting Students Up for Success

INTRODUCTION

Write right now on the following prompt: "If you were king/queen/dictator/God for the day and could do one thing to improve higher education, what would it be and why?" Your writing does not have to be good, but you do have to keep going until I tell you to stop.

I (Laura) often start the first day of my writing course with this activity. In my many semesters of asking students to perform this task, I have never once had a student not be able to do it. I use this exercise to show students that they can write when they are passionate about something and not paralyzed by perfection. My discipline is higher education, but this prompt can be easily adapted to the big questions in other fields.

Students like this activity because it's fun to imagine yourself with the power to impact something you care about. Creating this positive association with writing on the first day goes a long way in counteracting the negative experiences students may have encountered with writing in the past. Writer's block, unhelpful feedback, and abandoned writing projects are just a few pieces of the baggage many of your students are likely carrying to your class. Just being aware of this baggage and taking a few steps to ease its weight can go a long way in helping students show up in a way more conducive to learning.

In this chapter, I will discuss the conditions that facilitate student success with writing in courses where writing is not the primary subject. In my experience, it is helpful to take some time to address the following topics in such courses: Reducing anxiety, helping students focus, developing a writing practice, and breaking down the components of prewriting, writing, and revising in ways that are clear and understandable for students. Before we can tackle these topics, however, we must begin with setting ourselves up for success as educators.

SETTING YOURSELF UP FOR SUCCESS

Allocating Time and Bandwidth

The first step in helping your students succeed is to create a system designed to give you the time and bandwidth you need to meet students' needs. For me, this means going through my calendar and setting aside time to give students quality feedback (a topic addressed in Chapter 3) within a week of each assignment that is due. This may sound like a simple and obvious idea, but I know very few faculty who actually do it! A full day of nonstop grading strains my attention span too much, so I typically set aside a couple of hours each day over the course of a week to devote to this task. However you do it, carving out both time and headspace is a good way to prevent feeling too overwhelmed to give students the guidance they need to improve their writing.

It's also a good idea to block some time on your calendar in the day or so before big writing assignments are due. Despite our many warnings not to procrastinate, we know some students will not heed these wise words so having the time set aside can make those last-minute questions more manageable.

Anticipating the Expert Blind Spot

Allocating time on your calendar is the easy part of setting yourself up for success. The more challenging part can be getting into the right mindset for helping students effectively. Part of why helping students with writing can be challenging has to do with what Wiggins and McTighe (2005) call "the expert blind spot." The idea is that we reach a threshold in which we become so skilled at a thing that it becomes second nature to us. Things that are second nature are difficult to explain. For example, I only recently learned how to cook and would therefore probably be pretty good at teaching a more novice cook how to make a dessert. I would be methodical in following the recipe and explaining things like, "to melt the butter, put it in the microwave on the 'soften' function and keep an eye on it." My stepmother (Lindy), not so much. She would say things like, "melt the butter," "throw in about a cup of nuts," "just leave the raisins out if you don't like them," and so on. Lindy has been cooking long enough that she doesn't think about how one might blow up a stick of butter in one's microwave if they did not have a sense of how long it would take to melt (hypothetically).

Most faculty are to writing what Lindy is to cooking. We say things like, "write a solid thesis statement" and "this is unclear" because we know what these things mean. For some students, this is like saying, "melt the butter." They don't know things like how long that should take or what potential pitfalls to avoid. Similarly, when Lindy says to throw in "about a cup" or "just leave them out," I don't know if that lack of precision applies to all the ingredients or just these two. This is why our students ask questions like "How many pages? What font?

What size font? Single or double-space?" It's the same as me asking, "How long do you melt the butter? What setting? What is 'about' a cup? Can I also leave the flour out to make it gluten-free?"

We don't know to anticipate these problems because we haven't experienced them ourselves for a long time. Annoyance and frustration can result when we feel caught off guard by these "expert blind spot" challenges. If we don't understand "the expert blind spot," it's easy to make assumptions about the students asking these kinds of questions. I have heard many faculty lament that "students today have no tolerance for ambiguity" or "student just want me to spoon-feed it to them." The "expert blind spot" offers an alternative explanation with solutions baked into this more useful conceptualization of the problem.

Addressing the Expert Blind Spot

Now that we know the expert blind spot creates a gap in teacher-student understanding, why wouldn't we do everything we can to preempt it? Think about a skill you currently lack and the kinds of things that would help you as you were starting to learn it. The first thing that would *not* help would be judgment. We can say students should already know how to write (or, for that matter, that 50-year-olds should already know how to cook), but "should" doesn't really matter in getting the job done. I used to be surprised and even somewhat judgmental about what some students did not know, but I quickly realized the uselessness of that attitude. I now embrace that the buck stops with me; it's honestly less work and more fun to approach teaching from this perspective.

So what *does* help? For me, it's been useful just to have the language to describe the phenomenon of the expert blind spot because naming a problem is often the first step in addressing it. Instead of getting frustrated and judgmental about students' mistakes, I try to reflect on what is obvious to me and explain it if necessary. For instance, I do tell graduate students that "Jesus wept." is a sentence and that "Although Jesus wept," is not a sentence. So far, no one has gotten mad at me for this kind of refresher. I also aim for precision in my feedback. I do not write vague statements like "unclear" on students' work. I might say something more like, "I'm not sure why you're talking about appreciative inquiry here when this paragraph seems to be about student mental health issues." It takes longer to write more words, but it's generally more effective in helping students understand what I mean. I'll talk extensively about effective and efficient ways to offer feedback in Chapter 3.

Models and examples are also useful for addressing the expert blind spot. The first thing most of us do when learning a new skill is look for models. When I was learning to cook, I watched a lot of videos to observe what success might look like. Similarly, I keep a file of excellent student papers and post them (with the students' permission, of course). There are those who deem this practice as coddling or cheating in some way, but why wouldn't we offer students models when this is generally how beginners learn? I'm careful to emphasize to students that the examples I post are not templates; in fact, I post multiple papers so the students can see there are many ways to write well. Sharing models reduces the guesswork for students, thereby also reducing their anxiety.

SETTING STUDENTS UP FOR SUCCESS

Reducing Anxiety

Addressing anxiety is a big, but often underappreciated aspect of helping students with writing. More typically described as writer's block, anxiety can be the culprit when students procrastinate. It's daunting to face a major writing project when there are easier, more conquerable tasks on one's to-do list. Helping students name and develop strategies for reducing anxiety can go a long way in setting them up for success.

Mindset

One way to begin to help students name and address anxiety is to give them a primer on Carol Dweck's work on mindset. In her research on academic performance, Dweck (2008) identified two types of learners: Those with what she called fixed mindset and those with what she called growth mindset. Individuals with fixed mindset believe talent is innate and therefore difficult to achieve through work. They tend to seek easy tasks because struggling with harder challenges may reveal their genetic stupidity. Conversely, those with growth mindsets see talent as achieved through practice. These students gravitate toward challenging material because they are not threatened by the fear of being discovered as lacking. Students with growth mindsets understand that mastery requires stretching oneself.

Fortunately, the fixed mindset can be changed. Just naming it can help students understand that there is an alternative to feeling defeated and/or defensive in the face of a difficult task. When a student tells me they're a "bad writer," I assure them there are no bad academic writers, only people who haven't mastered the skills yet. Students also seem to feel better when I tell them there are no academic writing prodigies; people improve with practice. I also share that I love animals, but the dumbest human is smarter than the smartest dolphin so I absolutely believe they are up to the task. Humans can write. Period. Students have told me on many occasions that knowing I believe they can do it really helps.

Weirdly enough, the fixed mindset can also present problems for students who have either self-proclaimed or been labeled as "good writers." These students tend to become defensive when asked to work at the frontiers of their abilities because they do not want to lose their status. Stone et al. (2010) speaks of this phenomenon as "identity peril," conflict that results from a real or perceived threat to an aspect of one's identity. This is why it is so important to convince students to disavow thinking about writing as something people are just "good at" or "bad at"; people naturally become anxious when their identity is on the line. Conversely, people are more motivated to try something they believe they can do.

Puzzle

Lowering the stakes for one's writing performance can reduce the anxiety that stifles students. Langer (2016) presents this idea by asking readers to consider why people willingly work on hard puzzles and play difficult sports but describe taking the SAT and GRE as terrible experiences. Langer's research shows that assessment often acts as a demotivator in that it inhibits the kind of risk taking necessary to improve our skills. In contrast, people thrive when they feel like they are just tinkering or playing around for the fun of it.

Educators can do a lot to capitalize on this aspect of human nature. Sitting down to write a paper rarely feels like fun because students often feel inhibited by questions like: Is this right? Is this what the professor wants? How do I know what to cite? Exercises like the one at the beginning of this chapter can help students push past these questions and treat writing more like a fun puzzle they can begin to crack. They will eventually have to address some of these questions, but they can't get to the revision process until they have a draft. Therefore, I encourage students to treat their first pass like throwing pasta on a wall and seeing if it sticks. The more we can free students from the anxiety of judgment, the more we can access the internal motivation it takes to help them get going.

Another reason the puzzle is a good metaphor for approaching writing is that we do not expect ourselves to have the puzzle worked out when we sit down to do it. Unfortunately, many of us feel pressured to have our thoughts and arguments fully formed before we get started on a writing project. Though that feels intuitive, the reality is often the opposite: It's the writing that gets us to the thinking, not the other way around. The popular Wordle puzzle is a great example of this phenomenon because you start this puzzle with literally nothing but empty squares. You have to just throw something into the first round of the puzzle before you can get any clues as to what the word might be. You don't approach the puzzle with the target word in mind; there is no way to know what it might be in the huge universe of possible words. Instead, you play around with it, moving from chaos to clarity as you make attempts. If we can convince students to treat writing like a good puzzle, they will experience the satisfaction of clarifying their thinking in the process.

Focus

Ok, we've convinced the students they can write and we've gotten them to start writing. Now our challenge is to teach them the art of focus. This is an increasingly difficult endeavor in the world of digital distraction and multitasking. If you have the time in class, it's worth sharing some research on these topics or at least posting them on Blackboard or whatever platform you use. I've found it can be helpful for students to understand exactly what has been happening to all our minds over the past decade or so. Sharing this scholarship is not about creating nostalgia for the good old days; it's more about letting students know they are not alone in their struggle to focus. There are large, well-funded forces working constantly to gain and keep our attention, mostly for consumer purposes (Foer, 2018). We need to be able to name and describe how digital life affects us. Carr (2020) offers a vivid account of his own observations of his mind adapting to technology's encroachment into his daily life:

> The very way my brain worked seemed to be changing. It was then that I began worrying about my inability to pay attention to one thing for more than a couple of minutes. At first, I thought it was a symptom of middle-age mind rot. But my brain, I realized, wasn't just drifting. It was hungry. It was demanding to be fed the way the Net fed it—and the more it was fed, the hungrier it became ... I missed my old brain.
>
> (p. 16)

Carr's work is part of a robust body of literature on the ways in which the digital world changes our minds. Much of it is disturbing because technology companies design platforms that function like casinos, delivering the small amounts of dopamine that get us hooked and hold our attention so they can sell us more products. The good news is that students do not necessarily need a deep dive into this scholarship to get the point. Simply naming the problem allows students to understand what is happening to them. The other good news is that there are simple, no-cost strategies students can use to launch a preemptive strike on the elements that limit their attention span.

Strategies for Helping Students Focus

Focus Apps

Perhaps ironically, technology companies have created apps like SelfControl and RescueTime to help people avoid toggling between time-wasting sites and the work they are trying to accomplish. When I was working on my dissertation, I used to just shut off my wireless connection, but this was a hassle when I needed to jump on a useful website like the library database page. Apps like SelfControl allow students to access the sites they need while in effect grounding them from the time wasters.

It's easy to think that a couple of seconds on Instagram doesn't waste much time, but unfortunately the research is clear that the time it takes our brains to shift from one task to another costs more than those few seconds (Cardoso-Leite et al., 2015). When we toggle, we engage in cognitive overload and thus exhaust our mental capacity more quickly. Sometimes, our urge to toggle functions is a signal that we need a break. In that case, it's best to take a real break, preferably by doing anything other than looking at a screen. Sometimes, toggling means we're looking for a simpler task than the challenging one of writing. In that case, it's best to power through until it's time for a break (a topic discussed in the next section).

Most of us know we need to avoid sites like Instagram and Wine.com when writing, but it can be harder to turn off our thoughts about other tasks that need to get done. We may also need to block other sites like our email, Blackboard, and whatever else we use in our work.

Pomodoro Method

Students seem to grasp the importance of focus, but understandably have a hard time acting on this understanding. Part of the reason is related to the points we discussed earlier about digital culture, but part of it also seems to be due to an imbalanced view of focus. Many of our doctoral students talk about having a "writing day" in which they imagine working on their dissertation for an eight-hour stretch. I say "imagine" because the reality is that few of us can concentrate for that long. Different studies mark the optimal concentration time with some variation, but the average seems to be about 45 minutes. This makes sense as a lot of things are scheduled for about an hour give or take—classes, work out sessions, and therapy, as examples. Our brain's ability to focus for about 45 minutes is why an eight-hour writing day usually turns into a few attempts at writing interspersed with email, laundry, and other tasks that are easier to knock off a list.

The Pomodoro method offers a simple but effective way to address our limited focus. I encourage students to experiment with what works for them. For me, it's 50 minutes on task, 10 minutes off task, two rounds/day, 4–6 days/week depending on how much I need to write. I no longer literally set a timer, but I do look at my computer's clock and time myself. I marvel that this method works for me and seems to work well for most people if they actually do it. I think the trick is knowing that even if you're having a bad writing day, you've done your part if you at least tried for 50 minutes. And if you really do not let yourself do anything else for those 50 minutes, you will write something even if only out of sheer boredom.

Messiness

Getting started seems to be the most challenging part of writing, which is why I have focused so much on it in this chapter. The phenomena I have discussed to this point—uncertainty about how to write, anxiety about past writing failures, and challenges with focus—all contribute to the problem of getting the first words onto that blank screen. Another challenge worth mentioning at this point is perfectionism and the resulting inertia. I have some very smart, hardworking students who suffer mightily from procrastination because they have a hard time getting messy. They love to get on the library website, download their sources into well-organized Zotero folders, and color-code their planners with pristine timelines. They think, read, and take notes like nobody's business. They are waiting for that perfect moment when they will know exactly what to say and will write it beautifully and all will be glorious.

The problem is that this almost never happens. Thinking, reading, organizing, and planning are all important skills, particularly as students delve more deeply into what they are writing. But that first draft is about trying things out, being experimental, and tinkering. Young children are awesome at this; I used to love watching my neighbors' toddlers try out random feats of strength such as parkouring off various pieces of furniture on their deck. Sometimes the kids made it; sometimes they crashed and burned, but either way, they were always learning and developing their skills. They did not learn to walk, run, and jump by sitting around in neatly pressed dresses with their hands folded all day. They got messy, and this is what we need to give our students permission to do in their writing. (They will, of course, need to clean up the mess, but they can save that for the revision process, a topic discussed later in this chapter.)

Developing a Writing Practice

Breaking Stuff into Smaller Tasks

If "write dissertation" or even "work on history paper" is on a student's to-do list, they are likely to skip right over that and accomplish tasks like "renew driver's license" or "read article for class" instead. Vague and/or daunting tasks stimulate procrastination because we don't know how to get started. This is why the previous discussion about messiness is so important; students need to understand that a big part of writing requires leaning into ambiguity and just trying some things. Unfortunately, ambiguity feels uncomfortable for many people so they avoid it. Fortunately, we can teach students some skills for navigating ambiguity.

One way to negotiate ambiguity is to impose some order on it. For example, instead of putting "write dissertation" on one's to do list, I recommend breaking this huge task into things that feel clear and are easy to cross off a list. I would go as far as skipping the list entirely and instead writing things like "read three articles and annotate them" and "write 200 words of problem statement" in my calendar. This way, my brain knows what to do and when. This process seems to work especially well for my Type-A students (who also like to cross things off lists, so they report keeping both a list and calendar. I am not that Type A, but whatever works)!

Type-B students do better with ambiguity, but probably need to pay greater attention to making sure they create and stick to a writing schedule. I often find myself reminding students that their papers will not write themselves. I know they know this, but my Type-B students sometimes behave as if writing will just magically happen. Some of my Type-A students also experience this problem because they tend to read, take notes, buy fun office supplies, and get ready to write without actually writing. Both mellow and tightly wound people generally need a plan if they are going to get to the actual writing. So what is the best approach?

Blocking Time for Deep Work

In his widely read book, *Deep Work*, Newport (2021) lays out the case for drawing a sharp distinction between work requiring a high degree of focus and other kinds of activities. He defines deep work as "professional activities performed in a state of distraction-free concentration that push your cognitive capacities to their limit" (p. 2). Newport advocates heavily for the importance of this kind of work in an age when the forces of automation are making low- and medium-skilled jobs obsolete. Newport argues even highly skilled workers are at risk due to the twin forces of employers being able to recruit from a global labor pool due to remote work and outsource many tasks to artificial intelligence. He maintains that the only way to stay employable is to be the best and the only way to be the best is to carve out the time and bandwidth necessary to perform at the frontiers of one's abilities.

One of the hardest things about being a professor is that most of my job is about two fundamentally different things: Being present and available to students and producing scholarship. Once I realized this (partly with the help of *Deep Work*), I started building guardrails around my scholarship (aka "deep work") time. The obvious benefit is that constructing my time in this manner allows my brain the time and space it needs to do the difficult work of writing. The less obvious, but equally important benefit, is that I am more present and available during my non–deep work time because I'm not constantly thinking, "I should be writing. Please stop talking to me so I can get back to writing." By the end of my deep work time, my brain is tired of all the heavy concentration and solitude so I'm more than happy to interact with others. I encourage students to draw these kinds of boundaries so they do not have to feel pulled constantly between writing and other responsibilities. Though there is no perfect answer to the quest of time and space, the deep work framing seems to help.

Though Newport (2021) shares stories of people blocking days and even weeks for deep work, I discourage students from planning "writing days" or even "writing mornings/afternoons" because I fear they will experience diminishing returns with that plan for the reasons regarding our brains' ability to focus as discussed earlier in this chapter. Sometimes, students are reluctant to believe me because they imagine writing happening in a large, uninterrupted block of time when genius can occur. The reality, however, is that we almost never find that kind of time. Also, waiting too long between writing sessions often means spending a lot of time getting one's head back into the work. For these reasons, I encourage students to set aside even an hour a day to devote to their writing.

For me, the best time to write is after my morning swim and first pass at the day's email. Some people find that opening the email first presents what Leroy (2009) coined "attention residue" problems. "Attention residue" occurs when one experiences difficulty moving on to a new task because an old task lingers in the back of their minds. This will be an issue for some students, so it is useful to give them language for it. For those like me, wondering what fresh hell might lurk in my email presents the bigger distraction, so I need to know what's there before I can focus on something else. Some students write most effectively at the end of the day when everything is behind them or even late at night. I have a student who writes at 3 and 4 am because he needs the assurance that no one will be trying to get a hold of him while he writes. I encourage my students to experiment with what works best for them and keep adjusting as their responsibilities and schedules change. Being proactive establishes a sense of control and agency, which builds the confidence students need to be successful in their writing practice.

Topics to Cover

In addition to the previously discussed material about mindset and scheduling, many students benefit from at least a brief primer on the following topics. For a deeper dive into these ideas and additional skills to teach, see Chapter 4: "Developing a Writing Course." As I mentioned in the introduction, today's students generally receive less writing instruction and feedback than past generations. This means that educators should anticipate the need to provide some guidance for students as they prepare to work on writing assignments. What follows is a list of some of the topics I have learned over my many years of helping students write.

Reading Strategically

Perhaps surprisingly, some writing challenges can be traced to reading problems. This is an issue I have experienced myself as someone who loves to read. I read articles on multiple devices and in print form. My books are spread across many digital and physical locations. As a result, my notes exist in digital and paper forms all over the place, which is maddeningly inefficient. Hence, I confess that this topic is more preaching than practicing in my case.

My smarter colleagues and students use Zotero, RefWorks, Mendeley, or one of the many reference guides out there to store their sources and notes. I am working on this process myself, but I struggle because my mind and eyes want to keep moving forward without ever stopping to take stock of all my readings. I do at least store my frequently cited materials and organize them fairly well. The more you can encourage your students to develop a solid note and source organization system, the less time they will waste shuffling and searching.

The one thing I do competently in this realm of reading strategically is following Dorothy Duff Brown's (personal communication, November 13, 2009) method of reading with an eye toward a single question: "How will I use this?" The elegant simplicity of this method cuts down on all the random highlighting that rarely has meaning a day or two after I've read something. That quick, but substantive question, "How will I use this?" hits the sweet spot of making things stick without taking up too much time and keeping me from reading on. My students report that this guiding question helps them stay focused, though most of them will not give up their highlighters!

The bigger issue with reading, of course, is that students often struggle with it on a more fundamental level. Some pundits speculate that young people have reading challenges because they do it less than previous generations (Pappano, 2018) while others dispute that notion, arguing that this claim rests on stereotypes rather than data (Kim, 2018). There is evidence to suggest that reading comprehension levels have declined at elementary and secondary levels (NAEP, 2022), a trend that shows up in postsecondary education as well. As Bosley (2008) explains, "Students often read at surface level; if they do not 'get it,' they give up rather than engage in the difficulty of the task" (p. 286). I have observed this phenomenon on many occasions and admit to feeling unsure what to do about it. For one, I did not want to insult my students by suggesting that they were not reading adequately. Additionally, reading instruction is not my expertise so I felt unsure about my qualifications to teach reading.

In this book, we take the position that all college educators should play a role in helping students write. I've come to see that it would be helpful to adopt this view when it comes to reading as well. As Manarin et al. (2015) assert, "Some postsecondary instructors may assume that students receive critical reading instruction in their first-year compositions class. And while such classes do provide close attention to texts, they cannot be expected to bear either burden alone" (p. 36). Whether the culprit is less reading, more digital distractions, or something else, the reality is that many college students seem to struggle with reading, so it is incumbent upon college educators to offer some instruction.

Fortunately, the idea of critical reading can be useful in helping students engage more deeply with texts. Bosley (2008) describes critical reading as a metacognitive process that involves readers' active interaction with the text. Critical reading activities include mentally talking to the author, raising questions, making predictions, forming connections with prior knowledge and experiences, interrogating assumptions, noticing silences/omissions, transforming information for new purposes, constructing new knowledge, and considering how one's own positionality informs how the reader receives the text. This identification of precise aspects of critical reading helps make it tangible for students. Framing the activity as critical reading more specifically (as opposed to general reading comprehension) also avoids the potential for patronizing students as very few people have been introduced the concept of critical reading and therefore cannot be expected to already know this information.

Whether educators introduce the idea of critical reading, challenges of focusing in the age of digital instruction, or take some other approach, I recommend at least opening the floor for students to discuss and troubleshoot reading challenges. In my experience, deeper reading helps students develop the observational and analytic skills they need for more effective writing.

Prewriting, Writing, and Revising as Distinct Processes

I don't recall the moment I stumbled upon this idea of identifying prewriting, writing, and revising as distinct processes, but I do recall my and my students' lives getting a bit easier once I started explaining things this way. One of the big challenges with writing is that it involves so many different activities, minimally: Researching, reading, organizing, planning, thinking, structuring, expressing, creating, arguing, anticipating counterarguments, and editing. The good news is that these are such different skills that it's almost certain there will be at least a few to which students gravitate. Some students are big-picture thinkers who love that initial phase of brainstorming ideas. Others are more detail-oriented and enjoy the editing process. In both cases, it can be a sharp turn between all the tasks involved with writing so parsing them out can make the process less overwhelming for students.

For this reason, I encourage students to separate writing into prewriting, writing, and revising processes. In most courses, this takes the form of how I assign papers. I have each part of the paper due as a small assignment building up to the bigger paper. This structure generally helps students take smaller bites out of the assignment.

Crafting a Working Abstract

The first proverbial bite I require students to take is a working abstract. I call this part of the prewriting process because students don't have to commit fully to what they write in their abstract, but they need something to get them started. This assignment serves as a nonthreatening way to ease into the writing due to its short length (75–150 words), but it packs a lot of punch because it requires students to get going on their ideas. I emphasize that they can and probably should revise the abstract as they dive more deeply into their writing, but the act of providing an initial thumbnail sketch of what they are thinking is essential to starting the writing process. The other advantage of starting with this bit of prewriting is that I get to see what students are thinking about and help them troubleshoot without having to read thousands of words of writing in this first round. I make this assignment due very early in the semester as a preemptive strike on procrastination.

Working from an Outline

I require students to produce broad outlines of their work to get them thinking about the main points and subpoints they may make in their papers. Again, this document will likely need revision as students' thoughts develop, but a preliminary guide helps them start moving. Sometimes students confuse the outline with whatever they had to do in middle school English class, so I make it a point to share that I still work with outlines myself. I explain that my outline helps me keep the forest of my work in mind while I'm working on writing the single trees. A lot of what makes writing hard is the constant movement between big and small picture; what reads as unclear is often the result of too much detail that doesn't make sense or lack of context. Outlines can be useful in helping the writer connect these dots for the reader. For example, my first outline for this chapter looked something like this:

Intro
Setting Yourself Up for Success
- Time Management
- Attention Management
- Expert Blind Spot

Setting Students Up for Success
Anxiety
- Mindset
- Treating Writing Like a Puzzle
- Inculcating Focus

Strategies for Focus
- Apps
- Pomodoro Method
- Messiness
- Developing a Writing Practice

- Breaking Work into Smaller Projects
- Deep Work

Topics to Address in Student Writing
- Reading Strategically
- Prewriting, Writing, and Revision as Separate Processes
- Using Sources

Conclusion

As I wrote each section, my outline changed to reflect what actually happened in the writing process. For example, there were areas where I had more to say than I had originally anticipated, so I broke up those sections. This is the kind of thing I do naturally as an experienced writer, so I used to have the "expert blind spot" problem when trying to help students to be clearer and more structured in their writing. Now that I have considered this challenge more intentionally, I can articulate "forest and trees" issues more clearly to students and hopefully ward off some of them with the use of an outline.

Effective Researching

Students generally seem to start on Google Scholar, which I frequently use myself as a starting point. The problem is that there does not seem to be much between the very easy, but overly simplified world of Google Scholar and the sometimes arduous to navigate, but more substantive world of library databases like ERIC, PsychInfo, and others. If you are blessed with reference librarians like ours, you can outsource much of this education to them as they really are the experts at both doing and explaining research. If you are not so blessed, here are a few tips to help students research effectively.

First, the key to making library databases less onerous is to develop effective search terms. Showing students how to use the thesaurus feature in these databases will go a long way in getting them to use the sites. Students appreciate other quick tips like limiting searches to get to the most recent data, filtering out nonacademic sources, and finding seminal works. They are also grateful for a tour through services that allow them to avoid the paywalls they encounter on Google Scholar and receive materials free through services offered by their library.

Students also benefit when we take the time to point out tutorials for reference management systems (like Zotero, RefWorks) and style manuals (like APA, MLA, etc.). It is helpful to remember our expert blind spot here and recognize that things that may seem easy to faculty are often difficult for students in terms of navigating library websites. Taking a few minutes to show students these features as well as subject and course guides, how to access their subject librarian, and the full array of services can preempt students' claims like "there's nothing on my topic." There almost always is a robust body of work on their topic, but students won't always be able to access it without some guidance.

Writing a Clear Thesis

This seems to be one of the hardest aspects of writing for most students. They often describe their paper topics in vague language like "issues for first-generation students" or "problems with Greek life." These are not bad starting points for delving into the literature, but students need help moving from general topics to specific positions. Some students express reticence to this idea, worrying about being called out for taking the wrong position or not having enough evidence to substantiate a claim. Others are hesitant to commit to a thesis until they have all their ideas fleshed out, not realizing you often have to start with a clear idea before you can get to all the counterarguments. Finally, some students have been told that they are not experts and therefore have no right to make a claim. In all these cases, educators may have to disavow students of these notions to help them get unstuck enough to try out an idea.

As with many aspects of writing, one way to do this is to offer examples. Here are some examples I recently shared with my Diversity in American Higher Education students:

1. True commitment to racial justice necessitates "banning the box" and expanding formerly incarcerated individuals' access to higher education.
2. Have identity centers outlived their purpose as initiatives designed to promote inclusivity on college campuses?
3. The elimination of Greek Life would heavily reduce sexual assault and other forms of misogyny on college campuses.
4. Does removing statues and other tributes to human rights violators make a difference in marginalized students' sense of belonging on college campuses?

I instruct students about why these are pretty good thesis statements. They are clear and specific arguments around which it is easy to build a strong case for significance. They are complex enough to suggest counterarguments for the author to anticipate and address. They are simple enough to achieve the scope and scale of the assignment (about 5000 words).

Making the Case for Significance

Teaching students how to make the case for significance in their writing requires some diplomacy. Presumably, the student cares a great deal about their topic to have chosen it out of the universe of potential areas of study. Hence you do not want to quash their passion when pointing out that the world might not need another review of the literature on appreciative advising, for example (a very hot and over-researched subject in my field. Enough already). I recommend treading gently here, but still doing the delicate work of helping students both choose important topics and articulate the significance in their writing.

Some topics seem to have the significance baked in; for example, suicides on college campuses. You would be hard pressed to find a person who did not find this to be an important topic, but it still may have some weaknesses. For example, is this a heavily researched phenomenon and, if so, is there a new angle the student could bring to the discussion? Is suicidality well researched generally, but have the mental health concerns unique to specific populations been overlooked in the literature? These are the kinds of questions that you can use to help students communicate to the reader why their paper merits consideration.

Other topics may seem less significant on the surface, but the case can be made when students are intentional about articulating significance. For example, one of my students wanted to write a paper about how student athletes experience marginalization on college campuses. At first, this seemed trivial to me. Not only are student athletes not a protected class (like students of color, women, and LGBT students, for example), but one could argue they experience privilege depending on the sport and level of play. My student pushed back, though, arguing that many student athletes miss out on their education due to excessive athletic demands and thus have limited career options given that so few go on to play their sport professionally. When the student could express her concerns with this level of precision, she could start to build a case for her thesis. Further, she moved into more interesting territory about a group that experiences both privilege and marginalization, which helped her build an even better case for a more nuanced understanding of student athletes' challenges.

Developing Structure and Organization

Students seem to have received very little guidance when it comes to structuring and organizing their work. My guess is that this is because these topics are difficult to explain. When it comes to clarity, we kind of know it when we see it. I have not developed the perfect recipe for teaching structure and organization myself, but there are a few things that seem to help.

First, I always remind students that the audience is often an overlooked aspect of writing. If they can imagine who might be interested in reading their work, they will do a better job of thinking about things like what terms need definition, what context is necessary to convey a point, and what transitions might help the reader make connections between points. Second, working from an outline of headings and subheadings helps the writer see and articulate how big ideas and supporting evidence work together to produce a logical thread. Finally, reminding students of the introduction-supporting evidence-conclusion-transition to the next idea paragraph structure they learned in junior high school can go a long way in facilitating the writing organization process.

The other challenge that comes with structure and organization is that some students will be so daunted by it that they never sit down to write while others will word vomit on the page and turn it in. For this reason, I encourage students to seek a balance. When writing a draft, it's fine to just get it out in whatever messy, loosely structured way allows them to move their ideas from their head to the page. Students can then keep crafting and organizing as they write, doing a final assessment for clarity as part of the editing and revising process.

The young neighbors I mentioned earlier have proven useful for illustrating the importance of structure and organization in clear communication. I enjoy talking to them because they are entertaining, but their storytelling often goes something like this:

> Hey! We went to the zoo because we're three and we got to have McDonalds on the way which we never get to have and we both had nuggets and Daddy locked his key in the car and said a bad word like a really bad one so Mommy was mad and it was okay cause the A guy came and we saw a giraffe and we eated snowcones.

Note how the youngsters express all their points with equal emphasis, never explaining how one idea connects to another. This particular report was delivered while I was walking my dog by their house, so not only were the words pretty random, but they were not delivered in the context of joining a conversation. The kids just belt things out, which is how student writing can feel without the skill of offering context and acknowledgment of previous thinking on the topic. All of this makes the kids' line of thinking entertaining, but difficult to follow.

In contrast, their parents would tell the story more like this:

> Thanks for telling us about those discount tickets to the zoo; the girls had such a good time there this weekend. They loved all the animals, especially the giraffes. It was mostly a lovely day, though Mike did lock his keys in the car. It's always something, but that's how it is with family fun.

Note how this report began with a reference to a previous conversation on the topic of going to the zoo. Observe, too, how the adult version left out some extraneous details unnecessary to the story. Also, adult speech tends to include natural introductions, supporting details, conclusions, and transitions. These kinds of examples can sometimes help students see the difference between writing that is chaotic and wandering like the kids' story and structured and organized like the adult's story. The kids' version is not such a problem in a report delivered purely for fun, but it's easy to see how it would present challenges when trying to convey more complex material. The connections in the adult version create clarity, one of the most important elements in academic writing.

Writing Clearly

Students sometimes push back on structure and organization feedback, lamenting, "Can't you just grade my idea instead of whether the writing is right?" This question used to annoy me because I didn't know how to answer it. Then I realized that the answer is about clarity and curation being the value-added elements authors add to our knowledge through their writing. Without structure and organization, why should I read your paper when I could just Google key words related to your topic? Structure and organization add clarity, an entity lacking from the chaos of Google.

In addition to structure and organization, clarity is achieved through some specific and fairly simple practices. First, I find many students need to be disavowed of the notion that smart/academic equals complicated. Somewhere along the line, students seem to have learned that big words, multi-clause sentences, and long paragraphs constitute writing that sounds scholarly. I tell students that when faculty write "unclear" on their papers, one of these things is often the problem. The good news is that these are easily solved issues. Write shorter sentences, compose structured paragraphs that take up no more than half a page (double-spaced), and use the shorter word when it will do the job. In other words, write how most of us speak and you will achieve greater clarity in your writing.

Another enemy of clarity in writing is the long quote. I always make it a point to differentiate between citing (which should happen frequently) and quoting, which should happen sparingly as quotes interrupt the flow of one's work. Students are tempted to quote because quotes fill up word count and sound better than the student's own words (or so they think). I work hard to disavow them of this second notion. I tell them quoted material sounds good because they are reading it in the context of that author's work. Paraphrasing with appropriate citation is almost always a better choice for maintaining voice continuity in one's writing.

Achieving Depth, Precision, and Concision

I only have one goal in the first draft of a work: Get it out. Consequently, I write first drafts frenetically. I crank out a thousand words in an hour, which feels very productive. I both pat myself on the back and remind myself that these thousand words are not necessarily good words. I need to go back and add depth and precision to my work because these are the things that add value for the reader.

For example, the section on "Developing Structure and Organization" could have been much shorter. I could have written something like: It is important to have structure and organization in one's work. Teach students to work from an outline and write transitions between their ideas. These are not bad points, but they neither capture what is difficult about structure and organization, nor offer ideas about what how to solve the problem. I had to stew over this challenge for a few days, then remembered what I really do in class when trying to convey this material. I frequently invoke the toddlers next door as foils for clear communication because they demonstrate the point in a way that is relatable. Most people have talked to young children and experienced the long and winding labyrinth of their stories. Therefore, I included this story to flesh out how one might explain the complicated topics of structure and organization in a way that is more tangible.

Elaborating on fewer points rather than skimming the surface of more ideas is often a useful strategy for achieving more depth and precision in writing. Stories and examples provide helpful vehicles for achieving this goal. The trick is to provide depth and precision without falling into the trap of simply adding filler to achieve a wordcount. I try to spend some time explaining the difference to students, adding that I would rather have them turn in work that is under wordcount than replete with filler. It's easier to suggest places where they could expound on a point rather than work through tedious sections of rambling just to take up space.

Using Sources

Using sources, too, is an area in which balance is key. Some students have been told they must cite a source for nearly every assertion they make while others rarely feel the need to back up a claim. Here is where it can be helpful to remind students that they are joining a conversation with their writing. The audience needs to understand how the student's work connects with, departs from, and extends the current thinking on their subject. Many of my students are extroverts, so their understanding of verbal conversation can be a useful metaphor upon which to build this idea. I explain that they wouldn't sit down to a dinner party, ignore everything that had been said, and plop their idea out there with no context or acknowledgment of others' thoughts. More likely, they would listen to what has been said, draw some themes among the topics, and use those ideas as context for what they might contribute.

Negative examples often provide sharper (and more entertaining) images of this point. Many of my students grew up watching *The Big Bang Theory*, so I sometimes use Sheldon's obsession with trains to illustrate this point. There are funny moments when the other characters will be discussing another topic and Sheldon will try to wedge a commentary about trains into the conversation, becoming increasingly agitated when the others won't change direction. Even if the characters had been discussing trains, Sheldon would likely have inserted his thoughts and opinions without acknowledging what had already been said, a behavior consistent with his signature confusion about how interpersonal relationships function.

Unlike Sheldon, my students demonstrate a lot of interpersonal competence in discussions. In class, they tend to frame their contributions in terms of what had already been said up to that point. If we were discussing the recent Harvard affirmative action case, for instance, a student might add something like, "I can see Maria's point about the anti-Asian bias discussed in the article we read for today, but it seems like people could be using that a cover to be against affirmative action without coming off as racist." In verbal conversation, there is a natural positioning of one's thoughts in the bigger context of what has already been said. We can use this aspect of oral communication as a model for helping students make these connections in their writing.

As with many aspects of writing, examples from our own work can help students learn when and how to integrate sources. I can take any section of this chapter, for instance, and use it to show students how I decided to include a source. As I was thinking about my points regarding focus, I realized those ideas did not originate in my own mind. I had certainly thought about the challenges of focus before, but I didn't really clarify my thinking until I dove into the literature on this topic. I therefore needed to cite this scholarship both to acknowledge other people's work and to let my readers know how I was contextualizing my own contributions regarding this topic.

Once students understand sources as more than simply CYA (Cover Your Ass) measures, they start to get a feel for when they should include them.

Speaking of CYA, a frank discussion of what constitutes plagiarism is warranted in any course with writing assignments. It can be challenging to both cover the basics and neither overwhelm nor antagonize students. To accomplish this delicate balance, I briefly explain that plagiarism is claiming someone else's work as your own, then focus more on why people do it. Usually, the culprit is stress about not knowing how to complete an assignment or running out of time. I then assure students that all other strategies—coming to office hours, going to the writing center, throwing oneself at the mercy of the instructor—are better options than being referred for academic dishonesty. We will delve into specific aspects of plagiarism—generative AI and cultural differences around citation—in subsequent chapters, but for now the main point is to acknowledge why it happens and offer alternatives to the problems for which people use this unwise and unethical strategy.

Revising

This is the part of writing many of my students feel free to skip, so I go into this topic knowing I'm fighting an uphill battle against the forces of procrastination and just wanting to be done. I understand these impulses because I feel them myself. Revision can be boring and tedious if attempted too close to the end of the writing process itself. This is why I craft both draft and revised versions of writing assignments: To force the revision process!

The way this works is to make sure students understand that "draft" does not mean "crap I threw together the night before," but "the very best I could get the work on my own." As with anything, I get a range of drafts, some closer to the former and others closer to the latter. Really drilling down on my definition of "draft," though, does seem to stimulate more effort, especially when I explain that some students will do such a good job that they can basically coast through the revision process and not have much to do for the rest of the semester. This will be true or mostly true for about 10–20% of students in my masters-level classes.

The other 80–90% of students will need to make substantial revisions to their work. By assigning separate points for revision, I try to sell this as a bonus because they're getting points for writing they already completed. Now they just have to make it better. I can't honestly claim the students cheer at this news, but they do appreciate the chance to improve their work with some feedback and guidance. Students talk about how frustrating it is to work on something and not get the opportunity to improve it based on what they learned, so this process addresses that concern.

I capitalize on my students' extroverted tendencies in the revision process by strongly encouraging them to read each other's work and offer feedback on where things were clear/unclear, where ideas needed more structure, and any elements they found to be missing. I appreciate how daunting it can be to put one's work out there, so I preface this assignment by acknowledging the vulnerability inherent in both giving and receiving feedback. I remind them about growth mindset and try to cultivate a spirit of collaboration in helping one another improve. I emphasize that it's difficult to see one's own writing weaknesses because we're too close to our own work and generally need a fresh set of eyes to see where improvements are needed. Finally, I instruct students to point out strengths as well. There is an obvious psychological benefit in positive feedback, but it's also instructive to know where we're thriving so we can keep building on those strengths.

In sum, distance from their draft, feedback from the instructor, peer feedback, and attention to strengths as well as growth areas can help students navigate the revision process successfully.

CONCLUSION

In this chapter, we took a tour through the various challenges that confound educators and students alike when it comes to academic writing. Resources for addressing common writing issues like time and bandwidth management, expert blind spot, anxiety, and focus were provided. We discussed how to anticipate and address writing skill concerns like strategic reading, effective researching, and breaking writing projects into discrete phases such as prewriting, writing, and revising. In the next chapter, we'll move from the general overview offered in this chapter to a deeper dive into the art of giving feedback.

REFERENCES

Bosley, L. (2008). "I don't teach reading": critical reading instruction in composition courses. *Literacy Research and Instruction*, *47*(4), 285–308.

Cardoso-Leite, P., Green, C. S., & Bavelier, D. (2015). On the impact of new technologies on multitasking. *Developmental Review*, *35*, 98–112. https://doi.org/10.1016/j.dr.2014.12.001

Carr, N. (2020). *The shallows: What the Internet is doing to our brains*. WW Norton & Company. https://doi.org/10.1177/0094306111425021d

Dweck, C. S. (2008). *Mindset: The new psychology of success*. Random House Digital, Inc. https://www.penguinrandomhouse.com/books/44330/mindset-by-carol-s-dweck-phd/

Foer, F. (2018). *World without mind: The existential threat of big tech*. Penguin Press. https://www.penguinrandomhouse.com/books/533937/world-without-mind-by-franklin-foer/

Kim, J. (2018, September 3). Is NY Times correct that college students don't read books? *Inside higher ed*. https://www.insidehighered.com/blogs/technology-and-learning/nytimes-correct-college-students-dont-read-books

Langer, E. J. (2016). *The power of mindful learning*. Hachette UK. https://www.hachettebookgroup.com/titles/ellen-j-langer/the-power-of-mindful-learning/9780738219097/

Leroy, S. (2009). Why is it so hard to do my work? The challenge of attention residue when switching between work tasks. *Organizational Behavior and Human Decision Processes*, *109*(2), 168–181. https://doi.org/10.1016/j.obhdp.2009.04.002

Manarin, K., Carey, M., Rathburn, M., & Ryland, G. (2015). *Critical reading in higher education: Academic goals and social engagement*. Indiana University Press.

NAEP (2022). NAEP reading assessment highlights. https://www.nationsreportcard.gov/highlights/reading/2022/

Newport, C. (2021). *Deep work: Rules for focused success in a distracted world*. Grand Central Publishing. https://www.hachettebookgroup.com/titles/cal-newport/deep-work/9781455586691/?lens=grand-central-publishing

Pappano, L. (2018, August 2). The iGen shift: Colleges are changing to reach the next generation. *The New York Times*. https://www.nytimes.com/2018/08/02/education/learning/generationz-igen-students-colleges.html

Stone, D., Patton, B., & Heen, S. (2010). *Difficult conversations: How to discuss what matters most*. Penguin Group. https://www.penguinrandomhouse.com/books/331191/difficult-conversations-by-douglas-stone-bruce-patton-and-sheila-heen-foreword-by-roger-fisher/

Wiggins, G. & McTighe, J. (2005). *Understanding by design*. Association for Supervision and Curriculym Development. https://www.ascd.org/books/understanding-by-design-expanded-2nd-edition?variant=103055

Chapter 2

Giving Solid Feedback

INTRODUCTION

One of the most daunting yet overlooked aspects of faculty life is giving feedback on student writing. What should we say to students? How do we communicate clearly and directly without hurting students' feelings? How do we determine whether a piece of writing is legitimately wrong or just not the way we would do it? When should we deduct points and when should we just make suggestions? How detailed should we be? How can we do our due diligence without spending our lives grading? I will address these questions and offer strategies for doing right by our students while maintaining some semblance of work-life balance.

PREPARING STUDENTS FOR FEEDBACK

Carless and Boud (2018) assert "The most powerful single influence on achievement is feedback," (p. 1315), a statement I have found true in both my many years of teaching and as a lifelong learner. In fact, it occurred to me while writing this chapter that feedback I received over a decade ago played a central role in my ability to write this book.

The year was 2007. I had recently graduated with my doctorate and was trying to get a manuscript from my dissertation research published. I thought of myself as a good writer, having received consistently positive feedback from teachers and professors on my work. Hence I was puzzled as to why I could not generate any interest in my manuscript. After several rounds of rejection, I considered giving up. Fortunately, Dr. Kathleen Manning, who was the editor of the *Journal of Student Affairs Research and Practice* at the time, made the painstaking effort of sending me specific, thorough, and useful feedback. I felt both overwhelmed and vulnerable by her extensive notes; these feelings could have thwarted my ability to see the gift that Dr. Manning had offered me.

Luckily, I was an instructor by then, so I knew the considerable time and energy it took to craft feedback at that level of both quantity and quality. I also knew that feedback of that caliber signaled not disgust, but faith that the work could be improved. Why else would someone go to that kind of effort?

Student Feedback Literacy

Unfortunately, students do not often have the luxury of being able to see feedback through the faculty lens. Therefore, we have to lay the ground for students by teaching what Carless and Boud (2018) call *student feedback literacy*, which "denotes the understandings, capacities and dispositions needed to make sense of information and use it to enhance work or learning strategies" (p. 1315). They describe student feedback literacy as a four-step process: (1) appreciating feedback, (2) making judgments, (3) managing affect, and (4) taking action.

The first step of appreciating feedback requires students and faculty alike to conceptualize learning as an interdependent phenomenon. In practice, this means moving beyond the traditional paradigm of professors as active givers of notes on strengths and weaknesses and students as passive recipients of said notes. As the authors point out, the professor plays an important role in sharing feedback, but only the student has the power to act on this feedback to improve their own learning. Articulating the interdependent nature of education inculcates an active learning mindset in students who see feedback as part of that process.

The second step, making judgments, requires students to be able to understand and communicate standards for quality writing. In order for feedback to be effective, the student has to (1) know what good performance is, (2) be able to see the gap between their performance and the standard, and (3) understand how to close the gap (Sadler, 1989). If students do not grasp these elements of good performance, they are likely to feel frustrated and unmotivated.

Developing and communicating standards in writing is difficult for several reasons. The first and most obvious is that writing is not like math or other fields where there is a clear right and wrong answer. Nonetheless, there are elements that make writing better or worse and we can help students identify these criteria through the use of a rubric such as this one that I created for my courses (see Table 2.1).

In addition to a rubric with specific criteria, students benefit from exemplars when learning to make judgments about quality writing. Exemplars are thoughtfully curated examples of student work used to help students understand assignment expectations. When students ask, "What are you looking for? What do you want?" exemplars can be useful in reducing some of the anxiety behind those questions (Yucel et al., 2014). As discussed in Chapter 1, some faculty worry that students will use exemplars as templates, but I have found that can be preempted with a warning not to do so. I also provide several exemplars to

Table 2.1 Grading Rubric

Criteria	A	B	C–F
Thesis	The thesis is clearly stated. All sub-points contribute to a well-defined main point.	The thesis is clear, but the writing wanders at times.	The thesis is buried in extraneous points the author has failed to connect for the reader.
Significance	The author makes the case for significance through contextualizing the topic in the big picture and providing supporting evidence. The author considers a specific audience.	The author hints at significance, primarily by stating that the topic is important.	The author fails to make the case for significance either by not mentioning it or being sloppy in really explaining why the topic matters.
Content	The author balances description and analysis in the essay. Word choices are varied and interesting.	The author mostly balances description and analysis, but at times leans too far one way or the other.	The essay reads either like a book report (too much description) or a heated letter to the editor (too much argument).
Organization	Paragraphs follow a topic sentence-supporting evidence-conclusion-transition to the next idea model. The essay itself has a clearly defined beginning, middle, and conclusion in which transitions are made between global issues and detailed points.	Most of the elements in the "A" portion of this criterion are followed, but not entirely consistently.	Few of the elements in the "A" portion of this criterion are followed.
Grammar/Mechanics	All sentences are well constructed and contain very few (if any) errors. Run-on sentences and sentence fragments are completely absent.	Most sentences are well constructed and contain few errors.	Sentences are awkward, cumbersome, and difficult to follow.
APA	The paper adheres to APA7 guidelines, especially with regard to effective headings/subheadings.	The paper generally adheres to APA7 guidelines, with some deviation.	It is not clear that APA7 was consulted in the creation of this paper.

(*Continued*)

GIVING SOLID FEEDBACK

Table 2.1 Continued

Criteria	A	B	C–F
Quoted Material/ Cited	Quoting is minimal; citing is frequent. Quoted and/or cited material is incorporated seamlessly into the author's overall point.	Quoted and/or cited material is mostly appropriate, but may at times be used as a substitute for the author's voice.	Quoted and/or cited material appears to occur haphazardly. It is not clear to the reader how this material supports an overall point.
Evidence	Writing reflects sophistication in determining what claims require evidence. Evidence is consistently provided to support the argument being made.	Writing reflects attention to evidence, but at times provides too little (more likely) or too much (less likely, but it does happen).	Evidence is missing and/or provided seemingly at random. Writing claims too much without substantiating the claims.

illustrate that excellent writing can occur in many different forms. Students also tell me that showcasing great student work is aspirational in that it allows them to see more concretely how past students have succeeded in the course. Finally, asking students for permission to use their work for future students honors and recognizes their accomplishments, which heightens motivation.

This point about motivation leads to the third part of the student feedback literacy process: Managing affect. As Värlander (2008) found in her analysis of the literature on emotions and learning, students often experience strong emotional responses to feedback that can vary widely depending on how the feedback is delivered (a topic explored later in this chapter). Negative feelings like defensiveness and despair—two common responses to critical feedback—can sap students' motivation and ability to persevere. Student feedback literacy includes the ability to anticipate and address the affective dimension of feedback so that one is not blindsided by it and can thus respond in ways that are productive rather than self-defeating.

When affect is managed effectively, students feel the empowerment necessary to complete the final step of the student feedback literacy process: Taking action. Clear criteria and positive emotions assist enormously in the feedback process; however, students will only move from theory to practice if they know how to do so. This requires self-efficacy, defined as "people's judgements of their capabilities to organize and execute courses of action required to attain designated types of performances" (Bandura, 1986, p. 391). In other words, students need to believe they have the capacity to act on the feedback they receive. Self-efficacy is deeper than cute proclamations kids give about how they're going to be president some day; self-efficacy involves both evidence that we can accomplish a goal and a plan to make it happen. Students with higher levels of self-efficacy in writing set higher goals and work harder to achieve them (Ekholm et al., 2015).

Student feedback literacy plays an important role in setting the stage for feedback to be effective. We can inculcate a positive attitude toward feedback and that foundation is necessary, but it will not get the job done if we do not give our students the kind of feedback that propels them toward action (and away from paralysis). It helps to start with an effective definition of what feedback really is.

Defining Feedback

Although feedback is a frequently used term in education, it defies simple definition because it is a complex activity to which educators take many different approaches. Feedback has traditionally been conceived of as a corrective product communicated down one way from active expert to passive learner. This conception of feedback both reflects and reinforces instruction that Freire (1970) labeled "the banking concept," that is, education that positions students as empty vessels to be filled by omniscient teachers.

While attitudes toward education have shifted away from the banking notion, sometimes students and faculty alike find themselves stuck in conventional ideas about feedback. Price et al. (2011) describes this phenomenon as occurring when educators view feedback as a *product* to be consumed. Student engagement with feedback given in this framework is minimal because faculty have "little interest in the response to it, perhaps only an expectation of 'passive' engagement (in the sense of listening but not thinking), involving at best a behavioral response rather than a cognitive one" (p. 881). Price et al. (2011) contrasts the feedback-as-product concept with the notion of feedback as a *process* requiring active engagement and communication within the context of an actual relationship between student and teacher.

Students' language about what they want in communication from educators about their work reflects the feedback-as-process model. Li and De Luca (2014), for example, found that the feedback most desired by students is "personal, explicable, criteria-referenced, objective, and applicable to further improvement" (p. 390). Students are especially concerned with this notion of feedback as personal, that the professor "had actually read the work and was making comments specifically about it" as the students in Dawson et al.'s (2019, p. 32) study put it. It was noted in this same study that students and faculty alike saw feedback as a much richer process than simply words justifying grades.

Despite valuing feedback as a substantive exchange taking place in the context of a meaningful relationship, the current moment in higher education presents ideological and practical challenges to this respect for the feedback process. This phenomenon is variously referred to in the literature as *academic capitalism, corporatization, neoliberalism*, and *privatization*; the precise term is less important here than the idea that contemporary higher education has experienced massive public divestment in recent years. One of the most significant consequences for our purposes is the shift from conceptualizing students as people in which the public invests as future citizens to consumers investing in their own future earning potential as individuals. Bunce et al. (2017) found that students who identified more strongly as consumers of higher education took a more passive, instrumentalist approach toward learning. This passivity and instrumentalism translate into the diminishment of feedback (process) and elevation of grades (product).

The related challenge worthy of at least brief mention here is the push toward automated grading. An exhaustive discussion of the use of artificial intelligence (AI) to enact the academic capitalist agenda of ever-increasing revenue generation via larger class sizes is beyond the scope of this book. However, this is a trend of which it is important to be aware as it will affect our ability to provide the kind of thoughtful and personalized feedback advocated in this chapter. AI may have positive roles to play in education; some research indicates student and faculty satisfaction with its ability to provide prompt feedback efficiently to large groups of students (Rutner & Scott, 2022). Other researchers have found large limitations, including failure to provide quality feedback on coherence and relevance as well as failure to prevent students from gaming the AI (Ramesh & Sanampudi, 2022).

This last point about gaming the system also warrants discussion as ChatGPT exploded on the scene at the time of this book's writing. With students able to get robots to write their work and faculty able to outsource their feedback to learning management systems, are we entering an era in which humans will simply instruct their respective machines to talk to one another? If so, where does that leave human development? Will humans become the pampered pets of robot overlords as Apple co-founder Steve Wozniak imagined (Gibbs, 2015)? Again, these questions are beyond the scope of this book (though full disclosure, I am writing about them elsewhere), but they are issues with which we'll need to grapple.

I believe we will need to elevate the role of intrinsic motivation as technology makes it easier to game the system. If students want to develop technical workarounds to education, I don't know that I'll be able to stop them. What I can do, however, is make a case that what I'm offering is better. For one, I respect students' agency as human beings and do not see them as consumers, pampered pets, or the frequently used term I've come to despise, "butts in seats," a concept that reflects the rise of the neoliberal ethos in higher education. As Boud and Molloy (2013) assert, students will only follow guidance if they themselves believe the changes to be necessary to improve their work.

Relatedly, students will (and *should*) only participate in the feedback process if they see *intrinsic* value in the work itself. Helping students see this value often starts with educators expressing their appreciation for students' voices regarding the important issues in their field of study. If we ask students to simply go through the motions of writing a paper because that's what we think school is, then why shouldn't they just crank out the ol' ChatGPT in response? Students put their trust in us by going first in the feedback process, sending their words to us with little idea of how we might respond. The onus is on us to respond in ways that do justice to that act of faith.

THE ABC'S OF EFFECTIVE RESPONSES TO STUDENTS' WRITING

I started writing this chapter toward the end of an academic semester, the season educators dread for its endless grading. I felt this sense of anxiety often in my early years of teaching until I realized much of the angst could be avoided through shifts in my approach and planning. In terms of approach, I now focus more on feedback and less on grades. By decoupling these tasks to some extent, I no longer waste time fretting over whether a paper is a 98 or a 97 or even a 95 or 90. I assign numbers in fairly big swaths, so it's pretty much A, B, or C (and even sometimes D/F, which do require more work, but are blessedly rare with graduate students). Because I provide a grading rubric, the reasons for the grade are spelled out clearly for the students. This process allows me to focus less on writing feedback that justifies the grade and more on focusing my energy where it can help the students move forward in developing their writing skills. Scholars refer to this approach as formative feedback, an idea on which I will elaborate in the following section.

Approaching Feedback as Formative

Feedback can be conceptualized as summative (performance review of past work) or formative (guidance as to how work might be improved in the future) (Sadler, 1989). An indirect but significant benefit to formative feedback lies in the structure it requires to be effective. Summative feedback works with the traditional long paper due at the end of the course, a project that hangs heavy over students and faculty alike. Formative feedback is most effective with smaller, lower-stakes assignments that build over the course of a semester. For example, my students turn in topic descriptions, condensed annotated bibliographies, 100-word abstracts, 300-word introductions, and other shorter assignments that build to a first-draft paper due around the middle of the semester. To illustrate, I have included an excerpt from a recent syllabus describing this approach:

Assignment Descriptions and Due Dates

1. **Compelling Opening Sentence:** Write a compelling opening sentence to a topic about which you're considering writing for this course. DUE: 1/23/23
2. **Mini Annotated Bibliography:** Find 5 articles relevant to your topic and write a mini annotated bibliography of these sources. DUE: 2/6/23
3. **Abstract/Introduction:** Write the abstract and introduction for your paper, being sure to embed a strong case for significance. This document should be about 500 words/one single-spaced typed page. DUE: 2/13/23
4. **Draft:** Do not be fooled by the word, *draft*. This assignment must be a solid and complete first attempt at your final paper written in APA style. This work should be between 5000–7000 words (20–30-ish pages, 40+ references. References included in wordcount). DUE: 3/13/23
5. **Final Paper:** This paper will be the final, polished work for this course. DUE: 4/3/23
6. **Revision Sheet:** This document will serve as a guide to the revisions you made to turn your draft into the final paper. DUE: 4/3/23

Shorter, lower-stakes assignments benefit students and faculty alike by anticipating and addressing the procrastination that often accompanies large, high-stakes tasks. Giving feedback on shorter assignments is less daunting, so I can turn these papers around quickly and help students start improving on their work right away. The "lower stakes" is as important as the "shorter" in this plan; students get the chance to try out ideas and get a sense of the expectations without being paralyzed that whatever they write won't be good enough. It may not really be good enough, but that's easier to take when the point value is relatively low.

The most important aspect of this strategy is to inculcate the formative feedback mindset through this process. I communicate to the students that I *expect* them to need a lot of help in the beginning because, if they already knew everything, they wouldn't need the course! Communicating the formative approach and baking it into the structure of the course goes a long way in helping students accept the feedback that is necessary for improving their writing. That said, part of why it can take so long to write feedback is that we spend a lot of time wordsmithing in hopes of avoiding defensiveness, a topic I'll address next.

Anticipating and Preempting Defensiveness by Modeling an Alternative

There is nothing quite as effective as modeling when it comes to anticipating and preempting the natural defensiveness that comes from critique. This is why I keep a "Greatest Hits of Critical Reviewer Feedback Laura Has Received Lately" document to read to my students before I send them my first round of comments on their work. I emphasize the "Lately" in my document lest they think there is some state of perfection that I have achieved that makes me unsympathetic to how hard it is to write a piece, only to have someone say my work needs improvement. I let them know that I understand both the challenges of writing and the sting of criticism in a way that has not been dulled through years of mastery. If there was a way around critique's bite—I tell my students—I would find it and spare us all.

Criticism often stimulates the fight/flight/freeze reaction, but fortunately, we quickly realize that criticism is a paper tiger. I provide proof of this fact when I stand before them reading words that made me cranky for a moment but did not kill me. I *fought* with these critical reviewers in my mind, "You don't know what you're talking about!" I silently shouted in response. I also proverbially *flew* from them, "I'll just take this paper elsewhere if you want such major revisions!" But most often, I *froze*. I felt overwhelmed by the sheer volume of comments and didn't know where to even begin the revision process. Or I was confused by what reviewers meant and didn't know how to fix an issue I couldn't even identify as a problem. In short, I was tempted to either quit or make a halfhearted attempt and hope for the best in response to my critics.

By this point in my story, most of the students are nodding their heads and some begin to tell their own stories about being paralyzed by feedback from teachers. Interestingly, students almost always reference K-12 teachers because they receive so little feedback from college professors. This last point plays its own role in necessitating our anticipation and preemption of defensiveness; namely, many students have not had much practice in receiving feedback. We might want to label this phenomenon as "not my problem," but we have to address this skill gap if we are to help students improve their writing. This can be daunting because we as college educators are unlikely to have received much guidance in this department ourselves. Fortunately, there are a few tried and true measures that can help us prepare our students to receive feedback effectively.

Building on Strengths

The most obvious, but often overlooked strategy is to start with what students are doing well. This isn't simply a matter of protecting egos, though it serves that purpose as well. The deeper pedagogical purpose in focusing on strengths is that starting from the positive allows students to achieve what Csikszentmihalyi (1991) defines as flow: That state in which we can lose ourselves in the pleasure of activity for the intrinsic worth of the experience. While this sounds like a lofty goal, it is important in writing where too much focus on critique creates paralysis (think writer's block). Leveraging strengths gives students the boost they need to lose the soul-crushing critique and find their voice by relishing in and building on their strengths.

Identifying strengths also gives students that all-important home base to which they can return when they feel lost and overwhelmed. Here is an example of how this process works. Last semester, I had a student I'll call Maryam whose first full draft was a mess. It was tempting to write "this is all over the place" and "unclear" on every page. While this would have been accurate feedback, it is unlikely the student would have known what to do with it. Just hearing that our work is bad or wrong offers little direction. Confusion, in turn, saps motivation because it's daunting to face a difficult task when you have no idea where to begin. The final step in this vicious cycle is loss of confidence, a state from which it is hard to bounce back when you lack motivation and direction.

Returning to Maryam, there was no getting around the need to give her some constructive feedback about the lack of clarity and structure in her work. But I had to do that against a backdrop of hope and vision about what she could do better. Before I typed a single comment on her paper, I reread it with an eye toward the positive. I gave myself permission to read over all the errors with the assurance that I would return to those later. As I reread, I noticed that a lot of Maryam's lack of structure seemed to come from her need to include every piece of scholarship she had read on her topic. She was quoting and citing all over the place, which made for disjointed writing, but which also reflected a passion for her topic and a diligence in researching it thoroughly. So I started my feedback with: "Your passion for your topic comes through in your writing. You also did a great job of presenting key scholarship relevant to your work." Students need our help in articulating their strengths as sources of both hope and direction as they develop in their writing.

Model Sentences and Paragraphs

The first step in approaching feedback is to start with students' strengths. The next step is to be as specific as possible so students can not only feel the positive emotions that come from a pat on the back, but also use their strengths as a springboard for improvement. In Maryam's case, the next sentence in achieving this goal was something like: "For example, on page 2, you introduced Duckworth's seminal work on grit and explained her research clearly and concisely to the reader." The key is to craft comments designed to generate more of what you would like to see the student do. This is not the place to add a "but" because that qualifier both diminishes the praise and adds potential confusion. For example, reviewers have written things to me like "This work has merit, but lacks cohesion" to which I find myself responding, "Well, which is it?" Contradictions often occur when we are attempting to soften criticism. In natural conversation, statements like "I agree the coat is pretty, but maybe it's not the best color for you" serve this dual purpose of conveying both critique and sensitivity.

In writing feedback, however, feedback that contradicts perplexes students, so I try to keep my positive and constructive feedback distinct.

Another strategy for assisting students in building on strengths lies in pointing out specific sentences and paragraphs for them to use as models in the revision process. Even weak papers have bright spots that can be highlighted as examples to help students improve their work. The key is to state as clearly and specifically why a particular sentence or paragraph works. This practice also serves the purpose of tempering constructive feedback without contradicting the point you are trying to make. Here is an example of the kind of feedback that can achieve this purpose: "This paragraph is great because you cite one work and really develop your analysis of it rather than mentioning many studies without much context. Use it as a model when revising this work for the structure I mentioned in my other comments." Pointing out model sentences and paragraphs empowers students with solutions to the problems identified in the constructive feedback.

Clarifying Growth Areas

Admittedly, identifying students' strengths is the more fun part of the feedback process. Hopefully, the previous sections have offered some ideas for how to set your students up to receive constructive feedback not as an indictment of past performance but as a map for future growth. As previously discussed, couching critique in vague language in order to spare egos often results in confusion and frustration so being clear has to take precedence.

I have been commenting on students' papers for so long now that it is difficult for me to not jump to judgment when reading a student's work. Our minds have evolved to see patterns quickly and evaluate accordingly. This patterned, swift judgment results from evolutionary processes that generally serve us well as a species (Lazarus, 2021). Unfortunately, bias and overgeneralization are byproducts of this ability. Hence, I tend to look at a paper and quickly deem it good or bad before identifying the qualities that led me to one conclusion or the other. This is a problem even when my initial assessment is positive because that positivity becomes the biased lens through which I read the paper. Once I have identified the paper as good, my eyes gloss over mistakes and problems, a phenomenon known as *confirmation bias* (Kahneman, 2011). I literally fail to see the negatives because my brain automatically dismisses them as outliers, having committed to the mental model of "this paper is good."

Consequently, we need to slow down when reading students' work and focus more on the details than sweeping good/bad judgements, at least during the initial read. It's fine to identify patterns, such as Maryam's tendency to include a lot of details without context. The trick is to avoid the all good/all bad filter lens. Even the "all good" lens is limiting because students need to know specifically what they are doing well so they can keep building on their strengths. The "all bad" lens presents even more problems because it leads to a sense of defeatism for both the teacher and student. I confess that when I used to open papers and deem them "all bad," I felt anxiety at the prospect of giving feedback. Where does one even begin with the "all bad" paper? It feels impossible if we stay in the proverbial forest of the "all bad" paper, so it's important to get into the trees.

Painfully Clear and Detailed Feedback

I have found it helpful to resist the urge to get lost in the big picture and dive right into the details of the not-so-good paper. This approach serves several functions. First, it forces me to just get started. Rather than trying to fix a seemingly hopeless paper, I'm just commenting on a sentence here and there. This strategy seems to approximate The 5-Minute Rule, a trick in which you tell yourself you just have to do something for five minutes, then can stop. The idea is that once you get started, you'll keep going because getting started is the hardest part of the unpleasant task. Another benefit of the detailed approach is that once I start commenting on specific aspects of the paper, I can see how it might be improved. That glimmer of hope becomes motivational for me which, in turn, helps me motivate the student with formative feedback. My mental model of the paper goes from "all bad" to "some bright spots that can be built upon with specific fixes."

Admittedly, it's easier to stick with the all good/all bad binary because this allows us to write either "good job!" or "needs improvement" on the work and call it a day. Feedback that is precise enough to be useful to the student takes time to write. I acknowledge the luxury I have in teaching reasonably sized classes of motivated graduate students; I know this is not the case for everyone reading this book. Therefore, I have compiled my "greatest hits" of frequently given feedback you are welcome to use/modify in whatever way works for you. I have organized these stock comments as alternatives to the overly general, vague comments students tell me they often receive on papers. I realize the potential hypocrisy of offering examples in the good/bad binary, but students have told me that this stark framing is useful for them in the initial stages of grappling with writing challenges. Hence, I offer the following examples in this dichotomy, but feel free to edit for whatever works best for your students.

Saving Time with Stock Comments

One final caveat: Stock comments can alienate students if they read like stock comments. I discourage the checklist approach because students view them as an indicator of professors' unwillingness to read their work and respond respectfully (Price, Handley, Millar, and O'Donovan, 2010). That said, it can be frustrating to write the same thing over and over again so I advise aiming for a delicate balance of avoiding wheel reinvention while keeping the comments personalized and specific.

Instead of "unclear":

Try not to have more than two clauses in a sentence.

> **Bad**: The ecosystem provides a useful metaphor for understanding the systems approach to organizations, which states that each part is not an independent unit, but rather part of an interdependent organization in which each component cannot be viewed separately as in Taylorism, an idea that organizations are simply machines made up of discrete parts.
>
> **Good**: The ecosystem provides a useful metaphor for understanding the systems approach to organizations. The interdependence conveyed in the ecosystem model contrasts with Taylor's vision of organizations as machines that can be reduced to discrete parts.

Instead of "tighten up the organization":

Aim for shorter, crisper sentences that hold an idea together with the use of transition words.

> **Bad**: Although we might commend Hamlet for his introspection, his excesses in this area caused him to hesitate too much, thereby failing to avenge his father's death, which created space for his uncle to move in on his mother and wreak havoc in Denmark.
>
> Although we might commend Hamlet for his introspection, his excesses in this area caused him to hesitate. In turn, his hesitance led to his failure to avenge his father's death. This omission created space for his uncle to move in on his mother, wreaking havoc in Denmark.

Instead of "work on structure":

Each paragraph should introduce a new idea, provide supporting evidence, conclude, and transition to the next idea.

> **Bad**: Erikson posited that people face developmental tasks at various points across the lifespan. Erikson developed these stages in the 1950s and 1960s. He was born in Frankfurt, Germany to a young, Jewish mother who was a single parent for much of his childhood. He thought that if people do not complete a developmental stage in the time allotted, they could not move onto the next stage, but could complete that stage at a later time. There are many critiques of Erikson's ideas about development. Erikson was very influential as a psychoanalyst having worked at esteemed institutions such as Harvard Medical School and Yale University.

Good: Erikson posited that people face developmental tasks at various points across the lifespan. Beginning with Trust vs. Mistrust occurring at ages 0–1.5, the idea is that people face a psychosocial crisis that results in a corresponding virtue if they resolve it successfully. For example, Hope is the virtue associated with the Trust vs. Mistrust stage. Although Erikson believed people could achieve success in a developmental stage beyond the time allotted, he did not believe people could move on to the next stage until the previous one had been completed. This idea is highly influential, but also controversial.

Critiques of Erikson's work began almost immediately after the publication of ...

Instead of "lacking balance":
Be sure to anticipate and address counterarguments in your work.

Bad: Climate change presents the single greatest challenge to humankind and should therefore trump all other issues when it comes to budget priorities. Some may argue that it is too costly to transition to a green economy, but what difference will money make if people don't have clean air, water, and so on? People cannot eat money, so the priorities need to follow Maslow's Hierarchy of Needs in preserving the Earth for our most basic needs. Those who argue otherwise are ignorant of the issues or so steeped in capitalism that they are willing to sacrifice others' wellbeing for their own selfish financial gain.

Good: Although there is consensus in the scientific community about the grave risks of climate change, political will seems to be lacking when it comes to addressing the problem. Climate change has direct impacts like death and destruction, but also indirect impacts like contributions to the refugee crisis and increases in food prices leading to greater poverty. Despite these highly significant consequences, only 20% of US voters rank climate change in their top five priorities when considering candidates (Frank, 2021). Similarly, climate change accounts for less than 5% of airtime in political debates. Fortunately, there are places where communication strategies have increased public response to climate change. Two of these examples will be presented as case studies in this paper.

Instead of "insufficient evidence":
Be sure to anticipate and include the kinds of information your reader will expect given your topic.

Bad: Child abuse is a problem that was exacerbated by the pandemic. People having to stay at home and school in confined spaces increased child abuse due to frustration and lack of witnesses. There is a difference between child abuse and punishment, which is allowed by law. Some people disagree as to what constitutes child abuse and states can even differ in their rules, such as 19 states not allowing corporal punishment while the rest do.

Good: Several recent studies indicate a 10–20% increase in child abuse occurring during the height of pandemic-induced quarantining between late 2020/early 2021 (Farquar, 2023; Jenkins & Roberts, 2022; Massey, 2021; Neely & Jones, 2022; Phaly, 2021). The National Association of Social Workers (2001) defines *child abuse* as "an act that causes physical or severe emotional harm to a child" (para 23).

Instead of "unclear/weak thesis":

There is a balance to be struck between papers that read like editorial rants (such as the previous example) and those that read like instruction manuals. Sometimes students choose the latter approach because they are not sure what they can assert. This tendency toward caution is not a bad thing; it will remind you to back up your assertions with sources. However, you do need to take a position in your paper because this is the value you're adding for the reader. Taking a position in writing doesn't necessarily mean holding a political view like pro-choice/pro-life; it's more about positing a potential answer or solution to the central question or problem raised in your work.

Bad: Employers consistently rank liberal arts graduates higher than students with other degrees (Washington, 2022). Communication skills, ability to adapt to change, and writing competencies are the three most frequently cited reasons employers prefer students who studied liberal arts majors (Johnson & Chang, 2021). Students report job attainment as their Number One reason for going to college (Resser, Jacobs, & Lee, 2021). Students choose liberal arts majors with less frequency than they did in the past, according to a 2020 study of students' degree programs (Michaels, 2020).

Good: Employers consistently report higher levels of satisfaction with liberal arts graduates higher than graduates with other degrees (Washington, 2022), yet student enrollment in these programs has been on the decline for the past 20 years (Michaels, 2020). This phenomenon is puzzling given that students cite job attainment as their top reason for attending college (Resser, Jacobs, & Lee, 2021). In this paper, I will analyze the scholarship about perceptions of liberal arts degrees and present recommendations for marketing these programs more effectively in the context of career readiness.

Instead of "weak analysis":
Fully develop a point before moving on to a different point.

GIVING SOLID FEEDBACK

Bad: The majority of students never have a Black male teacher in their K-12 education (Williams, 2020), a problem that is only slightly improved in college where students report having on average 1.3 Black male professors (Henry & Young, 2019). Black men are underrepresented in the college student population, comprising 6% of the overall population and 4% of college students (Jenkins, Richards, & Rodriguez, 2021). This number has been on the decline for the past decade, partially due to tracking of Black youth toward vocational programs (Butler, 2021). Black male K-12 students receive disproportionately harsh disciplinary measures as well, according to a 2022 study by the NAACP.

Good: The majority of students never have a Black male teacher in their K-12 education (Williams, 2020). The underrepresentation of Black men in education is an underexamined phenomenon in the literature documenting disparities in Black male educational attainment. While scholars have examined issues such as harsher disciplinary measures directed toward Black male youth (NAACP, 2022) and tracking toward vocational programs (Butler, 2021), few have discussed these issues in the context of the dearth of Black male voices in K-12 schools. The failure to connect these dots has resulted in misdirected policies and practices that have, in some cases, only exacerbated the problem. In this paper, I will review the literature on the causes and effects regarding the lack of Black male representation in the teaching professions, identify key implications, and offer policy and practice recommendations for addressing the problem.

Instead of "so what?":
Make the case for significance explicit for your reader. Even if this seems obvious (for example, topics like suicide where the issues are dire), the reader need to know why your specific work matters. [Note: This paragraph provides an opportunity to offer both positive and constructive feedback. The student's last point is novel and may provide the seed for an improved work.]

Bad: Alcohol is a significant problem on college campuses. Drinking heavily is correlated with judicial referrals, poor academic performance, and financial hardship (Herman, 2011). Martin's (2021) research on sexual assault showed that most victims were inebriated when violence occurred. Patterson and Orson's (2016) findings indicated college students use alcohol to self-medicate when experiencing mental health issues such as stress, anxiety, depression, and grief. Many students miss class due to hangovers and other consequences resulting from alcohol abuse. This was proven in Ortega's (2019) study on student success. College campuses have done a lot to reduce alcohol abuse, but nothing seems to work according to Matthews and Cain's (2022) recent research on the topic.

The binge drinking rate remains stuck with 60% of students reporting they engaged in this behavior at least once during a two-week period (Matthews & Cain, 2022). Binge drinking plays a significant role in reducing positive outcomes like academic performance and retention (Miles, 2020) and increasing negative outcomes like financial hardship, disciplinary referrals, and mental health challenges (Casey & Rye, 2020). Given the severity of the problem and years of effort toward addressing it, why have college campuses not make more progress in addressing this issue?

Some scholars argue there have been inadequate human and financial resources allocated toward alcohol prevention efforts. Peterson and Harris (2021), for example, found that the average mid-size public university spends approximately $82,000 in programming and personnel dedicated to alcohol issues while losing nearly 2M in disciplinary and retention concerns related to student alcohol abuse. Given the loss of public funding, declining enrollments, and other economic hardships faced by the vast majority of public universities, there is considerable financial incentive that augments the health and safety reasons for addressing alcohol issues more effectively.

(Note that all references in the previous examples are made up.)

The Revision Sheet

Finally, consider requiring a revision sheet when students submit revised copies of their work. Having such a sheet allows you to locate students' changes more efficiently, but it also serves deeper pedagogical purposes. First, it holds them accountable for responding to the feedback you took the time and effort to write. I allow my students to push back on my feedback, but I require them to provide an explanation on the revision sheet in a way that is similar to professional publication processes. This practice allows me to convey respect for students as independent thinkers while requiring them to do the intellectual work of defending their choices.

I offer (with permission, of course) the following excerpt from one of the best revision sheets I have received from a student (Jill Harmon, Ohio University).

Page 19

HARRISON: *Avoid the "we" construction as it sounds like you and a team did the research. Referring to the sentence An applicant's chances of gaining admission to medical school can be greatly influenced by the amount of social capital one possesses; however, we find that minority and disadvantaged students typically have less social capital than their applicant pool peers*

HARMAN: removed the words "we find that"

Page 20

HARRISON: *This sentence is confusing. Also, don't do 2 howevers in a row. Referring to However, they are either choosing not to study medicine or maybe they are on the path to becoming a physician.*

HARMAN: Rewrote the sentence to read This suggests that students from lower S.E.S. families attend our colleges and universities but are not on a path that would lead them to the medical school application pool.
Removed the second sentence starting with However...

Page 21

HARRISON: *Whenever you say "literature suggests," it's convention to cite some. You've done such a good job providing thorough research here that you can simply make the assertion since you've been backing it up well to this point.*

HARMAN: Added citations from (Puddey et al., 2017; Bennett & Phillips, 2010; Senf et al., 2003)

Page 24

HARRISON: *Those last two points are super interesting and worthy of elaboration if you feel so inclined.*

HARMAN: Thank you for the suggestion. I did choose to elaborate and added the text below:

Mosley's points about the cost of applying and interviewing have been explored earlier in this paper. However, her points about letters of recommendation and unpaid internships are worthy of more exploration. ...

As is hopefully clear from this brief excerpt, revision sheets can help both professor and student achieve greater precision in their communication throughout the revision process. Although it takes time to comment with this level of specificity, I have found this upfront expenditure of effort pays dividends later because students tend not to repeat mistakes when they are required to respond to them.

I have focused on written feedback because that is the format I use, but I should note that video and audio alternatives do exist and can be equally effective if delivered with attention to personalization and specificity. In fact, some studies conducted when audio feedback was first gaining prominence suggest students preferred it because it felt more personal than written feedback (Sipple, 2007; Warnock, 2008). Subsequent scholars like Bilbro et al. (2013) have pointed out that the research on students' preferences for audio feedback is consistent, but that studies do not necessarily demonstrate that it is more effective than written feedback. Hence, I conclude that the medium does not matter as much as the quality, clarity, and positive spirit reflected in the content of feedback.

The chapter has focused on conceptualizing feedback as an interactive process, building the rapport and skill set needed for students to participate effectively in the feedback process, and communicating feedback clearly and efficiently through the use of rubrics, exemplars, and revision sheets. These theoretical and practical tools have been offered with the professor-student relationship in mind; however, peers can also play a powerful role in the feedback process. The final section of this chapter will highlight the ways in which faculty can introduce and support peer review.

PEER REVIEW

As helpful as faculty feedback can be, there are some benefits unique to peer review, which Armstrong and Paulson (2008) define as "an activity that is more focused on holistic concerns, rhetorical issues, and issues of meaning and audience appropriateness" (pp. 400–401). When executed skillfully, peer review creates benefits for the reviewer and reviewee alike because it encompasses more than students merely helping each other catch editing errors. In fact, some research suggests that providers of peer feedback reap greater benefits than receivers (Cho & Macarthur, 2011). The act of formulating feedback on another person's work provides a powerful learning opportunity because it requires moving beyond one's limited perspective. Heinert (2017) captures this process, describing it as students mastering the ability "to offer an evidence-based critique of peer work that goes beyond their opinion" (p. 296). Thinking deeply about someone else's work and articulating the kinds of comments that will help them demands students take a more active role in learning (Ion, et al., 2019).

Receivers of peer feedback also benefit from the process. For example, students in one study reported that having been reviewed by peers "forced them to pay attention their own writing and gave them space to reflect on their writing process..." (López-Pellisa, et al., 2021, p. 1307). Reflection enhances cognitive development by increasing metacognition, a vital skill for supporting the growth in self-efficacy discussed earlier in this chapter. This makes sense intuitively because agency is baked into the peer review process; peer review's role in increasing self-efficacy has also been demonstrated empirically (for example, Bürgermeister et al., 2021). As is the case for givers in the peer review process, receivers also benefit from having their perspective widened. As Ramage et al. (2015) explained:

> One of the best ways to become a better reviser is to see your draft from a reader's rather than a writer's perspective. As a writer, you know what you

mean: you are already inside your own head. But you need to see what your draft looks like to someone outside your head.

(p. 519)

Peer reviewers pull us out of ourselves, potentially increasing motivation by offering a real audience to whom our work might offer some value. Chaktsiris and Southworth (2019) found "soft skills" benefits like motivation in their study on peer review. More specifically, their findings indicated that peer review helped students overcome procrastination because they had to account for their peers' role in the writing process. In this same study, peer review also created a powerful opportunity to confront and therefore overcome some of the anxiety students expressed about critique. Hence, the literature shows that peer review enriches student learning in a variety of ways on which educators can capitalize by incorporating it into their courses.

Preparing Students to Be Successful in the Peer Review Process

While peer review can produce myriad positive outcomes, there are barriers to anticipate and preempt if it is to be conducted effectively. Students sometimes doubt their own and/or peers' competence, preferring feedback to come from the professor (Holt, 2019). This is not surprising given the traditional notion of education as knowledge imparted by teachers upon students. Communicating respect for the knowledge students bring to the learning enterprise is good pedagogical practice generally and it is particularly important for inculcating faith in peers' ability to provide thoughtful feedback. Creating rapport among students is also vital to overcoming reticence; we rarely take intellectual risks outside the support that comes from being in relationship. Finally, students need to know they have the foundational skills necessary to give and receive feedback with confidence. It is incumbent upon us to make sure they have the tools they need to do the job.

That said, I understand there is limited time in non-writing courses to teach writing skills more generally, much less the intricacies of peer review more specifically. Hence, I offer what I think is a decent scaled-down version of the guidance needed to prepare students for a successful peer review process.

Strategies for Facilitating Peer Review

Successful peer review begins with clear instructions about what you want students to do (and not do!) in the process. Role clarity helps address students' hesitance to accept feedback from peers. I make it a point to explain that the peer reviewer is not the grader of the work; that is my job as the professor. I position the peer reviewer as a friendly reader offering an extra set of eyes on the work. This seems to mitigate concerns about expertise.

That point about "friendly" is key because praise has been shown to motivate students to implement the feedback they receive from peers (Patchan, et al., 2016). Hence, I encourage students to be generous in their peer reviews, both for this motivational reason and for the point I made earlier in the chapter regarding building on strengths. As with the writing assignment itself, I provide examples of peer reviews done well so students have models from which to work. The models show effective feedback should go beyond error flagging (marking issues without offering guidance as to what the error is and how to fix it). There should be a heavy dose of localized comments (delivered in markup in close proximity to the error) with suggestions for fixing errors. I also require end comments that sum up strengths and growth areas.

This level of direction works well with my students, but I only teach graduate students and imagine many undergraduates may need more structure. Research suggests supports like procedural facilitation are useful with more novice students. Burgermeister et al. (2021) defines procedural facilitation as "instructional support that reduces potentially infinite sets of choices (e.g. in formulating sentences) to limited sets and provides aids to memory" (p. 387). Prompts, sentence stems, and templates are examples of these support mechanisms.

Although some scholarship suggests multiple reviewers yield more substantive feedback (Anderson & Flash, 2014), others argue too much feedback creates a cognitive load that can be burdensome for students (Holt, 2019). Therefore, I generally facilitate peer review in pairs with the goal of students using this initial coupling as a springboard for branching out and reviewing more fellow students' work when possible. I also try to incorporate shorter, in-class opportunities for students to discuss their work and benefit from other perspectives on it. In these activities, my goal is to empower students to continually develop confidence as writers specifically and agency as learners more generally.

CONCLUSION

In this chapter, we explored the vital role feedback plays in helping students write with greater skill and competence. It is always heartening to me how much students crave feedback, even when they might initially find it intimidating. My first-year masters students recently told me that they look forward to my comments on the assignments they turn in via Blackboard, which they apparently check frequently in hopes of more feedback. I found this interesting and asked them what they liked about feedback; the answers were mostly something like, "It's just nice to feel heard—like someone really wants to know what you think." I appreciate these students sharing their experience of my feedback because it motivates me to keep writing it!

As I reread and revised this chapter many times, it occurred to me that this issue of motivation served as a subtext in many of the themes I discussed. Writing is certainly about technical skill, but it is equally about motivation. I've had many students who were brilliant writers, but who timed out of the dissertation process because they lost motivation. Similarly, I've had many students who struggled with writing skills, but who persevered through sheer will. The students in this second group had something to say and this vision drove them to be resilient in the face of adversity. Sometimes, the difference between the first and second group of students came down to something as simple as enjoyment of the writing process. I believe enjoyment is a wildly underappreciated but vital part of the motivation necessary for learning to occur. I appreciate Hung et al.'s (2010) framing of motivation as "the need to do something out of curiosity and enjoyment" (p. 1082). The connections we make with our students through feedback can enhance their enjoyment and thus their motivation to keep expressing their voice through their writing.

REFERENCES

Anderson, N. O., & Flash, P. (2014). The power of peer reviewing to enhance writing in horticulture: Greenhouse management. *International Journal of Teaching and Learning in Higher Education, 26*(3), 310–334. http://www.isetl.org/ijtlhe/

Armstrong, S. L., & Paulson, E. J. (2008). Whither "peer review"? Terminology matters for the writing classroom. *Teaching English in the Two Year College, 35*(4), 398–407. https://www.proquest.com/scholarly-journals/credits/docview/220965130/se-2

Bandura, A. (1986). *Social foundations of thought and action A social cognitive theory*. Prentice-Hall. https://doi.org/10.4135/9781446221129

Bilbro, J., Iluzada, C., & Clark, D. E. (2013). Responding effectively to composition students: Comparing student perceptions of written and audio feedback. *Journal on Excellence in College Teaching, 24*(1), 47–83. https://eric.ed.gov/?id=EJ1005171

Boud, D., & Molloy, E. (2013). Rethinking models of feedback for learning: The challenge of design. *Assessment & Evaluation in Higher Education, 38*(6), 698–712. https://doi.org/10.1080/02602938.2012.691462

Bunce, L., Baird, A., & Jones, S. E. (2017). The student-as-consumer approach in higher education and its effects on academic performance. *Studies in Higher Education, 42*(11), 1958–1978. https://doi.org/10.1080/03075079.2015.1127908

Bürgermeister, A., Glogger-Frey, I., & Saalbach, H. (2021). Supporting peer feedback on learning strategies: Effects on self-efficacy and feedback quality. *Psychology Learning & Teaching, 20*(3), 383–404. https://doi.org/10.1177/1475725721101660

Carless, D., & Boud, D. (2018). The development of student feedback literacy: Enabling uptake of feedback. *Assessment & Evaluation in Higher Education, 43*(8), 1315–1325. https://doi.org/10.1080/02602938.2018.1463354

Chaktsiris, M. G., & Southworth, J. (2019). Thinking beyond writing development in peer review. *The Canadian Journal for the Scholarship of Teaching and Learning, 10*(1). https://doi.org/10.5206/cjsotl-rcacea.2019.1.8005

Cho, K., & MacArthur, C. (2011). Learning by reviewing. *Journal of Educational Psychology*, *103*(1), 73–84. https://doi.org/10.1037/a0021950

Csikszentmihalyi, M. (1991). *Flow*: The psychology of optimal experience. Harper Collins Publishers. https://www.harpercollins.com/products/flow-mihaly-csikszentmihalyi?variant=32118048686114

Dawson, P., Henderson, M., Mahoney, P., Phillips, M., Ryan, T., Boud, D., & Molloy, E. (2019). What makes for effective feedback: Staff and student perspectives. *Assessment & Evaluation in Higher Education*, *44*(1), 25–36. https://doi.org/10.1080/02602938.2018.1467877

Ekholm, E., Zumbrunn, S., & Conklin, S. (2015). The relation of college student self-efficacy toward writing and writing self-regulation aptitude: Writing feedback perceptions as a mediating variable. *Teaching in Higher Education*, *20*(2), 197–207. https://doi.org/10.1080/13562517.2014.974026

Freire, P. (1970). *Pedagogy of the oppressed*. Continuum. https://www.abebooks.com/9780826412768/Pedagogy-Oppressed-30th-Anniversary-Edition-0826412769/plp

Gibbs, S. (2015, June 25). Apple co-founder Steve Wozniak says humans will be robots' pets. *The Guardian*. https://www.theguardian.com/technology/2015/jun/25/apple-co-founder-steve-wozniak-says-humans-will-be-robots-pets

Heinert, J. (2017). Peer critique as a signature pedagogy in writing studies. *Arts and Humanities in Higher Education*, *16*(3), 293–304. https://doi.org/10.1177/1474022216652767

Holt, J. (2019). Grade-Accountable peer editing: Students' perceptions of peer-editing assignments. *Journalism & Mass Communication Educator*, *74*(1), 31–43. https://doi.org/10.1177/10776958187649

Hung, M. L., Chou, C., Chen, C. H., & Own, Z. Y. (2010). Learner readiness for online learning: Scale development and student perceptions. *Computers & Education*, *55*(3), 1080–1090. http://doi.org/10.1016/j.compedu.2010.05.004

Ion, G., Sánchez Martí, A., & Agud Morell, I. (2019). Giving or receiving feedback: Which is more beneficial to students' learning? *Assessment & Evaluation in Higher Education*, *44*(1), 124–138. https://doi.org/10.1080/02602938.2018.1484881

Kahneman, D. (2011). *Thinking, fast and slow*. Macmillan. https://us.macmillan.com/books/9780374533557/thinkingfastandslow

Lazarus, J. (2021). Negativity bias: An evolutionary hypothesis and an empirical programme. *Learning and Motivation*, *75*, 101731. https://doi.org/10.1016/j.lmot.2021.101731

Li, J., & De Luca, R. (2014). Review of assessment feedback. *Studies in Higher Education*, *39*(2), 378–393. https://doi.org/10.1080/03075079.2012.709494

López-Pellisa, T., Rotger, N., & Rodríguez-Gallego, F. (2021). Collaborative writing at work: Peer feedback in a blended learning environment. *Education and Information Technologies*, *26*(1), 1293–1310. https://doi.org/10.1007/s10639-020-10312-2

Patchan, M. M., Schunn, C. D., & Correnti, R. J. (2016). The nature of feedback: How peer feedback features affect students' implementation rate and quality of revisions. *Journal of Educational Psychology*, *108*(8), 1098–1120. https://doi.org/10.1037/edu0000103

Price, M., Handley, K., & Millar, J. (2011). Feedback: Focusing attention on engagement. *Studies in Higher Education*, *36*(8), 879–896. https://doi.org/10.1080/03075079.2010.483513

Price, M., Handley, K., Millar, J., & O'Donovan, B. (2010). Feedback: All that effort, but what is the effect? *Assessment & Evaluation in Higher Education*, *35*(3), 277–289. https://doi.org/10.1080/02602930903541007

Ramage, J. D., Bean, J. C., & Bean, J. C. (2015). *The Allyn and Bacon guide to writing*. Pearson Education. https://www.pearson.com/en-us/subject-catalog/p/allyn--bacon-guide-to-writing-the/P200000002195/9780137477555

Ramesh, D., & Sanampudi, S. K. (2022). An automated essay scoring systems: A systematic literature review. *Artificial Intelligence Review*, *55*(3), 2495–2527. https://doi.org/10.1007/s10462-021-10068-2

Rutner, S., & Scott, R. (2022). Use of artificial intelligence to grade student discussion boards: An exploratory study. *Information Systems Education Journal*, *20*(4), 4. https://isedj.org/2022-20/n4/ISEDJv20n4p4.html

Sadler, D. R. (1989). Formative assessment and the design of instructional systems. *Instructional Science*, *18*(2), 119–144. https://doi.org/10.1007/BF00117714

Sipple, S. (2007). Ideas in practice: Developmental writers' attitudes toward audio and written feedback. *Journal of Developmental Education*, *30*(3), 22–31. https://www.jstor.org/stable/42775244

Värlander, S. (2008). The role of students' emotions in formal feedback situations. *Teaching in Higher Education*, *13*(2), 145–156. https://doi.org/10.1080/13562510801923195

Warnock, S. (2008). Responding to student writing with audio-visual feedback. In T. Carter & M. A. Clayton (Eds.), *Writing and the iGeneration: Composition in the computer-mediated classroom* (pp. 201–227). Fountainhead Press. https://redshelf.com/app/ecom/book/1711652/writing-and-the-igeneration-1711652-9781644854617-terry-carter-and-maria-a-clayton

Yucel, R., Bird, F. L., Young, J., & Blanksby, T. (2014). The road to self-assessment: Exemplar marking before peer review develops first-year students' capacity to judge the quality of a scientific report. *Assessment & Evaluation in Higher Education*, *39*(8), 971–986. https://doi.org/10.1080/02602938.2014.880400

Chapter 3

Troubleshooting

INTRODUCTION

Writing is a technology not natural to us as compared with orality (Ong, 2013). Communicating clearly with neither verbal tone nor nonverbal gesture creates the "need for exquisite circumspection that makes writing agonizing work" (p. 102). The agony referenced here makes troubleshooting difficult. On the one hand, it can be tempting to adopt a laissez faire attitude and there are several compelling reasons to do so. Lack of time, energy, and pedagogical training are just a few of the obvious. At the other extreme is the professor who is writing the student's paper for them.

I have fallen into this second trap on more than one occasion, including the time a student had to gently correct me. This situation occurred when I was a resident fellow at Stanford, helping out the peer writing tutor (Jessica) who was overwhelmed with the volume of students who wanted her to read and help improve their work. After Jessica and I set up shop in the student lounge, we were both inundated with student requests. The students' papers were so interesting that I found myself getting a little too enthusiastic, adding my own thoughts to their work rather than coaching them appropriately. Catching this behavior out of the corner of her eye, Jessica informed me, "Uhm, Laura, they told us in training not to write students' papers for them because they're supposed to be learning how to do it and also it's an academic integrity issue." Yikes!

A big part of helping students successfully troubleshoot writing challenges is understanding the nature of writing and why it can be so difficult. Students and faculty describe writing challenges with words like "perfectionism" and "procrastination," words that capture elements of the problem. But a deeper understanding of the true challenges of writing can suggest more substantive interventions, which are the foci of this chapter.

As Ong (2013) points out, writing is a technology not natural to us as compared with orality. Communicating clearly with neither verbal tone nor nonverbal gesture creates the "need for exquisite circumspection that makes writing agonizing work" (p. 102). This difficulty inherent to writing is exacerbated by the reality that today's students face challenges like less emphasis on writing in K-12 education (Applebee & Langer, 2009), heightened problems with focus (Carr, 2020), and imposter phenomenon (Clance & Imes, 1978). I will share some of the current literature on these topics as well as concrete strategies for helping students anticipate, identify, and overcome these problems. I will also provide profiles of typical student challenges and tips for addressing them.

TROUBLESHOOTING PROBLEMS STEMMING FROM THE NOVICE/EXPERT CONUNDRUM

I started writing this chapter in the middle of Spring Semester, 2023. My first-year master's students were making me bananas as they fretted frequently about the paper I had assigned. The due date loomed. Students' complaints fell into the following themes:

> "I don't know what to write about."
> "I don't know what you want."
> "I don't know how to do this."

If you have been teaching for more than a couple of weeks, these comments probably don't surprise you. Yet they may perplex you, as they did me. Regarding Comment #1, how could the students not be delighted with me for letting them choose their own topic? Isn't that so much better than making them write about something they don't care about? Comment #2: How do they not know what I want? It's right there on the syllabus. I posted examples. What more can I do? Comment #3 can't even be true. Of course students know how to write. They had English classes where they learned how to do this, right?

Wrong. I was engaging in what can be a design flaw if not managed thoughtfully; that is, issuing an expert assignment to novices. Remember in Chapter 1 when I discussed the expert blind spot? I shared my adventures as a novice cook, flummoxing my stepmother with questions and frustrations to which it was difficult for her to relate. "I know you know how to cook," she had to have thought, "You've been feeding yourself for decades." And it was true: I had made many grilled cheese sandwiches and the like. But it was a leap from the grilled cheese sandwich to dishes with many ingredients and steps involved. The way I started to learn was through imitating real cooks, mostly on Wikihow and YouTube.

Imitation is an underappreciated and even sometimes denigrated aspect of moving from novice to expert. We may tolerate culinary education via internet video, but we often view writing as too special or important to imitate. "Find your voice," we instead tell students. We may say it in the spirit of empowerment, but they may hear it as an impossible demand more like, "FIND YOUR DAMN VOICE!" I do want my students to find their voice in writing, but I now see that this can be daunting to a novice. It could be the culinary equivalent of someone demanding I become the next Alice Waters in a 15-week semester.

Sommers and Saltz's (2004) excellent piece, *The Novice as Expert: Writing the Freshman Year*, helped me both identify the expert-novice problem and discover imitation as an underappreciated aspect of academic writing. They liken this process to learning how to use the tools of a craft: "Freshmen might not be able to fashion their own tools or even know which tool to use under what condition, but they learn by holding the expert's tools in their hands, trying them out, imitating as they learn" (p. 135). Again, the cooking metaphor works here. I learned about mixers and Dutch ovens from repeatedly watching other people use them; they were in no way intuitive to me.

There may be creative writing prodigies, but I doubt there are academic writers for whom the enterprise is intuitive. As Sommers and Saltz (2004) go on to explain, "Writing development is painstakingly slow because academic writing is never a student's mother tongue; its conventions require instruction and practice, lots of imitation and experimentation in rehearsing other people's arguments before being able to articulate one's own" (p. 145). The key is to wrap one's head around all the complex processes that comprise academic writing so we can help students troubleshoot specific places where they might need clarification and guidance.

The novice provides a helpful way to frame most student writing challenges. First, the novice is a productive frame because it destigmatizes both students and faculty. It helps us refrain from defaulting to the "kids today!" kind of finger pointing that rarely leads to positive results. The novice frame can also help us not be too hard on ourselves because it is indeed challenging to teach skills in which one has developed expertise. Figuring out what's going to be difficult for novices is a big part of learning how to assist them more effectively in academic writing. In my experience, this involves helping students unlearn some of the misconceptions novices often have about writing. Fortunately, students will often help us help them, but sometimes they struggle to describe their challenges with precision and accuracy. Understanding our role as translators can be helpful in getting both our students and ourselves unstuck when working through some of the more common issues.

Writing as Thinking

As discussed in Chapter 1, one of the most common problems for novice writers is that they are often under the impression that they must know exactly what they want to say before they sit down to write. They will often express this problem with language like "writer's block" or "procrastination," but students overuse these terms so it's important to parse it out. I do this by asking diagnostic questions like:

1. What drew you to this topic?
2. Why does this topic matter?
3. Let's pretend there's no paper involved and that we're just friends having a conversation. What would you have to say about this topic?

If the student can respond even minimally to one of these questions, the issue is often more that they have a misconception about the writing process and less of a Big 3 problem. Students sometimes think they must have the entire paper figured out and that they will sit down and type when that happens. If they open their laptop and the words don't flow out of them, they must need to think more.

Students are not foolish to think this is the process; it does seem like one would know what they want to write before they write it. It's counterintuitive to imagine that the process is actually the other way around; writing gets us to thinking. Experts realize this because they have experienced it many times and are therefore more willing to noodle around, knowing that exploring will get them to richer and better material. Novices need experts to help them become more tolerant of the exploration phase of writing. Just naming and explaining my own process of tinkering has helped students understand and value this part of the process. Creating space for tinkering in class can be particularly useful because students see evidence for the process in both their peers' and professor's work. Students tell me they feel less ashamed and overwhelmed by what they formerly called writer's block or procrastination when they have space to talk through their own thoughts about their topic and hear about others' as well.

Speaking of writer's block, that third question, "Let's pretend there's no paper involved and that we're just friends having a conversation. What would you have to say about this topic?" seems to help students when they're stuck. They often relax into that question, telling me all kinds of ideas they have about their topic. I usually start taking notes to capture the gems, then hand them over at the end of the meeting. Students thank me, but I remind them that I simply recorded their words. Just a few words on a piece of paper can convince students that they really do have something to say.

In my many years of teaching writing, I've learned that students are often under the false impression that they are "not allowed" to include their own thoughts in academic writing. They often confuse the (correct) rule that claims require evidence with the (incorrect) notion that there is no room for their own analysis in scholarly work. I've struggled to explain this nuance to students, but recently stumbled into what I'll call the "boring book report vs. editorial rant" analogy. Students know what both things are: boring book reports they had to write where they merely described the plot, characters, and so on, and editorials written with too much emotion and too little factual content. They can see the excesses in fully descriptive reports and overly opinionated tirades, so this framing can help anticipate and address the novice misconception that they must only report or put forth fiery arguments (the latter is less common in my experience, but still sometimes an issue that requires nuanced language to explain).

Once students know they can and should include their own analysis in academic writing, sometimes they feel more confidence in getting started. They have the thoughts and feelings that can help them get started thinking, reading, talking, and writing about their topics. Moreover, sometimes the knowledge that their voice is welcome in their work makes the prospect more pleasurable. Admittedly, permission to include one's own ideas does not necessarily solve the problem of knowing how to get started so reflecting on and sharing one's own writing process can give students a helpful model from which to work.

Writing as Process

I learned about appropriate self-disclosure as part of my master's degree program in counselor education. While I no longer have occasion to use appropriate self-disclosure therapeutically, I find it has many educationally enriching applications. Appropriate self-disclosure simply means sharing one's own experience in a way that might be helpful to the client or, in this case, the student. The "appropriate" caveat is about making sure the experience to be communicated is truly helpful to students (as opposed to a random story one just feels like sharing). Appropriate self-disclosure can facilitate the practice of imitation as previously discussed in this chapter. Appropriate self-disclosure can help faculty modeling their own writing process so students can benefit from seeing a more visceral representation of what can feel like abstract notions of exploring topics and writing as thinking.

I started developing my ideas about appropriate self-disclosure and modeling when writing my first book with a student co-author, Monica Hatfield Price. Monica and I shared a cloud folder where we uploaded drafts, sources, and other material pertinent to the book. Monica described her experience of sharing a folder with me as akin to websites where you can watch your car being built. She observed how I start with an imperfect idea and get super messy as I write notes to myself, use placeholders that only I understand, and generate a lot of text that gets highly reworked or cut as the draft develops. I've been writing professionally for so long that these things seem normal and unnoteworthy to me, but it's these kinds of details that often help students get unstuck. For example, my use of placeholders includes notes such as "insert example" or "find article about x." Monica shared that seeing these notes helped her stop losing focus hunting down details, that she could instead made a note and keep writing before she lost the train of thought. I now make it a point to tell my students what I'm working on and how the process is evolving with the goal of both normalizing challenges and modeling ways to address them.

Free Writing

Unfortunately, most of us seem prone to paralysis when writing. This is especially true for students who have been standardized tested about rules so much that it's difficult to conjure up the free and playful space needed in the early stages of a writing project. Again, my cooking analogy works here. I have a friend (Beth) whose parents were both excellent cooks and compulsive neat freaks. They tried to teach her to cook, but she was so rattled by their constant patrol of messes—to the point where they complained if she left water droplets in the sink—that she gave up. Life went on. Beth never thought of herself as a good cook, but she forgot about how these early experiences shaped her until she met her husband, Matt. Matt is a laid-back person who is not afraid to get himself or the kitchen dirty while expressing his culinary creativity. She watched him being experimental and trying things out, sometimes producing masterpieces, sometimes failing, but always learning and having fun. She also learned messes are not scary and can be cleaned up in accordance with one's own standards of tidiness. As a result of all this messy practice, Beth is now a great cook!

As I stated in Chapter 1, students need permission to get messy if they are to ever get their thoughts out of their head. Freewriting is a useful path in this process. In his classic work on the topic, Elbow (1998) explains that freewriting is not just nice, but absolutely necessary because there is almost a sense of healing that needs to take place for many people before they can feel uninhibited enough to write. Much like Beth who internalized her parents' neuroses without even realizing it, students are frequently so blocked that there is an unlearning process required as a precondition for learning to write.

Elbow (1998) describes the process of articulation aptly, pointing out that people will often ponder aloud something like this, "I want to describe this person I met ... I wouldn't say he was mean, but maybe a little caustic ... no, that's not it ... under socialized. Yes! That's the word. Anyway ...." While it's common to allow this process to happen naturally with verbal speech, people are less comfortable with letting the wrong words get them to the right words in writing. Sometimes this reticence takes the form of not writing at all, just staring at that blank screen unable or unwilling to write the wrong words as part of the process of getting to the right ones.

Elbow (1998) digs more deeply into this problem, identifying how people lose not only their capacity to try out wrong words, but also their instincts about what even constitutes good writing in the first place. He describes this issue eloquently:

> ... some students who have had their words corrected over and over again come to lose all trust in their felt sense: "Why listen to my felt sense if it's just going to lead to what's wrong?" So gradually they learn not to *feel* any

sense of wrongness. As a result, they no longer judge the words they speak or write in terms of any felt meaning—only in terms of *outer standards*: their understanding of how language is supposed to go and what they think teachers and others are looking for.

(xvii)

It's sad to think students lose their own intuition when overcorrected, but fortunately free-writing can undo much of that damage. Before we turn to this solution, however, there is another hidden problem Elbow uncovers in his analysis; namely, that losing one's own sense of wrongness (and, accordingly, also one's own sense of rightness) can produce sycophantic writers who have "learned to spin out skilled and intelligent words and syntax—but the words and syntax are generated *only* by the rules for words and syntax, not by connection with felt meaning" (p.xvii). We all know this student, the one who thinks they are enticing us with their insufferable correctness but who is not in fact saying anything. Elbow correctly warns that "sometimes it's hard to notice the ungrounded quality to the words—especially if the verbal skill is indeed impressive" (p.xvii). This is true, but we must notice and challenge this phenomenon if we want our students to aim higher than appliance-instruction kinds of writing.

Freewriting therefore serves to free up both the underconfident and pedantic among us by silencing the critic and letting the inner voice emerge. Elbow (1998) recommends ten minutes of freewriting as a way of warming up, positing that getting started is often the hardest part of anything challenging. He also advocates assigning students a high volume of freewriting that is submitted to the instructor, but not graded. He then comments only on places he sees the student's voice coming through; this strikes me as a highly effective way of helping students build on strengths and not get stifled by critical feedback. I incorporated this practice into my most recent scholarly writing course and it did seem to help students feel less inhibited and more empowered.

Another benefit of freewriting is that it can catapult students over the main barrier they experience when toiling away at something difficult; namely, that it's not fun. Elbow likens this conundrum to learning to play the piano. Practicing scales over and over again is boring, so it's hard to stay motivated if the student must perfect the scales before attempting the more enticing activity of playing a song. Elbow's view is that it's better to let the student play the song imperfectly while continuing to work on the scales to get a glimpse of what they might achieve if they stick with it. I've seen this happen with both students and myself in the writing process and appreciate how Elbow gives language to the importance of building in this kind of inspiration to keep writers engaged. This strategy works when the student has some inclination toward the task at hand; however, we know that there are many students who would prefer not to write at all. It is to these students to whom I turn my attention in the following section.

TROUBLESHOOTING PROBLEMS STEMMING FROM DISLIKE OF WRITING

I once had a student I'll call Todd. I was teaching the seminar paper course in our master's program and Todd was my most challenging student. I'd had him in other courses where he'd been an absolute delight—always present, polite—a front-row student, even. His papers were never great, but he more than made up for it with his excellent presentations and consistent class participation. After missing several deadlines and submitting multiple substandard drafts in the seminar paper course, I summoned young Todd to my office for a visit. Since we had a nice rapport, I felt comfortable going for the direct approach.

ME: "Why aren't you responding to my feedback and using it to improve your paper? Also, why are you turning things in late?"
TODD: "Because I hate writing so much."

Todd did not even need a moment to deliberate before answering my question. On the surface, it could have easily appeared that Todd was experiencing writer's block or procrastination tendencies, but these can be mere symptoms of a deeper problem that must be addressed at its root cause. Still—though I appreciated Todd's candor about disliking writing—I wasn't sure what I could do with it. So we explored for a while and eventually started talking about our previous courses together. Todd had liked those courses because they required presentations, one of his strengths. As he talked about his enjoyment of public speaking, it occurred to me that Todd was an extrovert. I tried out an idea.

ME: "Do you think you like presenting because you have an audience?"
TODD: "Yeah, presenting is better because there are actual people there that you could impact. It's boring to be by yourself for hours on end writing something only one person is ever going to read. No offense."

Todd and I eventually agreed that he would submit some outlines for his paper in PowerPoint and start imagining it as something that could be repurposed for a presentation in the future. I am not going to claim that Todd produced an award-winning seminar paper, but it was solid and beyond passable. We were both proud of it and Todd remains humored that I have many occasions to tell this story.

The story contains a few lessons worthy of exploration when considering how to troubleshoot students' writing challenges. First, students need personalized attention when struggling, a topic I'll discuss more in Chapter 4. There is only so much we can do for a class when it comes to writing instruction; students have unique challenges that sometimes have to be negotiated individually.

In that negotiation, students need educators to ask them real questions in the spirit of brainstorming. When I asked Todd why he was turning in such bad writing, I truly had no idea what he would say. If he had cited inability to focus or mental health challenges, for example, the conversation would have gone in a different direction. Being open to each student's explanations requires a willingness to dive into uncertainty with them. As I tell my students when I invite them to office hours, I may not have the answer, but I'll get into the mess with them and try to help them sort it out.

The Perils of Extrinsic Motivation

Another lesson I want to discuss in Todd's story is this idea of disliking writing. Todd may be blunter than most in expressing it, but he is not alone. As Teresa, one of the student research participants in a study I conducted about academic struggle so aptly put it, "If you don't like what you're learning, it's hard to pay attention" (Harrison & Mathuews, 2022, p. 407). Unfortunately, (dis)pleasure is an underappreciated and undertheorized phenomenon despite the role it plays in intrinsic motivation. As a society, we have largely settled for extrinsic motivation as the answer when students dislike a task. Advice given in this domain includes exhortations like, "You may not like learning this now, but you'll need this skill later!" The corresponding treatment tends to be Skinnerean in nature, a piece of proverbial cheese for completion of the desirable behavior and perhaps a little shock for failure to stay on task.

There is also self-imposed external motivation like choice architecture, the strategy of designing one's surroundings to point oneself toward the goal and away from undesired behavior. An example of this approach might be stocking the kitchen with healthy food that is visible and easy to reach while hiding junk food or not keeping it in the house at all. The idea is to make the target choice easy and the tempting option inconvenient by design.

These kinds of strategies are embodied in the "nudge," a concept made famous by Thaler and Sunstein's (2009) popular book on the topic. The idea behind the nudge is that self-control is sometimes too difficult so we can create lower-hanging fruit to gently point our choices in the direction of our goals. Fitbits are a good example of this concept; subtle prompts to take more steps can add up to big strides toward long-term wellness goals. I was a resident fellow at Stanford when the Fitbit came out in 2009 and—as is the California way—the students were early adopters. I recall running into my neighbor with her very spirited three-year-old son and noticed he was wearing several Fitbits. "The students like to put their Fitbits on him because he racks up their step counts," she explained. This funny little story illustrates the limits of the nudge; namely, it can stunt the growth of internal motivation and encourage people to game the system.

I'm not going to say that these sorts of behavioral interventions never work because that would be hypocritical. For example, I have a sweater I call "Todd" because it resulted from the online shopping I allowed myself as a reward for getting through the first draft of his seminar paper. The Pomodoro method discussed in Chapter 1 also reflects a bit of behaviorism in its on task/on break design. It's been my experience that behavioral strategies work well when students (or myself) just need a push to get going. When we're convinced that the task at hand is worth doing, a little extrinsic motivation can help us get unstuck. For students like Todd and Teresa, however, extrinsic motivation alone often leads to attempts to game the system like the students were doing when they strapped their Fitbits to the neighbor kid.

Until recently, this kind of behavior was not too much of a concern in writing instruction because it was not particularly easy to game the system. Plagiarism has always been an issue, but we have tools to detect and deter it. The widespread availability of generative artificial intelligence (AI) like ChatGPT, however, could become the academic equivalent of cheating on one's step count. "But wait," you say, "surely Stanford students were smart enough to know they would not reap the health benefits of artificially boosted step counts." The students were indeed smart enough to understand this point and valued their health enough to continue to take their own steps while playing a fun game with my neighbor's child. That valuing of the thing itself rather than the points associated with it is key to understanding and inculcating the more effective and sustainable tool in education: Internal motivation. This is even more important in the era of generative AI, a topic that warrants elaboration as it is upending writing instruction at the moment.

Leveraging Generative AI as an Opportunity to Recommit to Intrinsic Motivation

I doubt that readers will need too much of an explanation of generative AI by the time this book comes out but, for the uninitiated, here is a brief explanation. You can now open ChatGPT or any of the other generative AI programs on the market and type in a prompt like, "Write a 3000-word essay on the merits of standardized testing. Use 20 references. Include a counterargument." The program will then spit out a document more or less matching the criteria. "More or less" ranges widely; I have tried several prompts and the quality has been both eerily good and comically bad. I don't want to say too much more about ChatGPT because it is evolving so rapidly that my description is sure to be obsolete by the time I finish writing this chapter. There are a few key issues that will likely endure, however, so it is worth discussing them here.

I have a colleague I lovingly call "Creepy Robot Guy" as a homage to his scholarly identity in the field of all things tech. His real name is Greg Kessler and he invited me to one of the many panel discussions created after ChatGPT came on the scene in early 2023. As we discussed the panel, Greg made an insightful remark that went something like this: "We're way too worried about students using ChatGPT to cheat. The bigger issue is that too much academic writing reads like it was written by robots anyway. If we're going to suck the life out of writing, why do we care if robots or people do it?"

I think Greg has the right approach to generative AI, which can neither be ignored nor used to undermine the importance of students learning to write. As a speaker at the University of California, San Diego Academic Integrity Virtual Symposium explained, the purpose of assigning writing is not to put more student essays into the world (Mills, 2023). The point—as mentioned earlier in this chapter—is that writing teaches thinking. Writing is central to the mission of higher education because of this vital function. Writing also teaches people how to persuade, an essential skill in a democratic society.

In her analysis of the limits of incentives, Grant (2011) asserts, "... [the] reason to be critical of social engineering is that it tends to inhibit processes of persuasion" (p. 138). Grant argues that social engineering (and its cousins, incentives and external motivation) obscures the power dimension by presenting it as a benign choice rather than an arrangement framed by the more powerful subject to an unwitting object. From defendants punished for not accepting pleas to countries extended loan offers in exchange for austerity measures, Grant offers a plethora of examples demonstrating how incentives too often function as offers disempowered entities cannot refuse. She positions persuasion as an alternative more appropriate in both its transparency and assumption of agency among involved parties.

It is in this idea of persuasion that I have had some success in helping students identify, use, and leverage their intrinsic motivation. Going back to Todd's case, the subject of his seminar paper was the issues transgender students face in campus housing. Some of these issues have been resolved in recent years, but Todd was writing at a time when it was not a given that most colleges and universities had a responsibility to meet the needs of transgender students. Todd worked in campus housing, so he had firsthand experience of students for whom gender-based room assignments and restroom use presented many problems. He had both the empathy and expertise to write a potentially uniquely compelling work on the topic. When we talked about his paper, he offered me a clue as to why he was having a hard time feeling motivated to write when he said "just for one person, no offense."

While it may aggravate faculty when students make comments like this, they do have a point. It *is* a giant hassle to do something you find frustrating when you think of it as just another hoop to jump through on your way to something better. Sometimes I feel a version of this myself when I'm grading papers and long to be working on my own scholarship. If I didn't see the value in providing students with detailed, personalized feedback, it would be tempting to slap a few stock comments on their work, assign some grades, and call it a day. Perhaps this is why grading/feedback is so often outsourced to teaching assistants or automation. Hence, clarity about one's "why" is important for students and faculty alike.

Selling Writing as Intrinsically Worthy

Why do so many students dislike writing? As someone who cannot ever remember not loving writing, this is a difficult question for me. I'm guessing this is true for most faculty who enter academic life knowing that most disciplines require a serious and sustained commitment to writing. Hence, it can be hard for us to troubleshoot motivational issues with student writing because it's difficult to empathize with a situation you can't really imagine.

It can therefore be useful to translate student concerns into another domain; for me, that would be math. I know I disliked math and therefore encountered motivational challenges in math courses, especially statistics which I had to take at the high school, undergraduate, master's, and doctoral levels. I never fell in love with statistics, but upon reflection I realize that my dislike for it decreased each time I took it. I recognize that this is partly due to the fact that all of my statistics instructors were excellent. It's like they knew they taught an unpopular subject and had to sell it a bit. Further, they were good at convincing students that failure to understand statistics could make one vulnerable to manipulation. While I didn't enjoy math, I did value critical thinking so this line of reasoning stimulated my intrinsic motivation.

Sommers and Saltz (2004) found that college students who made the greatest gains in writing: "(1) initially accept their status as novices and (2) see in writing a larger purpose than fulfilling an assignment" (p. 124). I discussed the novice topic earlier in this chapter; the "larger purpose" idea warrants some discussion here because it relates directly to the kind of intrinsic motivation that comes from a deeper place than simply meeting a requirement. Intrinsic motivation is what gets us to what Csikszentmihalyi (1991) called *flow* in his seminal work bearing the same title. As discussed in Chapter 2, flow describes that state in which we can lose ourselves in the pleasure of activity for the intrinsic worth of the experience. Flow is a highly desirable state for achieving the kind of focus necessary to produce meaningful writing.

Just as the widespread availability of generative AI heightens the need for faculty to tap into students' intrinsic motivation, Generation Z's lack of interest in some of the incentives that appealed to previous generations calls attention to the limits of external motivation in the zeitgeist of the 2020s. McMurtrie (2023) offered the following explanation of this phenomenon:

> But as many students continue to exhibit debilitating levels of anxiety, hopelessness, and disconnection—what one professor termed "militant apathy"—colleges are struggling to come up with a response beyond short-term solutions.

The standard curricula in higher ed—and the way it's discussed primarily as a path to economic success—can exacerbate those feelings. Students are told the main point of college is to move up the economic ladder so no wonder it feels transactional. And the threat of failure must seem paralyzing given the high cost of a degree. but what if students believed college was more than that? That it was a place to discuss the big questions bouncing around in their heads, learn a vocabulary to describe what's happening around them, engage with the messiness of the world, and navigate their place in it. That it was meaningful.

(para 4–5)

You may be thinking this is a bit off-topic, that a critique of higher education's instrumentalist bent is beyond the scope of a book about helping students write. I would have thought so, too, until I spent so much time listening to students' struggles with writing specifically and school more generally. Despite the robust scholarship demonstrating the connection between meaning, motivation, and learning, the dominant narrative about higher education too often pushes instrumentalist thinking. Today's students face monumental challenges that stimulate a heightened need for work that is relevant and meaningful. As McMurtrie (2023) goes on to discuss later in this article, Generation Z is less motivated by joining the status quo than previous generations so framing education as the path to success as defined by some mainstream standard does not speak to their hearts and souls.

The good news in all of this is that this generation can be appealed to by tapping into that rebellious and entrepreneurial spirit. I have found by Gen Z students to be more than willing to reflect and articulate the things that matter to them. The next step is to make space for students to mine this material with their own unique forms of expression.

Making Room for Students' Writing Styles

I never had this particular conversation with Todd, but I suspect that he liked speaking better than writing because there are fewer rules. When a student is discussing something they care about, no one interrupts them to demand a source or correct their grammar. They have the freedom to express themselves without an annoying authority figure critiquing their point. This is why students will write all day in text messages and chat boxes; no one hovers with a digital red pen in these spaces. The trick is to channel that free-spirited verbosity into writing assignments where students can develop a positive association with both writing and having one's work read without judgment.

One way I try to accomplish this task is through having students produce written reflections on the assigned readings before each class. Admittedly, my initial goal in assigning these reflections was to enforce reading so we could have more substantive class discussions. I feared the students would revolt, but it turned out that they liked writing these short papers. Students have told me on more than one occasion that they look forward to reading my responses because the exchange is very conversational rather than critical. They like that I react to what they're saying without commenting on grammar and spelling.

I wish I could say that I'm such an inspirational teacher that I had planned it this way, but the truth is that I had neither the time nor the bandwidth to correct the 75 or so papers collecting in my various assignment drop boxes each week. I also lack the time and bandwidth to worry too much about my own writing, so in effect the students and my comments to each other often read like text messages. Of course, this activity does not totally solve the problem of getting students to enjoy writing longer academic papers, but it can provide proof to students that they do have something to say and can say it. I knew I had struck gold on this point when my students were complaining about the 5000-word paper I had due in my class this semester and a student pointed out that it was just 10 reading reflections. Everyone knew that was not entirely true, but it was true enough to make them feel better!

Some people truly hate writing, but I suspect more people would like it or at least hate it less if they could do it sometimes without internal or external editors looming. As Lanham (2007) deftly put it in observation of U.S. writing customs, "We pare away all sense of verbal play, of self-satisfying joy in language, and then wonder why American students have a motivation problem and don't want to write" (p. 18). My students will tell you (loudly) that I have played Lanham's killjoy on too many occasions. I'm trying to strike a balance between my way too slacker reading of students' reflective writing and sometimes too uptight responses to their academic writing. Why not make more space for students' voices and styles in academic writing? The obvious benefit is that it may increase their motivation to write, which is reason enough given the strong relationship between intrinsic motivation and student success.

Reading for Voice

A significant challenge in helping students find their voice in academic writing is that they often don't know where to start. Students may not know how to produce a distinct voice, so starting with consuming voice more intentionally can be useful. We talk casually about "liking" or "disliking" a piece of writing, but we are not often encouraged to pinpoint what it it we're responding to. Sometimes, we simply agree or disagree with the argument, but other times it's the author's tone, diction, and/or a host of other stylistic choices that make something pleasurable or painful to read. Asking students to dig into these points with greater precision can help them begin the process of developing their own style.

A very simple way to begin is to ask students to bring in a piece of academic writing that spoke to them. By "academic," I include the *New York Times, Atlantic,* and other more mainstream publications because the writing is often more varied than that which can be found in most traditional academic journals. I give the students a list of things to look for like tone, word choice, inclusion of counter-arguments, and so forth and they generally do a great job of simply noticing these elements that we're all used to glossing over when we read. This is usually enough to get their wheels turning.

One variation on this assignment that I've found particularly instructive is asking students to find a piece with which they disagree, but that made them think. I've been using Gonzalez's, *Why Rich People Love Quiet* as my own example. The title alone jarred me from my lazy skimming, causing me to immediately object to the author's claims that loving quiet is a bit entitled and maybe even bratty. I fought with the author through every paragraph but, by the end, I could see her point. I felt challenged. Gonzalez was convincing in her vivid descriptions of feeling marginalized when she and her friends were constantly "shushed" for simply talking and laughing:

> I just hadn't counted on everything [in college] being so quiet. The hush crept up on me at first. I would be hanging out with my friends from orientation when one of our new roommates would start ostentatiously readying themselves for bed at a surprisingly early hour. Hints would be taken, eyes would be rolled, and we'd call it a night ... I soon realized that silence was more than the absence of noise; it was an aesthetic to be revered. Yet it was an aesthetic at odds with who I was. Who a lot of us were.
>
> (para 6)

Talking and laughing are two beautifully human activities that the world needs more, not less of. How could I have never thought about this perspective before? Why should some peoples' preference for silence always trump others' desire for merriment and connection? I had truly not thought of these questions before and was impressed by the author's ability to plant them in my mind. In a world with so much entrenchment of views, it felt intellectually satisfying to wrestle with genuinely new questions and viewpoints.

I ask my students to write a reaction paper to the pieces they select, so I wrote one myself in response to *Why Rich People Love Quiet*. I share this excerpt of my paper as an example of how this exercise can help demystify the writing process, allowing readers to identify and articulate language that moves them:

> In Gonzalez's story, I am the bad guy! If she is the drunken asshole in my story, I am the killjoy in hers. It's natural to center oneself as the protagonist in one's story, but how shortsighted, narrow, and rigid do we become if that's the only story we let in? Gonzalez's story made me revisit mine in light of hers. I maintain a dislike for noise; it's an objective fact about me at this

point. But I can see now that the circumstances by which I developed this trait are anything but neutral. I did not grow up rich, but I was raised in a part of the country where even lower middle-class people can afford land and space, both of which tend to attune us to quiet. Gonzalez's formative years were spent in a densely populated neighborhood where noise signaled people and connection. What we experience as noise, music, connection, peace, etc. varies accordingly.

I've learned through this assignment that I'm drawn to writing that gently, but powerfully, asks readers to consider a deeper or more nuanced view on either a topic that seems benign or a subject about which they've made up their mind. I went on to describe this process for my students:

Gonzalez's history lesson made me revisit some other memories that I had not thought too much about, such as when I lived in the super rich community of Palo Alto and residents tried to pass an ordinance requiring noise reduction mechanisms on leaf blowers. This seemed like a good idea to me at the time, but now I think about the almost 100% low-income immigrant workers operating the leaf blowers. Did they have to pay for new ones to accommodate wealthy people's need for quiet? Who accommodated their need for new equipment? More recently, a former student told me about a flight delay that was exacerbated by her rich community passing a noise ordinance wherein airplanes had a curfew placed on their landing times. So hundreds of people are forced to stay elsewhere overnight each time a plane is delayed so that others don't have to hear it land past 11pm?!? Gonzalez made me start asking questions about what had previously seemed normal.

I probably had some inkling of this idea before doing the assignment, but the exercise helped me identify and clarify my own goals as a writer. Consequently, I can develop my voice with greater knowledge and skill and model this process for my students. They, in turn, were eager to share their examples, discussing with greater depth and precision the kinds of writing that made them think new thoughts. It's edifying to watch students evolve past the "like/dislike" comment card–style evaluation of works into more thorough analyses of what inspires them as thinkers.

THE OVERDIAGNOSIS OF IMPOSTER PHENOMENON (SYNDROME)

I opened this chapter by naming writer's block, procrastination, and imposter syndrome as "The Big 3" overdiagnosed problems when it comes to students' writing challenges. I addressed the first two with deeper dives into the more precise barriers students experience when developing their writing skills and provided some strategies for overcoming them. The last of the Big 3 I want to begin discussing in this chapter's conclusion and transition to the next chapter is imposter phenomenon (more commonly known as imposter syndrome"). Imposter phenomenon has become too much of a good thing. Originally coined by Oberlin professors Pauline Chance and Suzanne Imes, imposter syndrome describes the experience of feeling uncertain or unconfident about one's abilities despite evidence of one's competence.

Chance and Imes developed their thinking about this idea in the 1970s as they observed many highly capable women paralyzed by fear of being discovered as not as smart as they had somehow tricked others into believing them to be. As an 80s child and 90s young adult interested in gender issues, I don't recall hearing this term, but it seems to have become part of the popular culture in the 2000s as many famous women raised its profile by diagnosing themselves with it on social media (Tulshyan & Burey, 2021; Jamison, 2023). Like many good ideas, many believe this one has gone too far, including Tulshyan and Burey, whose 2021 *Harvard Business Review* piece, *Stop Telling Women They Have Imposter Syndrome*, is widely cited as a counterargument.

Tulshyan and Burey (2021) object to the diagnosis of imposter syndrome because they view it as blaming individuals for structural problems. They argue that women—particularly women of color—feel fraudulent not because of some internal psychological problem, but because systems were designed to exclude them: "In truth, we don't belong because we were never supposed to belong. Our presence in most of these spaces is a result of decades of grassroots activism and begrudgingly developed legislation" (para 11). Chance and Imes agree with this critique, asserting that it was a problem when the term shifted from their original idea of *imposter phenomenon* to the more popular *imposter syndrome*. As Jamison (2023) discussed in her interview with Chance and Imes, "… the phenomenon is 'an experience rather than a pathology,' and their aim was always to normalize this experience rather than to pathologize it" (p. 31). In this interview, Chance also pointed out that imposter phenomenon was meant to give language to an experience and acknowledged that it was insufficient as a solution to the structural problem creating that experience, "When mothers came to Chance describing their imposter feelings, her advice was not 'Work on your feelings.' It was 'Get more childcare.'" (p. 31).

This is a truly important critique of imposter phenomenon/syndrome and one that I'm surprised my students don't express. They are all over similar criticisms of resilience and grit for their victim-blaming subtexts but seem to not see these qualities in imposter syndrome. In fact, they gravitate toward imposter syndrome and use it as a catch-all for all kinds of problems that would be more accurately described as lack of focus or annoyance with the reality that writing is just hard a lot of the time. The mislabeling wouldn't matter if it were simply a matter of semantics, but unfortunately inaccurate diagnosis leads to ineffective treatment, which is why I feel the need to draw attention to this issue. In my experience chairing doctoral students, nearly all of them cited imposter syndrome as an obstacle to their progress. Acknowledging that my diagnosis might not be better than theirs, I would still argue that the label really only applied to one of the 20 students I have chaired thus far. This student fits the profile of having writing proficiency and working hard yet flailing due to debilitating feelings of inadequacy. The others either didn't really struggle beyond what is normal effort for a task that is fairly difficult or lacked a strong educational foundation in academic writing skills.

This second point echoes Tulshyan and Burey's (2021) critiques of imposter syndrome masking challenges more correctly identified as rooted in structural inequality. We know that students receive vastly unequal K-12 educations due to unequal school funding but rarely think of this problem when troubleshooting academic challenges in postsecondary settings. I would imagine that most college faculty are aware of disparities resulting from students attending underresourced schools, but they either don't come to mind or we're not sure what to do with them when we see them manifested in students' papers. Maybe it's easier for *us* to chalk it up to imposter syndrome and send the student off to the counseling center rather than owning that the buck stops with us to at least try to level things out.

The inconvenient reality is that most of the quality differences I see in students' work stem from differences in their academic preparation, not their psyches. To be sure, the two phenomena are related. It's a lot easier to like school when your mind associates learning with reasonably sized classes held in clean, safe spaces led by caring and creative teachers. I experienced this myself when my parents took me out of underfunded and somewhat chaotic public elementary schools and put me in a quiet Catholic school where I benefited from a lot of personalized instruction. By the time I arrived at the doorstep of a university, I had written many essays. I had learned how to formulate a thesis, find sources, present sources, and write in a way that appealed to college professors. I could face increasingly challenging writing assignments because I had the foundational skills necessary to the task. As importantly, I knew that writing was still hard even with this good preparation, so I wasn't blindsided by the experience of words not always coming easily or quickly. I didn't—and still don't—get particularly frustrated or upset by writing challenges because I have the tools to handle them.

Imposter syndrome can be a self-defeating frame for students because there are not great tools for addressing it. Imposter syndrome also lets faculty off the hook because we can abdicate responsibility for the emotional realm. I wonder if our collective attachment to imposter syndrome functions as what Berlant (2011) called *cruel optimism*, "an attachment to something that is actually an obstacle to your flourishing" (p. 1). Instead of facing the harder problem of many students' underpreparation for college-level writing, we've bought into an explanation that allows students and faculty alike to do the easier work of cheerleading rather than the thornier task of leveling the playing field.

HIGHER EDUCATION'S EFFICIENCY MENACE

Writing for the Morehouse College student newspaper, *The Maroon Tiger*, an 18-year-old Martin Luther King Junior wrote, "Education which stops with efficiency may prove the greatest menace to society." The final issue I deem worthy of some troubleshooting is what I've been calling higher education's efficiency menace. Again, you may wonder why this topic warrants discussion in a book about helping students write, but the reality is that our work takes place in an institutional context. Both writing and helping students write are inherently inefficient undertakings. As such, there are hidden forces working against both our students' and our efforts. Suggesting systemic solutions would be beyond the scope of this book, but surfacing these mitigating factors so that we can be aware of them and perhaps combat them on the individual level has helped me and it is my hope that it will help you, too.

In *The Slow Professor, Challenging the Culture of Speed in the Academy*, Berg and Seeber (2016) warn that overwork can make faculty "hate students" (p. 50). "Hate" jolted me into the question of whether I've ever gotten to this point myself. "No, I have not," I calmly reassured myself, then thought of all the related terms that would not have let me off the hook so easily. I've definitely felt resentful of and overwhelmed by students and recall students' stories from my own research where participants talked about noticing these vibes from faculty. I was on sabbatical when conducting this particular study, so it was easy for me to be present and emotionally available when the 50 students I interviewed told me about their experiences of academic struggle (Harrison & Mathuews, 2022). I remember feeling surprised that so many of them specifically cited professors' impatience with questions as a challenge to their ability to navigate academic challenges. To be honest, I felt a little pearl clutchy as I imagined these insensitive professors being mean to the sweet young person sitting in front of me.

I finished up my interviews in February 2020, and we all know what happened the following month. By the next semester, I was scrambling to adjust to online school like the rest of the world. I was fielding a ton of questions both inside and outside my expertise. I had to fight my annoyance with turned-off cameras and constant demands to be flexible. I was relieved when life returned to (more or less) normal, thinking the relatively easy rapport I had always enjoyed with students would be there waiting for me.

I was in for a rude awakening on this point as were many others given the proliferation of articles in the *Chronicle of Higher Education, Inside Higher Education,* and similar outlets decrying the challenges of Gen Z. No one has determined an exact diagnosis and treatment of the problem, which is likely too complicated to warrant neat and tidy solutions anyway. But I think of Berg and Seeber's (2016) warning and the fact that they wrote it well before the pandemic. This theme of overwork runs through the *Chronicle of Higher Education* and other higher education periodicals but does not seem to intersect with the Gen Z-as-problem strain. I'm starting to think the two issues are more related than they might initially appear to be. What if today's students are reacting to years of neglect by overworked parents and teachers who do not have the time to offer the sufficient adult attention needed to develop resilience and focus on learning? This may seem like a counterintuitive notion given the concern that today's youth are pampered snowflakes, but indulgence is not the same as attention. In fact, treats and toys (especially of the digital nature) are often substitutes for being fully present.

I write all of this not to judge parents and/or teachers; we're all stuck in systems demanding more work to evade the precarity that comes from a declining middle class. Over a decade ago, I left an administrative position at Stanford University because I loved teaching and wanted to do it full time. When I started my faculty position at Ohio University in 2011, I mostly felt like I had the time and bandwidth to offer high quality, personalized teaching and advising to my students. And this was before I had tenure, so the pressure to produce scholarship was higher then than it is now that I am a full professor. Yet the last few years have proven the most difficult because the pressures for ever-increasing enrollment while faculty lines disappear are squeezing the majority of professors and staff who work closely with students. Class sizes and advising/counseling caseloads have increased with demands for more recruitment, marketing, and spreadsheet production eclipsing the time and energy we used to have for students. Those at the top making these kinds of decisions are largely out of touch with students and therefore do not see the effects of their actions.

Berg and Seeber (2016) write, "Being ethical may actually mean being inefficient at times" (p. 60). There is a lot to troubleshoot in student writing and the process is anything but efficient. It requires close attention, patience, and valuing what students have to say as important and worthy of our time and energy. While it's not likely we will find people on college campuses who openly declare that writing is not important, the reward structures and time demands would not indicate that it's a priority. Therefore, I've found it helpful to understand the choice I make to do the labor-intensive work of helping students write as a countercultural one.

This framing helps me to avoid unrealistic expectations of institutional acknowledgement, practicing what I preach in terms of intrinsic motivation. Having a clear-eyed understanding of the lack of institutional support for writing instruction at all levels also helped me see that developing a course on writing could serve as a corrective to this issue. The addition of our scholarly writing course has eased my time pressure as I am able to teach it on load and has helped out my colleagues by giving them more well-prepared students in the dissertation process. Ideas for developing a scholarly writing course will therefore be the topic of the next chapter.

CONCLUSION

I opened this chapter with a discussion of the importance of gaining a deeper and more precise understanding of the kinds of writing challenges students face in order to provide a more accurate diagnosis and treatment. While commonly referenced issues like imposter phenomenon, procrastination, and writer's block do exist, we run the risk of defaulting to these explanations when we are unaware of other challenges students face. Some of these challenges include not understanding writing as thinking, frustration with the seemingly subjective nature of writing standards, and the limits of external motivation. Individual and systemic interventions for addressing these challenges were discussed in the context of educational inequality. In the next chapter, I will expand on this idea with material about how to build writing courses centered around "new majority students."

REFERENCES

Applebee, A. N., & Langer, J. A. (2009). EJ extra: What is happening in the teaching of writing? *The English Journal*, *98*(5), 18–28.

Berg, M., & Seeber, B. K. (2016). *The slow professor: Challenging the culture of speed in the academy*. University of Toronto Press. https://utorontopress.com/9781487521851/the-slow-professor/

Berlant (2011). *Cruel optimism*. Duke University Press. https://www.dukeupress.edu/cruel-optimism

Carr, N. (2020). *The shallows: What the Internet is doing to our brains*. WW Norton & Company.

Clance, P. R., & Imes, S. A. (1978). The imposter phenomenon in high achieving women: Dynamics and therapeutic intervention. *Psychotherapy: Theory, research & practice*, *15*(3), 241.

Csikszentmihalyi, M. (1991). *Flow: The psychology of optimal experience*. Harper Collins Publishers. https://www.harpercollins.com/products/flow-mihaly-csikszentmihalyi?variant=32118048686114

Elbow, P. (1998). *Writing with power: Techniques for mastering the writing process*. Oxford University Press. https://global.oup.com/ushe/product/writing-with-power-9780195120189?cc=us&lang=en&

Grant, R. W. (2011). *Strings attached: Untangling the ethics of incentives*. Princeton University Press.

Harrison, L. M., & Mathuews, K. B. (2022). How students experience faculty responses to academic struggle. *Journal of College Student Development*, *63*(4), 399–413.

Jamison, L. (2023, February 13 and 20). Not fooling anyone: The dubious rise of imposter syndrome. *The New Yorker*. https://www.newyorker.com/magazine/2023/02/13/the-dubious-rise-of-impostor-syndrome

Lanham, R. A. (2007). Style: An anti-textbook. *Paul Dry Books*. https://www.pauldrybooks.com/products/style-an-anti-textbook

McMurtrie, B. (2023, February 15). Teaching in the age of 'militant apathy'. *The Chronicle of Higher Education*. https://www.chronicle.com/article/teaching-in-an-age-of-militant-apathy

Mills, A. (2023, April 18). Rethinking writing for assessment in the era of artificial intelligence [Conference presentation]. *Academic Integrity Virtual Symposium*, San Diego, CA. https://academicintegrity.ucsd.edu/events/virtual-symposium.html

Ong, W. J. (2013). *Orality and literacy*. Routledge. https://www.routledge.com/Orality-and-Literacy-30th-Anniversary-Edition/Ong/p/book/9780415538381

Sommers, N., & Saltz, L. (2004). The novice as expert: Writing the freshman year. *College Composition and Communication*, 124–149. https://eric.ed.gov/?id=EJ728781

Thaler, R. H., & Sunstein, C. R. (2009). *Nudge: Improving decisions about health, wealth, and happiness*. Penguin. https://www.penguinrandomhouse.com/books/690485/nudge-by-richard-h-thaler-and-cass-r-sunstein/

Tulshyan, R. & Burey, J. (2021, February 11). Stop telling women they have imposter syndrome. *Harvard Business Review*. https://hbr.org/2021/02/stop-telling-women-they-have-imposter-syndrome

Chapter 4
Developing a Writing Course

INTRODUCTION

If we really want to help students improve their writing, the best way to do so is to offer them an opportunity to focus on this skill without the added pressure of learning other material. Some elements of writing such as time management, writer's block, and feedback have been discussed in previous chapters so I will not elaborate on these when I mention them as part of curriculum development in this chapter. Here, I will focus on identifying skills students need and strategies for helping students learn them. I am fortunate to teach a culturally and linguistically diverse student population, so my thinking about writing course development is informed by this experience. I will leave more specific conversations about cultural and linguistic difference to my colleagues who dive deeply into this topic in Chapter 6, but I will address first generation, socioeconomic status (SES), and U.S. ethnic and regional dialect considerations in this chapter.

My experience is also informed by teaching at an institution where students have received a wide range of writing instruction before they get to my courses. Not surprisingly, both professors' and students' prior knowledge shapes their expectations, often in subtle and unconscious ways. On the faculty side, we tend to think we have a clear idea of what constitutes good writing, but we often find it difficult to convey in ways that are specific enough for students to understand. Similarly, students have different expectations of everything from instructor directiveness to the appropriateness of peer review based on their previous educational experiences. Unpacking these hidden dynamics and making them more explicit requires some work upfront, but it pays off in the long run when faculty and students can communicate their expectations and challenges more effectively, thus reducing anxiety and confusion. Hence my hope is to begin this chapter by shedding some light on the dispositions with which it is helpful to approach writing instruction. I will then show how these approaches are operationalized in the design of group instruction and individual coaching, the main components of an effective writing course.

PLANNING FOR "THE NEW MAJORITY" COLLEGE STUDENTS

"I don't know why these students need so much handholding." "Students don't come to office hours." "Students today seem less mature/pro-active/intelligent ...." These are some of the comments one hears on campuses and in periodicals like *The Chronicle of Higher Education* and *Inside Higher Education*. I think these comments are intentionally general, masking a more specific sentiment: Nostalgia for a time when professors only taught privileged "college-ready" students rather than the "new student majority" of first-generation and/or low-income students. Though generally not considered polite to state this desire directly and openly, I base my assertion on the sizeable body of research—my own and others'—showing frequent breakdowns in faculty-student communication. More often, these challenges are discussed in terms of generational divides, a more politically safe explanation than social class. Generational conflict undoubtedly contributes to the problem, but there are markers that suggest frustration with "new majority" students' real or perceived lack of assimilation into the middle/upper class norms of college culture is the bigger culprit (Ritter, 2023).

An exhaustive review of the literature explicating class tension in higher education is beyond the scope of this book, but it is important to understand how the problem plays out in writing instruction. First, those who are accustomed to teaching what we might call the "old student majority" could expect their students to arrive with what Conley (2007) called "college readiness." Traditionally, that term referred specifically to academic preparedness, but it is also understood as knowledge about collegiate norms, values, and customs. Of course, the situation was not always so simple, but many assumptions spring forth from this understanding. The main assumption is that students are (or should be) ready for the academic, cultural, and social world of college and that any problems reside in the students themselves. Unlike K-12 schooling where the onus for student success is on teachers, college educators have largely been socialized to imagine students are responsible for their own success in postsecondary education.

This may have been a fair belief back in the days when higher education was the domain of the privileged, but it is common knowledge that widening access requires a shift from demanding "college ready" students to creating "student ready" institutions (McNair, et al., 2022). Policy makers and higher education leaders are well aware of the need to support student success and have created scores of initiatives ranging from tutoring centers to enhanced advising to respond to the call. Yet faculty continue to receive very little pedagogical training generally, much less specifically on how they might work effectively with "new majority" students. To at least partially ameliorate this gap, I offer a synthesis of some of the themes that emerge in the composition studies literature on the topic.

Before diving into these highlights, I want to clarify my use of the term, "new majority" student. Traditionally, higher education scholars refer more specifically to first generation, working class, and/or students of color because these are more precise terms. There are disadvantages, however, in that precision fails to capture nuance in this case. For example, Student A's parents may have graduated from college, but worked full time and commuted, and thus do not have a lot of college knowledge to pass on. Student B's parents may not have gone to college, but they may have siblings who did, making Student B in some ways more knowledgeable about what to expect even though they technically fit the traditional definition of first-generation more closely. A related benefit of "new majority" terminology is that it captures intersectionality; students can be first generation and high income, for example. This more nuanced language allows the reader to focus less on parsing concrete categories and more on understanding what is salient about new majority students; that is, their attendance at institutions that were not designed with them in mind.

Differences vs. Deficits

Despite volumes of scholarship on diversity in higher education, there are still many challenges to even discussing differences, which is why it is sometimes avoided. This often-unconscious avoidance leads to what Alfano et al. (2023) call an "overrepresentation of the generic student" (p. 251) in our thinking, planning, and teaching. This generic student is almost always of the "old majority" population. Educators can count on them to understand unwritten rules; for example, the relatively autonomous and self-directed learning that characterizes post-secondary education. New majority students, however, are more likely to have been socialized to expect more hierarchical educational arrangements. As Carter and Thelin (2017) explained, new majority students "... have been educated in directive, mechanical ways while students from wealthier school districts have been allowed more creativity and are expected to engage materials in more critical ways" (p. 8).

This difference is not surprising given that a routinized curriculum is easier to deliver en masse and therefore more likely to dominate financially strapped schools with higher teacher-to-student ratios. Without this knowledge about the class differences in K-12 schools, a professor could mistake a new majority student's questions about what they are looking for in a writing assignment, how long it should be, and so on, as a desire to be spoon-fed, a common complaint among college faculty. Even with the best of intentions, college educators can unwittingly reify educational disparities if they are ignorant about what norms to expect in a truly diverse group of students. Awareness about diversity must include the less obvious work of decentering continuing generation/"old majority" students as the default standard bearers. Educators can unwittingly reify the bias that these students only have assets; Baird and Digler's (2023) study on students' writing strategies shows that continuing generations students often overestimate their abilities, leading to procrastination based on the belief that they had the skill to get by with all-nighters pulled right before due dates. The point is not to criticize either group, but to recognize the complexity of various students' adaptive and less-adaptive proclivities.

Knowledge about the diversity of educational environments that shape our students is the first step in teaching them more effectively. The next step is to truly frame this diversity in the language of difference rather than deficit. In the previous example, it might be tempting to feel sorry for the student who attended a more regimented school and thus see oneself as the fixer of the problem. In terms of writing instruction specifically, Bollig (2019) refers to the stories faculty might tell themselves in this vein as "narratives of transformation through literacy." These narratives position the professor as the savior who lifts the damaged student out of the working class and sets them on the better path of assimilation to middle/upper class sensibilities. Fortunately, there is an alternative to the assimilationist mindset that allows college educators to make the leap from trying to force students to change to meeting them where they are.

Transfer

A large part of what makes helping students write so difficult is that educators often start with how students *should* approach writing rather than how they *do* approach writing. Being prescriptive seems intuitive, practical, and efficient given the busyness of our lives; however, this practice ignores *transfer*, which Baird and Digler (2023) define as "the adaptation of writing-related skills, experience, and knowledge for use in new contexts" (p. 212). Writing instructors need to be interested in transfer because, as the authors continue, "writers rarely begin from scratch but draw on learning from other contexts" (p. 213).

Educators' ability to leverage the knowledge students bring to the classroom relies on their ability to manage class biases. Consider the following example that could appear on the surface to be an objective call on the part of the faculty involved, but which clearly demonstrates class bias:

> Our student participant Scarlet, who had one parent with an associate's degree, performed well when leading a group project but struggled to confront a professor whose course design prevented her from drawing on work experiences she deeply valued. On the other hand, personality benefited the continuing-generation student Steve, who used his charm and exceptional

persuasion to persuade teachers and students of the value of methods he had learned in previously completed undergraduate research projects.

(Baird & Digler, 2023, p. 212)

Students enter our courses with a lifetime of these kinds of incidents that inform the lens through which they experience our teaching. If we reinforce stereotypes—even subconsciously—we signal that some students belong while others do not. Further, we miss out on potentially rich opportunities to help the Scarlets build on their wealth of knowledge while reigning in the Steves who might need to focus a little less on networking and a little more on adapting to the task at hand.

In this same research on transfer, Baird and Digler found students' dispositions to be a salient factor in how well students could use previous learning. They found some dispositions to be generative, such as a participant whose familial expectations about the need to adapt empowered him to be able to reshape prior knowledge and apply it in new environments. In contrast, Baird and Digler offered an example of a student who had a disposition disruptive to feedback as she believed that "doing it right the first time" was the only acceptable path to success. This disposition may have worked for this student in other environments where being quick and immediately accurate were both possible and necessary for the task at hand. In the case of writing instruction, however, this disposition impeded the student's ability to value, accept, and integrate feedback non-defensively.

Awareness about the potential dispositions in the room can go a long way in helping instructors address students' vulnerabilities. Since learning about Baird and Digler's (2023) work, I make it a point to tell students that revision can be tough for those who have been socialized with a "do it right the first time" ethos. I add that this is not necessarily a bad belief because it is useful in some situations. Communicating these seemingly small messages can help students and faculty alike anticipate some of the challenges in writing.

Conventions

Aull (2021) suggests several dimensions of a more helpful disposition for writing educators. First, she points out that "academic language is not anyone's mother tongue" (p. 3), a seemingly obvious point, but one that can be leveraged to position scholarly writing as a project about conventions, not absolute rights and wrongs. This orientation can mitigate the marginalization students experience when given the message that the way they were taught to communicate is at odds with the collegiate norms. Makmillen (2023) describes this as a push-pull dynamic between many of their African American students' home language conventions and what the students call the "proper" language of academia:

> In the context of my writing class, students are being pushed toward seeing their language use as a social justice issue—through readings, class discussions,

and assignments that address the topics of language, race, and power; they are also being pulled back in toward the proper English that has been and educational and, for many of them, a family value all their lives.

(p. 190)

While Makmillen (2023) discusses the pull toward "proper" English coming from the family, more often students experience that pressure in the reverse direction. Students receive overt and covert messages that African American, Spanglish, rural, and other linguistic variations represent deficits rather than differences. Educators must walk a fine line between reinforcing deficit and assimilationist norms and denying the standards expected in academic and professional settings.

I recall a first-generation student who shared in class that his Resident Assistant helped him figure out the rules for email communication with professors. Other students in my class objected, saying the Resident Assistant was behaving oppressively by encouraging him to conform to the college norm. The first-generation student challenged the rest of the class by explaining that he was grateful to the Resident Assistant for helping him understand the culture so he could navigate it successfully. As he explained, the Resident Assistant was not saying that his communication style was bad or wrong. She was simply translating a norm that was unfamiliar to him, an orientation we can take with our students by teaching academic writing as convention, not absolute rightness or wrongness.

COURSE PLANNING

Most courses live or die by the effectiveness of design; my experience is that this is particularly true for writing courses. A big part of the value-added for students is learning how to plan and manage writing projects so the design needs to be intentional and realistic. For me, this structure starts with clear, well-crafted assignments that meet students where they are and move them toward skill growth. I have mixed feelings about higher education's near obsession with "learning outcomes" because I know education is more art than science. If the light about how to write a strong case for significance comes on a week after the course ends, did I fail that student? If a student had a really great high school English teacher and shows up already writing like a whiz, do I get credit for that student? The learning outcome craze oversimplifies the complex reality of student learning and should therefore receive less veneration.

The stilted language of learning outcomes can also suck the joy out of learning. Ross Gay (2022) makes this point eloquently in his essay, *Dispatch from the Ruins*, in which he describes learning outcomes in the following manner:

It [the learning outcomes statement] is a forceful, Nostradamic moment in the document [syllabus], anticipating what will happen by the end of the fourteenth or fifteenth week ... if it makes you feel a little bit claustrophobic or bored, you are not alone. In fact, I think you are in the company of just about every humanities professor I have spoken to, who to a one rolls their eyes or shakes their head 'no' or makes a hissing sound when this part of the syllabus is mentioned, because they know that real learning is unpredictable, improvisatory, and by definition, confounding. By definition, if the learning is real, the outcomes are unfathomable.

(p. 146)

I share this point to distinguish between the boring "students will be able to" institution-speak that fails to acknowledge the personal and dynamic nature of learning from course objectives, which serve the useful function of creating broad end goals. Course objectives provide a balance between the rigidity of learning outcomes and the laisse faire approach that masks disorganization in the language of student-centeredness and/or critical pedagogy. Students learn little from either regimentation or free-for-alls, so I advocate balancing structure and flexibility in course design.

Starting with the End in Mind

Starting with the end in mind helps delineate what can be accomplished in a 15-week semester so I recommend thinking through what success will look like for you and your students, broadly speaking. Conventionally, we think of defining success for the students without considering what success means for the instructor. I therefore think it's worth defining our aims more specifically than vague hopes that students got something out of our course. The Council of Writing Program Administrators used the National Survey of Student Engagement (NSSE) best practices for deep learning to develop standards for examining high-quality writing curricula. I offer Addison and McGee's (2010, p. 153) summary as benchmarks for faculty to consider when developing a writing course:

> Prewriting Activities: How much students got feedback from faculty and others about their writing ideas and drafts.
> Clear Expectations: How much instructors provided clear expectations of the goals and criteria for the writing assignments.
> Higher-Order Writing: How much students wrote assignments involving summarization, analysis, and argument.
> Good Instructor Practices: How much students collaborated with classmates, reviewed sample writing, and were assigned practice writing tasks.
> Integrated Media: How much students included numerical data, multimedia, and visual content in their writing.

I appreciate these guidelines as general enough to be broadly applied, but specific enough to be clear. I have discussed elements of these criteria throughout the first three chapters of this book but will focus with greater depth on the second point of clear expectations in this section of the chapter at hand.

Clarity of expectations starts with the learning objectives, which I recommend stating clearly so that students do not have to work hard to decipher them. Here are the learning objectives I developed for my scholarly writing course:

1. Learn the foundational skills necessary to produce quality scholarly writing. Examples include researching, writing a clear thesis, making the case for significance, and concluding with takeaways for the reader.
2. Practice these skills through assignments.
3. Receive feedback from the professor, writing coach, and peers to improve work.
4. Develop good writing habits, particularly regarding time management. Solid writing takes time, focus, and perseverance.

Wiggins and McTighe (2005) developed a useful model for course planning known as *backward design*. The idea is to start with the end in mind; educators need clarity about what success looks like before they can effectively plan instruction and course activities. This may seem like an obvious point, but most of us have experienced a class that feels thrown together in a haphazard fashion. The instructor might have been a knowledgeable scholar and skilled lecturer, but students quickly feel lost if they cannot see how each part of a class connects to an overall design.

There is sometimes a reticence to explain our logic to students, especially when they demand it in the form of a "why do I have to do/know/learn this?" question. Admittedly, those kinds of questions can feel whiny, but there is often a genuine need behind them. If students sense they are being asked to do something that is random or perfunctory, it's difficult to find the motivation to complete that task. Even for those who will just comply for the grade, not knowing the reason for a feature of the course can be a detriment to student learning. This is why Bain (2004) advocates for instructors to both create an intentional design and articulate it clearly to students. Bain conducted extensive research uncovering themes in excellent college teaching and identified this quality as essential among them.

Crafting Meaningful Assignments

For these reasons, it is safe to say that the first step in effective course design is starting with the end in mind. Once these course objectives have been established, the next step Wiggins and McTighe (2005) recommend is asking yourself,

"How will I know if the learning goals have been met?" Asking this question truly helps with crafting meaningful assignments that move your students toward an end goal. In the absence of this guiding question, educators sometimes develop assignments without much intentionality, leaving students to feel like they're doing tasks that seem arbitrary and perfunctory. Students use words like, "random," "busy work," and "jumping through hoops" to describe activities they find uninspiring. It is therefore worth the effort to create assignments that communicate purpose.

As we have discussed, another good practice to employ when developing assignments is starting with easier, lower stakes activities and moving to more complex work. This helps with both skills building and anxiety reduction. The following table provides a list of some of the assignments I used the last time I taught our scholarly writing course:

1. <u>Good Writing Example:</u> Bring an example of nonfiction writing you find to be clear, compelling, and powerful. It doesn't have to be from an academic journal, but it should be from a serious publication (For example, *Chronicle of Higher Ed*, *Atlantic*, *NY Times*). Write a 300-ish word reflection on at least three specific elements that made you choose this piece of writing.
2. <u>Five Scholarly Writers on LinkedIn:</u> Find five scholarly writers to follow on LinkedIn and be ready to discuss their work throughout the semester.
3. <u>Compelling Opening Sentence:</u> Write a compelling opening sentence to a topic about which you're considering writing for this course.
4. <u>Mini Annotated Bibliography</u>: Find five articles relevant to your topic and write a mini annotated bibliography of these sources.
5. <u>APA Quiz 1:</u> You will take a quiz on the APA reading assignment for the 10/17 class session.
6. <u>APA Quiz 2:</u> You will take a quiz on the APA reading assignment for the 10/24 class session.
7. <u>Abstract/Introduction</u>: Write the abstract and introduction for your paper, being sure to embed a strong case for significance. This document should be about 500 words/one single-spaced typed page.

COURSE CONTENT

One of the best gifts that comes from a writing course is the time and space to slow down and think about writing in a focused way. When I do this, the first question that always comes to mind is, "What is good writing?" These follow up questions form quickly, "How do I know good writing when I see it?" and "How do I explain it to students?" Thus, this section begins with Aull's (2021) work on civility and coherence as goals toward which to strive in academic writing. I then move into the research and revision elements of academic writing, having covered in Chapter 1 many of the other topics like managing time, writing thesis statements, and attending to structure. These topics warrant attention in any course requiring writing but can be covered with greater depth in a course focused on writing. Instructors rarely have time to cover research and revision in non-writing courses, so my recommendation would be to allocate serious time to these activities in a writing course. Hence, I will provide resources for teaching these processes after addressing the art of articulating what constitutes high-quality writing.

Civility and Coherence

The answers to "What is good writing?" can be framed as broad categories of civility and coherence (Aull, 2021). That is, we deem writing worthwhile when it includes evidence and multiple perspectives (civility) and flows logically (coherence). "Civil" and "coherent" are more useful descriptors than "good." However, Aull points out that they do not solve the challenge of explaining more explicitly how to write with civility and coherence, "The bad news is that often, students and instructors cannot connect these characteristics to written language in a systematic way. They cannot connect labels like civil or coherent to common choices in their reading and writing" (p. 37).

Hence, students need practice in identifying these qualities in others' writing before they can produce them in their own. Aull (2021) draws on Vande Kopple's (2012) assertion that understanding writing does not necessarily require long and boring forays into forcing more precise rules for attaining civility and coherence. Instead, students can learn effective writing by starting with "analysis of authentic written language, including how it attends to the readers' needs" (Aull, 2021, p. 39). Simply slowing down and asking students to observe good (and maybe even bad) writing gets them thinking about the idea more thoughtfully and intentionally.

Aull (2021) does us a great service by offering some specifics as to what we can look *for* in studying writing that is both civil and coherent. She identifies textual and epistemic markers that convey openness (civility) and connection (coherence). Hedges like "might" and "somewhat," for example, signal caution, inviting the reader to feel some doubt. Boosters like "definitely" and "clearly" offer less invitation to the reader and therefore tend to produce writing that can read as novice or unnuanced if not used judiciously. Text connectives like "however" and "consequently" offer bridges to the reader, helping them follow the writer's logic. An initial assignment asking students to circle hedges, boosters, and text connectives can be useful in helping students understand with greater precision what constitutes clear and effective writing.

Critical Thinking

Another way to make the vague idea of good writing more concrete for students is to employ Paul and Elder (2019) standards of critical thinking. I have adapted their points both as qualities to look for when analyzing others' writing and aims to achieve in one's own writing:

1. Is the writer's purpose clear and justifiable?
2. Does the writer ask sound questions?
3. Does the writer cite accurate and relevant evidence?
4. Does the text reflect the complexity of the issue given its scope and scale?
5. Does the text show a sensitivity to what the writer is taking for granted or assuming?
6. Does the writer acknowledge alternative points of view?
7. Does the writer develop a line of reasoning explaining how they arrived at their main conclusion?

I've reworked the language in these questions many times over the years, and this iteration seems to be the one students most comprehend. This list lends itself to interactive in-class activities, especially at the beginning of a semester when students are more comfortable critiquing authors who are not in the room rather than themselves or peers. As students develop rapport, this activity can be repurposed to allow students to gain fresh perspectives on their own ideas. For example, I often ask students to write their thesis statement and brief case for significance on the white boards in our classroom. Students then walk around the room and make notes for each other on the first question: Is the writer's purpose clear and justifiable? Whether the answer leans toward "yes" or "no," I encourage students to: (1) explain their assessment and (2) offer ideas for how to build on the strength or address the weakness.

Here is where I may need to remind the reader that I teach graduate students in a helping profession, meaning they tend to be both thoughtful and mature enough for this exercise. I have attempted to craft this chapter with undergraduate students in mind, drawing almost exclusively on literature addressing undergraduates. That said, this may be the kind of exercise the reader considers adapting for younger students. For example, more guidance and/or privacy may be needed. However you choose to incorporate them, the standards for critical thinking can be useful in giving students more concrete and consistent language for what constitutes good academic writing.

The Search Process

When I started teaching our writing course, I made a lot of assumptions about what students know in terms of research, time management, and writing conventions. I also assumed that students would ask questions and/or come to office hours if they were confused. I quickly learned students can become so lost that they don't even know what to ask or how to pull themselves out of what can feel like quicksand. Therefore, my starting point in the writing course is helping students anticipate, learn to tolerate, and navigate ambiguity.

Nowhere is this more important than in the search process, an often-overlooked aspect of writing instruction. Carol Kuhlthau has studied students' search strategies extensively and found emotion—particularly anxiety—plays a large and underappreciated role in how students locate and use information. For this reason, Kuhlthau (2004) deems conventional approaches to teaching and learning about the search process inadequate, explaining "The bibliographic paradigm is based on certainty and order, whereas the user's constructive process is characterized by uncertainty and confusion" (p. 8). Students seem to have an intuitive sense of this uncertainty and confusion, often seeking to resolve these uncomfortable emotions by asking a lot of pointed questions about requirements.

We all look for models and direction when venturing into new territory, so it makes sense that students seek clarity about what is expected of them. The problem arises when students get so concerned about meeting assignment specifications that they cannot loosen up enough to explore broadly before getting into details. When students feel stressed, they often scramble to feel a sense of relief by simply getting the task off their plate. This phenomenon results in quick, shallow digital searches that do not always yield the most accurate and/or relevant information. Hence, Kuhlthau, Heinström, and Todd (2008) advocate for instructors and librarians mentoring students through the search process.

This kind of mentoring involves helping students understand searching as a process deeper than gathering information for an end product. When students frame searching more holistically, they shift "from simply collecting and compiling information to please teachers; rather, they become involved in thinking processes that require extensive exploration of ideas and formulation of thoughts before developing their own deep understanding of their topics and presenting it" (p. 17). Kuhlthau (2004) developed a six-stage search process based on the primary task students need to accomplish at each stage: Initiation, selection, exploration, formulation, collection, and presentation. Explaining these stages to students goes a long way in helping them comprehend the involved nature of the search process. Further, students often experience a reduction in anxiety when we help them anticipate and plan for points of frustration and confusion along the way. Finally, students benefit when we serve as coaches in the search process, helping them think through strategies. I like to do this in a flipped classroom portion of some class sessions throughout the course of a semester. Students report finding it useful and comforting to have an instructor present for questions and even celebratory moments they experience along the way.

Revision

It may seem odd to jump from searching to revising; I include a good deal about the writing process in my class but covered much of that material in the previous chapters so I will not revisit it here. When I have the luxury of teaching writing by itself without other course content to cover, I can focus more on the often-skipped bookends of the writing process: Searching and revising. Revision is as important as creation, yet it is an overlooked part of the writing process for several reasons. Sometimes it is skipped entirely, falling victim to the whirlwind of procrastination. Other times, we are so enamored with our work that we resist re-examining it with fresh eyes. We can anticipate and address these common problems with effective course design. Simply naming the issues and requiring revision (with assigned point values) will largely solve these problems.

A less obvious challenge with revision is that it is not as simple as we think. Revision is deeper than copyediting or proofreading, both of which are necessary, but more technical and detailed than the more global work of revising. Thomson (2023) states that revision begins by being able to imagine a reader other than oneself. Building on Germano's (2021, p. 131) assertion that "you can't know what's missing until you know what you're looking for," Thompson suggests that diagnostic reading is the first step in an effective revision process. This is why students need ample practice reading and analyzing other texts for specific examples of what works (and what does not work) in academic writing.

The revision process can be daunting if not broken into smaller, more concrete tasks to make it more manageable. Thomson (2023, p. 60) provides a helpful set of questions students can ask themselves when rereading their completed work for the first time:

1. What is the problem or puzzle I am investigating?
2. Why is it important to know about it?
3. What literatures have I used to construct my study? What are the building blocks to situate, design, and analyze my study?
4. How did I go about my study? What did I do, with whom/what, why, how and when?
5. What do I and the reader now know that we didn't know at the start of the project?
6. What is the evidence to show we know it?
7. What does this add to existing knowledges?
8. What does this new understanding mean for research, policy, and/or practice?

Students may become confused by the word "study," so it's good to add that this word encompasses literature reviews as well as original research. Encouraging students to think of a literature review more methodically has the added benefit of reinforcing sound search practices as they should be explained at least briefly in most academic writing. Another side benefit of this list occurs with Question #5, which can serve as a gentle reminder to students that an academic paper should not be a rant about one's own views. Having to answer Question #5 can serve as a check on students whose writing takes on a preachy tone by reminding them to think more intentionally about the value their work should add for the reader. Questions #7 and #8 also provide a potential corrective to students whose passion eclipses reason in their writing. Question #2 can serve a similar function for the student who leans more toward facts without telling the reader why they should care about them.

Once students know how to do this kind of initial reading of their work, they can move into the more specific terrain of analyzing how their work conveys meaning for the reader. Murray (2014) explains that revising starts with examining one's work for information, emphasizing that good writing is "built from specific, accurate, and interesting information" (p. 612). Writers then need to move on to looking for meaning in this information; Murray argues that "the specifics must build to a pattern of significance. Each piece of specific information must carry the reader toward meaning" (p. 612). Grounded in this idea of checking one's work for meaning, Thomson (2023) provides a clear and concise checklist students can use as a tool in this process:

1. Information: Does the text contain enough information?
2. Meaning: Does the writing convey something of significance?
3. Audience: Does the text connect with the reader?
4. Form/Genre: Is the writing appropriate to the genre?
5. Structure: Is the text well structured?
6. Development: Is there enough information in each section?
7. Dimension: Do the parts make the whole?

Depending on students' skill level, they may need more guidance with one or more of these broad questions, but they provide a useful guide to reading one's work with an eye toward conveying meaning. However one mentors students in the revision process, the key is to emphasize concreteness and depth. It is difficult to look at one's work with a fresh set of eyes, so we tend to gloss over pages unless given clear direction. Finally, I find it useful to allocate class time to revision so that students are not distracted by other tasks and can seek my and their peers' assistance if they need help.

INDIVIDUAL COACHING

One of the many gifts of a course dedicated to writing is the time and space to work individually with students. Students benefit from the sounding board we can provide as they build on their unique strengths and growth areas. I've found the initial conversation often needs structure; "come to office hours" does not always cut it for students who need more direction. I require all students to meet with me at least once throughout the course of a semester. Making this time mandatory rather than optional levels the playing field for students who may see office hours as either remediation and/or an imposition on my time, a particularly common phenomenon for new majority students who are sometimes unclear about the purpose of office hours.

I hesitated to require students to meet with me individually until I had a particularly challenging class and realized I needed to try something new. I passed around a sign-up sheet in class and noticed that no one seemed to mind setting up a one-on-one meeting with me. I also noticed a lot of lights coming on for students in these individual meetings, particularly for a student I had taught in previous courses. I shared this observation, to which she responded that she finally understood her mistakes after meeting with me one on one. I asked her why she didn't go to office hours in our other classes together and she explained, "I felt weird about it, but having that sign-up sheet made it just a normal thing to do." This may seem odd to faculty, but I recommend just accepting it and normalizing individualized help by building it into the course design.

Exploring Together

I schedule individual coaching meetings after students have received their first round of feedback from me. I ask them to prepare questions and comments in response to my feedback, which gives us a nice starting point. Students consistently express appreciation that they can ask me what I meant by certain suggestions; this conversation goes a long way in helping demystify the process. We tend to start with the specifics of their paper, then move into more broad areas like what they love/hate about writing or even how they are doing more generally. These can be rich conversations, inviting the kind of metacognition that helps students learn.

Individual conversations can also surface dispositions like the one just discussed regarding a student's ambivalence about feedback. It is monumentally helpful to get a sense of what each individual student brings to the course so I can tailor instruction accordingly. If I know a particular student is not well-versed in the academic convention of feedback, I can talk that through with them and hopefully gain their trust to try out a new way of being (see Chapter 2 for a more extensive discussion of Student Feedback Literacy). The key to making this work is conveying respect and a non-deficit attitude. Sometimes I do this simply by joking that academics speak in ways that are not common in regular life. We wouldn't normally tell someone directly that their shirt doesn't look great with those pants, for example. But academia has its own language that sometimes requires translation. Letting students know they can learn it without abandoning their native tongue can go a long way in warding off some of the cultural disconnects "new majority" students experience when feeling forced to assimilate.

Finally, individual conversations benefit students because they are opportunities to be listened to, an experience that is becoming rarer with the advent of online instruction and bigger classes. I will refrain from a tirade on this point, except to say that the payoff for meeting with students individually is well worth it. The previous example of Scarlet and Steve illustrates this point. In class, it is likely that Steve exhibits the charm and confidence upper-class students have been socialized to express while Scarlet might await instructor direction as is characteristic of students from lower-class families (Lareau, 2011). In group situations, the Steves of the world dominate faculty attention, often reaping the rewards of greater engagement that pays off in positive perceptions that can be exchanged for letters of recommendation and other perks. Scarlets can slip by unnoticed and maybe even judged as less participative. These are not mere speculations; the literature shows that new majority students interact less with faculty and thus miss out on some of the educational and networking rewards that accompany strong faculty-student relationships (Raposa et al., 2021). Making space to get to know students individually has a potentially equalizing effect wherein Scarlet may benefit from a more proactive invitation for connection and Steve may receive some gentle instruction on moving from style to substance.

Dissertation Chairing

I am in the process of writing this book with two doctoral students and one alum, all of whose dissertations I chaired. They have pointed out that I am the only author of this book to have chaired dissertations, so they assigned me this topic. Obviously, dissertation writing is a big enough topic to warrant its own book and there are several good ones on the market. I won't rehash them here, but I will offer some tips on this special topic of working with doctoral students on their dissertations. Because this specific topic is not the focus of the book, I will confine my analysis to the writing itself rather than getting into all the aspects of the research process more generally.

When I reflect on my own experience as a doctoral student, I recall mostly enjoyable experiences on the foggy, hilly campus of the University of San Francisco. I struggled neither with coursework nor the data collection process, so I was blindsided by how overwhelmed I felt when I finished my transcriptions and sat in my office with so much data to analyze and write up. I was intrinsically motivated and liked writing: What was my problem?

Role Clarity

Like many doctoral students, one reason I chose to pursue a terminal degree is that I had always done well in school. People don't usually sign up for more of something that they fear they cannot do, especially when it entails the kind of time, energy, and financial investment associated with doctoral studies. Consequently, students are sometimes in for a rude awakening because the dissertation is its own unique beast for many reasons. I will focus on a few of the more common challenges I've seen and share some tips for addressing them.

The first conundrum many doctoral students encounter is lack of role clarity. I had a student I'll call Samantha who experienced this issue. Like many students who are drawn to helping fields like mine, Samantha has strong interpersonal and networking skills with which she can solve most problems. In our work together, however, these skills quickly became the proverbial hammer with which she was turning every problem into a nail. When I answered her questions, she would ask more questions without trying to move forward on her own. We found ourselves in a frustrating vicious circle wherein I felt I had answered her questions and needed her to be more independent and she felt lost and confused.

Fortunately, Samantha and I both have counseling skills and could use them to dive into our communication conundrum. We eventually figured out that Samantha did not realize how many of the decisions were hers to make as the author of her dissertation. Once we had clarity on this point, I could tell her directly which choices she should make, and which ones required my consultation. I now make it a point to be more explicit about the role of decision-making in the writing process when I teach the scholarly writing course at the doctoral level.

Clear Expectations

Another common challenge doctoral students experience lies in the shift from structured coursework to independent dissertation writing. Most programs attempt to address this transition by offering a proposal writing course, which can do wonders in inculcating good habits. Still, the time eventually comes when doctoral students must navigate the intimidating task of creating a system for managing the many moving parts of the dissertation process. My experience has been that students often either underestimate this work, engaging in magical thinking like "it will get done" or schedule the work in rigidly unrealistic ways. One odd but common issue I've seen is students who compulsively set up plans, deadlines, and meetings instead of getting to the real work of writing. This makes sense in that it can be self-soothing to fuss over color-coded schedules instead of doing the harder and more ambiguous work of the actual writing.

I do two things to address this issue, one of which may seem a bit controversial. The noncontroversial strategy I employ is drawing attention to the possibility of this distraction and warning students not to waste too much time making plans that will likely change because we never really know how long it will take to write a chapter, what work/family issues may arise, and so forth. Yes, it's important to have a plan, but it should be broad, flexible, and not too time consuming to produce.

The more potentially controversial strategy I use is that I mostly avoid discussing students' timelines, plans, and so on with them. I decided on this approach after too many students wanted to discuss their partner's lack of help with the kids, employer's demands, and so forth when the reality is that I have no jurisdiction over these aspects of their lives. Rather than getting stuck in the uncomfortable role of the priest to whom students feel the need to confess, I have extricated myself by setting the expectation that my role is to read and respond to writing. That is the area in which I can be of assistance. My goal is to free my students of guilt by refusing to be the arbitrator of whether their child's piano recital was more important than getting Chapter 1 to me by a deadline they set. Not knowing this deadline is key in the process!

What I *do* want to discuss with my students is their writing, so I am sure to communicate my availability, turnaround time, and resources I think can help them along their journey. I take the time to introduce students to other students and faculty with shared intellectual interests so they can expand their thinking in collaboration with them. I prioritize my chairees over other commitments, often dropping what I'm doing to respond as quickly as possible to them (always within a week). I make a commitment to students I'm chairing that they will not be held up because of me. It's easier for students to do their part when they can trust us to do ours consistently.

Collegiality

Another aspect of the dissertation process I feel is worth mentioning is the benefit of socializing students into how to engage productively as a community of scholars. I've seen too many students get derailed by jealousy and competition when they could have had a more productive and pleasurable experience by understanding their classmates as colleagues. People don't like to think of themselves as jealous or competitive, so it's easy to overlook this potential problem. Simply telling students that sometimes the pressure cooker of doctoral work stimulates these feelings can help students guard against them. It's not so much of a moral issue as a practical one; I've had more than one student feel so deflated when another student graduates before them that they get overwhelmed by insecurity when that time and energy would be better spent getting to the finish line themselves.

Speaking of the finish line, there is a common expression that "a good dissertation is a done dissertation." Again, I have no moral judgment about this sentiment, but I have found it to be a highly impractical attitude. When students obsess over "just being done," they tend to waste time and energy turning in substandard work. The time it takes to keep fixing the same mistakes resulting from lackluster commitment would be better spent on an actual break that could restore the student and get them re-energized. For this reason, I encourage students to shift from the "have to" to the "get to" mindset when it comes to dissertation work. If this requires time off to recharge oneself and return to more inspired work, the investment almost always pays off.

There are obviously many other aspects to the dissertation chairing enterprise that are beyond the scope of this chapter, but the main point is to enter this process with intentionality. It's a substantial commitment worth some thoughtfulness upfront. It can be easy to make assumptions about what students know and become frustrated with either them or ourselves when these things aren't just common knowledge. It is better to have an honest conversation about appropriate topics for discussion, reasonable turnaround time for feedback, and our respective roles and responsibilities rather than being caught off guard.

I want to close with a note about the importance of celebrating small successes along the way and the big success at the end. Too often, we're so busy that we immediately start the next task before taking a moment to recognize our students' achievements. Again, I find this personally uplifting, but there is also a practical element to congratulating our students when they achieve the smaller milestones on the way to graduation. I invite the reader to think back to the last time someone acknowledged a job well done, even in a small way. My guess is that you felt encouraged, motivated, and inspired to do more of that thing. When we do this for students, we both build their confidence and help them (and ourselves) stay in touch with the transformative promise of education.

CONCLUSION

I began this chapter with some considerations about new majority students, followed by conceptual frameworks (differences vs. deficits, transfer, and conventions) for meeting them where they are. I moved from this foundation to a discussion of course planning with an emphasis on starting with the end in mind. Next, I explored some content areas for developing course materials: Answering the question of what constitutes good writing, searching, revising, and chairing dissertations. I intentionally got into the weeds in this chapter with the intent to offer the reader a clear picture of what I do in my scholarly writing course. My goal was to be specific enough to provide tools, but general enough that ideas can be adapted to each individual reader's unique needs.

This chapter concludes Part 1 of this book where we focused on themes broadly applicable to improving writing instruction. Part 2 was written by my student and alumni co-authors who offer a wealth of knowledge and experience about working with specific populations of students. In these chapters, you will gain invaluable insight into how we can tailor our instruction to meet the needs of an increasingly diverse student population. To this end, the authors curate scholarship and mine their experiences in truly creative ways that make the material come alive for the reader. When you finish Part 2, I hope you feel as inspired as I did by all the ways we can engage diverse students in the meaningful work of expressing their good ideas clearly and powerfully.

REFERENCES

Addison, J., & McGeee, S. (2010). Writing in high school/writing in college: Research trends and future directions. *College Composition and Communication*, 62(1), 147–179. https://www.jstor.org/stable/27917889

Alfano, C. Formato, M., Johnson, J., & Newby, A. (2023). Research-Writing pedagogy as sustaining first-generation college student identities in a bridge program. In Ritter, K. (Ed.), *Beyond fitting in: Rethinking first-generation writing and literacy education* (pp. 251–266). Modern Language Association. https://www.mla.org/Publications/Bookstore/Nonseries/Beyond-Fitting-In

Aull, L. (2021). What is 'Good Writing?': Analyzing metadiscourse as civil discourse. *Journal of Teaching Writing*, 36(1), 37–60. https://journals.iupui.edu/index.php/teachingwriting/article/view/26240

Bain, K. (2004). *What the best college teachers do*. Harvard University Press. https://www.hup.harvard.edu/books/9780674013254

Baird, N., & Digler, B. (2023). Writing transfer strategies of first-generation college students: Negotiations as a metaphor for adaptive transfer. In K. Ritter (Ed.), *Beyond fitting in: Rethinking first-generation writing and literacy education* (pp. 211–232). Modern Language Association. https://www.mla.org/Publications/Bookstore/Nonseries/Beyond-Fitting-In

Bollig, C. (2019). 'People like us': Theorizing first-generation college as a marker of difference. *Literacy in Composition Studies*, 7(1), 22–43. 10.21623/1.7.1.3

Carter, G. M., & Thelin, W. H. (Eds.). (2017). *Class in the composition classroom: Pedagogy and the working class*. University Press of Colorado. https://upcolorado.com/utah-state-university-press/item/3161-class-in-the-composition-classroom

Conley, D. T. (2007). *Toward a more comprehensive conception of college readiness*. Academia. https://www.academia.edu/48506115/Toward_a_More_Comprehensive_Conception_of_College-Readiness

Gay, R. (2022). *Inciting Joy: Essays*. Algonquin Books of Chapel Hill. https://www.rossgay.net/inciting-joy

Germano, W. (2021). *On revision: The only writing that counts*. University of Chicago Press. https://press.uchicago.edu/ucp/books/book/chicago/O/bo115834535.html

Kuhlthau, C. (2004). *Seeking meaning: A process approach to library and information services*. Greenwood Publishing Group. https://www.bloomsbury.com/us/seeking-meaning-9781591580942/

Kuhlthau, C. C., Heinström, J., & Todd, R. J. (2008). The 'information search process' revisited: Is the model still useful. *Information Research*, 13(4), 13–28. https://informationr.net/ir/13-4/paper355.html

Lareau, A. (2011). *Unequal childhoods: Class, race, and family life*. University of California Press. https://www.ucpress.edu/book/9780520271425/unequal-childhoods

Makmillen, S. (2023). First-Generation students at a historically Black sniversity talk about "Proper English". In K. Ritter (Ed.), *Beyond fitting in: Rethinking first-generation writing and literacy education* (pp. 189–210). Modern Language Association. https://www.mla.org/Publications/Bookstore/Nonseries/Beyond-Fitting-In

McNair, T. B., Albertine, S., McDonald, N., Major Jr, T., & Cooper, M. A. (2022). *Becoming a student-ready college: A new culture of leadership for student success*. John Wiley & Sons.

Murray, D. M. (2014). The maker's eye: Revising your own manuscripts. In J. Klausman (Ed.), *Writing about writing: A college reader* (pp. 610–614). Bedford/St. Martins. https://robertnazar.files.wordpress.com, 2018/09

Paul, R., & Elder, L. (2019). *The miniature guide to critical thinking concepts and tools*. Rowman & Littlefield. https://rowman.com/ISBN/9781538134948/The-Miniature-Guide-to-Critical-Thinking-Concepts-and-Tools-Eighth-Edition

Raposa, E. B., Hagler, M., Liu, D., & Rhodes, J. E. (2021). Predictors of close faculty – student relationships and mentorship in higher education: Findings from the Gallup – Purdue Index. *Annals of the New York Academy of Sciences, 1483*(1), 36–49. https://pubmed.ncbi.nlm.nih.gov/32242962/

Ritter, K. (Ed.). (2023, February). Beyond Fitting In: Rethinking First-Generation Writing and Literacy Education. Modern Language Association. https://www.mla.org/Publications/Bookstore/Nonseries/Beyond-Fitting-In

Thomson, P. (2023). *Refining your academic writing: Strategies for reading, revising and rewriting*. Taylor & Francis. https://www.routledge.com/Refining-Your-Academic-Writing-Strategies-for-Reading-Revising-and-Rewriting/Thomson/p/book/9780367468767

Vande Kopple, W. J. (2012). The importance of studying metadiscourse. *Applied Research on English Language, 1*(2), 37–44. https://doi.org/10.22108/ARE.2012.15453

Wiggins, G., & McTighe, J. (2005). *Understanding by design*. Association for Supervision and Curriculym Development. https://www.ascd.org/books/understanding-by-design-expanded-2nd-edition?variant=103055

Part 2
Helping Specific Populations with Writing

Chapter 5

Helping ESL Students with Academic Writing

INTRODUCTION

There is no doubt that the purpose and experience of writing varies depending on geographic location and the language written. Written communication is both offered and received through the lens of culture within the language and society you reside in. Teaching in higher education institutions in the United States, we might assume that all of our students understand the writing culture of English in the United States. But for many of our students who speak languages other than English, this may be the first time that they have experienced a reader who approaches their writing from the lens of American English writing culture.

In this chapter, we (Becky and Oumarou) will focus on supporting students with academic writing for whom English is not their first language. This group of students is diverse and can include heritage speakers, refugees, native-born citizens, international students on student visas, naturalized or permanent residents, and others. We will first provide an overview of terminologies that are used to refer to learners for whom English is not their primary language. Although English may be the second, third, fourth, and so on, language for some students, we will refer to these learners as English as a Second Language (ESL) students.

We will also discuss different writing styles in different languages. For example, in English, writing tends to be very linear. We tell our audience what we will write, then we write it, and finally, we remind our audience of what we just wrote. However, French is a descriptive language, and Francophones tend to write long and complex sentences, which can often show the author's mastery of the language. As a francophone, I (Oumarou) usually find myself writing wordy sentences that irritate some of my professors in the U.S. academic context, which is part of the differences in writing styles that this chapter will address. With an understanding of the complexity of language, culture, and writing styles of ESL students, we will also share a variety of practical tips for providing helpful and constructive support to assist ESL students with academic writing.

We will begin with an overview of the various of lexicons often used to describe students for whom English is not their first language.

Defining ESL

There are many ways to refer to students whose native, or first, language is a language other than English and there is a fair amount of discussion around what terms are most appropriate in this context. You may have heard any number or combination of a variety of acronyms in reference to multilingual students whose first language is not English. Each of these acronyms has a slightly different meaning or nuance and might be used in different contexts for different purposes. In this section, we will provide an overview of the implications of these various acronyms and clarify our use of "ESL students" in this chapter.

To begin, TESOL (Teaching English to Speakers of Other Languages) refers to the profession. ELL (English Language Learners) and MLL (Multilingual Learners) refer to the students themselves and are sometimes used interchangeably. The acronyms ESL (English as a Second Language) and EFL (English as a Foreign Language) can be differentiated by a student's geographic location. ESL implies that English is the primary or official language where the student is studying. EFL implies that English is not the primary or official language but instead a foreign language in the location where the student is studying. ESL and EFL might be the most commonly recognized acronyms for this student population.

Some have adopted the term ESOL (English for Speakers of Other Languages) as it takes into consideration that English may not be the students second language but may be their third, fourth, fifth, and so on, language. While this is a very important consideration, this term could be confusing since it implies that English is the skill being taught but this book is not specifically intended for professors who are teaching English language or composition directly. Instead, it is intended for those who have the desire to support their students writing within their content area. Therefore, for the sake of clarity and consistency, we will simply use the term ESL when referring to students for whom English is not their first language.

TOWARD AN UNDERSTANDING OF ESL STUDENTS' BACKGROUNDS

With the increased movement of college students from one country to another for the pursuit of postsecondary education opportunities across the world, colleges and universities in English-speaking countries like the United Kingdom, Canada, the United States (U.S.), and others, enroll a considerable number of students for whom English is not the primary language. For example, according to the Institute of International Education's (IIE) recent Open Doors Report on International Educational Exchange, the United States hosted 914,095 foreign students during the 2020–2021 academic year (IIE, 2021). It is important to note that some of the students in IIE's report referenced here might come from other English-speaking countries like Canada, Nigeria, Ghana, and others.

Also worth noting is a category of students referred to as "heritage speakers." According to Benmamoun et al. (2013):

> The term *heritage speaker* typically refers to second generation immigrants, the children of original immigrants who live in a bilingual/multilingual environment from an early age. Heritage speakers have as their dominant language the language of the host country, whereas first generation immigrants are dominant in the native language of their home country, although they may have undergone L1 [first language] attrition in specific aspects of their grammar.
>
> (p. 132)

Heritage speakers share linguistic characteristics of both native language speakers and second language learners (Benmamoun et al., 2013). As an example, my (Becky's) grandmother (first generation born in the United States of parents who immigrated from Italy) grew up in a home where both Italian (her heritage language) and English (the majority language) were used. English was used in the schools and community and quickly became her primary language while her mother maintained the use of Italian in the home. The use of language along this continuum of heritage language and majority language could impact, to varying degrees, a heritage speaker's language skills, perhaps speaking most notably.

ESL students studying at U.S. colleges and universities come from various countries worldwide (Institute of International Education, 2021). As such, many of these students bring with them a wealth of assets, including self-determination, distinct personal experiences, varied learning styles, and diverse cultural, educational, and linguistic backgrounds (Andrade, 2008; Baklashova & Kazakov, 2016; Cheng et al., 2010; Jean-Francois, 2017). Despite the various language proficiency entrance requirements (e.g., IELTS, TOEFL, Duolingo) in place at many U.S. colleges and universities, ESL students often arrive at their host institutions with different language skills and from various linguistic backgrounds. While these language proficiency requirements may vary from one institution to another, their main purpose is to ensure that ESL students are admitted with a language skill that is necessary for their academic success at U.S. colleges and universities.

I (Oumarou) am a graduate ESL student studying at a U.S. university. Like many ESL students, I have learned English as a subject in secondary school in my home country, Benin, a French-speaking country. I also obtained my Bachelor of Art in African Studies from the English department at the Université D'Abomey-Calavi in Benin, West Africa. I came to the United States with a lower TOEFL score. Based on the required TOEFL score at many U.S. postsecondary institutions, my TOEFL score (64) at the time meant that I did not meet the language fluency necessary to succeed at a U.S. college or university. Thus, like many ESL students, I had to go through an intensive English language program (for the spring and summer semesters) to be ready for and meet the linguistic requirement of my graduate academic program (Moussu, 2013). Some ESL students simply enroll at a language training center to learn English and TOEFL test-taking strategies for a period of time, after which they register to take their test.

ESL students studying at postsecondary institutions in English-speaking countries come from diverse cultural, linguistic, and educational backgrounds. Differences in education systems and (academic) writing conventions such as style, rhetorical organization, structure between ESL students' first language and English (their second, third, etc. language) could affect ESL students' writing in a second language. In some cases, because these students come from linguistically and educationally different backgrounds, it is possible that they may be unaware of or unfamiliar with the stylistic conventions and writing requirements in English or their specific discipline. The next section provides a discussion of cross-cultural and linguistic divergences in academic writing and potential implications for ESL students' academic writing.

CROSS-CULTURAL AND LINGUISTIC DIVERGENCES IN WRITING OR ACADEMIC WRITING ACROSS CULTURES

Writing culture, style, and structure can vary from one language to another. Students from culturally and linguistically diverse backgrounds may experience writing differently. Also, because of potential differences in writing systems, grammar, or rhetorical organization that may exist between the English language and other languages, academic writing in English may present some challenges for college students for whom English is not a primary language. For instance, according to Flaitz and Eckstein (2003), Francophone students trained in the French style of writing are not necessarily taught to use the direct and linear structure of English which often includes first telling your audience what you will write about, then writing it, and finally, reminding your audience of what you just wrote. When you write an essay in French, you can go off-topic a bit in order to explain and mention different aspects of the subject before giving your opinion at the end (Siepmann, 2006). Writing styles and organization can thus differ based on educational and linguistic backgrounds.

Students trained in French-speaking countries are frequently instructed to compose essays following a specific structure and flow of ideas. This structure entails initially identifying the problem and clarifying any ambiguous terms, followed by providing an explanation of their proposed approach to address the issue. The essay's body must adhere exactly to this outline/plan. Bridge sentences, which continue the argument's thread, serve as paragraph transitions.

The writer may briefly consider the problem's broader ramifications after presenting a solution or an opinion in the conclusion (Siepmann, 2006). In contrast, Siepmann (2006) stressed that in the Anglophone academic culture (e.g., U.S.), a paragraph should generally begin with a topic sentence that all subsequent sentences must logically support, and a closing sentence concludes a paragraph while facilitating a smooth transition to the next paragraph (see Chapter 2 for more insight and perspective on writing mechanics). It is also important to focus on the topic and avoid repetition and digression, as these are not encouraged in essay writing in the Anglo-Saxon academic culture. There are indeed some differences between the writing and organization of an essay in English and French.

Le (1999) suggested that there are significant differences in the use of paragraphs in academic writing between French and English cultures, which are influenced by their respective educational systems. In English academic writing, paragraphs are typically used to develop and support a specific argument, whereas in French academic writing, paragraphs are more commonly used as a means to construct the argument itself. In other words, English writers tend to use paragraphs as building blocks within their overall argument, while French writers use paragraphs to build the argument itself. As such, it is possible that college students for whom English is not a primary language transfer into English a specific rhetorical style to which they are accustomed in their first language, which may not be familiar to their college professor or reader, particularly if the latter is from a different linguistic or educational background. Thus, the potential consequences of language transfer could lead to confusion and misinterpretation of the intended argument by readers unfamiliar with the transferred rhetorical style. Additionally, language transfer issues could result in a disconnect between the student's writing and the expectations of their English-speaking professors, impacting the overall clarity and effectiveness of the communication.

In academic writing, the differences in a paragraph's use as well as its development by students writing in their first language can be explained by cross-cultural differences in thought and writing patterns, as well as the education systems of each culture. It is fundamental to understand this kind of difference outside the confines of a simplistic or binary "right-wrong" perspective, embracing a more nuanced understanding of students' diverse linguistic and educational backgrounds. Educators can transcend the confines of a strict "right-wrong" assessment approach for students' academic writing by recognizing the intricacies of their varied linguistic and educational backgrounds. Doing so is important because each student's approach to writing is shaped by a complex myriad of cultural factors, language proficiency, and educational experiences. For more information, please refer to our discussion on conventions in Chapter 4 of this book.

Differences in rhetorical styles or structures might present a potential obstacle among people from different linguistic and educational backgrounds. That is why we discussed and drew our readers' attention to the fact that academic rhetorical styles can differ from one language to another. We only use French as one example to illustrate the potential differences in rhetorical style. But these differences in writing conventions grounded in languages and educational cultures are true or even more magnified for ESL students whose first language is, for example, Arabic or Chinese, where the writing directions, alphabets, punctuation, and rhetorical organizations are completely different from English. Because students for whom English is not a first language generally come from educationally and linguistically diverse backgrounds, academic writing in English might present novel challenges for these students. In the following section, we turn our attention to the potential additional challenges ESL learners may face with academic writing.

Challenges for Students

For many students, perhaps for most people in general, writing a paper is challenging in terms of time commitment, depth of thought, organization of those thoughts, and perceived ability, to name just a few factors (see Chapter 3 for more insight and perspective on the many reasons why writing is so difficult). For ESL students, linguistic and cultural factors, in addition to content development, can be especially challenging. It may come as a surprise when an ESL speaker with a very high command of spoken language struggles with their writing. For example, heritage speakers who may sound native-like, might struggle with some English writing conventions. Additionally, speakers of languages with strong oral traditions, such as Arabic speakers, may have an oral proficiency that is stronger than their written proficiency while speakers of languages with strong written traditions, such as Chinese speakers, may demonstrate stronger skills in writing than in speaking. For many, challenges in spoken English may be easier to navigate through conversation with others than through the solitary efforts of writing. In any case, challenges surrounding the coherence of thoughts and ideas in a second language may be prevalent.

Ultimately, it is essential for writers to express their thoughts in a way that their reader can understand and follow. As Paul Silva (2007) very succinctly writes, "writing is a skill, not an innate gift or special talent. Like any advanced skill, writing must be developed through systematic instruction and practice" (pp. 5–6). As you may already imagine, this can be an incredibly difficult skill to master in a second (or third, or fourth, etc.) language. In a 2-year study of tenth-grade ESL students, Duff (2001) found the following:

> To succeed in class, students needed to participate in a variety of types of classroom discussion and reading and writing activities; they also needed a current knowledge of popular North American culture, mass media, and newsworthy

events; an ability to express a range of critical perspectives on social issues and to enter quick-paced interactions; and a great deal of confidence.

(p. 103)

This finding illustrates the complexity of what ESL students in high school face in their writing beyond the knowledge and use of linguistic features of language. It is possible that these complexities become even more complicated and necessary to address in college as the context and need for critical thinking continues to evolve. In this section, we will talk about challenges for ESL students related to developing knowledge of cultural context and use of linguistic conventions.

Cultural Context

Deardorff (2015) defines culture as the "values, beliefs, and norms held by a group of people which shapes how individuals communicate and behave, that is, how they interact with others" (p. 142). International students in university classes often bring certain cultural assumptions based on their home culture to classrooms where other cultural assumptions already exist. Elements of the culture from which a student is accustomed such as communication styles, classroom culture, nonverbal and behavioral expectations, and so on, may have an impact on your classroom.

Hofstede et al. (2010) differentiate culture from human nature and personality by identifying culture as something that is learned, as opposed to inherited, and belongs to a group, as opposed to being individual or universal (p. 6). They assert that basic feelings and emotions, connections with others, awareness of surroundings, and so forth are universal, or human nature. But "how one expresses fear, joy, observations, and so on is modified by culture" (p. 7). This can be seen through the four "*dimensions of culture*" that impact how people from different cultural contexts interact with each other: "*power distance* (from small to large), *collectivism versus individualism, femininity versus masculinity*, and *uncertainty avoidance* (from weak to strong)" (Hofstede et al., 2010, p. 31). Let's look briefly at each of these dimensions as well as different ways of viewing time and space and a variety of communication styles and preferences and how they might manifest in the classroom.

Power Distance

According to Hofstede et al. (2010), in cultures where a large power distance exists, the expectation is that the teacher holds full control and responsibility for the learning that happens in the classroom. In cultures where a small power distance is valued, the relationship between students and their teachers is more collaborative. Both the student and the teacher play a vital role in the learning process. Students in your class may fall anywhere on this spectrum in terms of their expectations related to student and teacher roles. By allowing for discussions that can inform you of the students' perspectives and expectations and them of yours, differences in power distance can be bridged with mutual understanding.

Collectivism vs. Individualism

The second dimension, centered around individualism and collectivism, can also be viewed as two ends of a spectrum. According to Hofstede et al. (2010), individualist cultures place high importance on concern for self with concern for others outside of close family being far less relevant. Collectivism on the other hand "stands for a society in which people from birth onward are integrated into strong, cohesive in-groups, which throughout people's lives continue to protect them in exchange for unquestioning loyalty" (Hofstede et al., 2010, p. 515). One example of collectivism versus individualism can be seen in how students view learning.

Hofstede et al. (2010) assert that, in collectivist cultures, "The purpose of education is learning how to do" while in individualist cultures "The purpose of education is learning how to learn" (p. 124). Culture is dynamic and, as with all dimensions and aspects of culture, it is possible to see some connection between collectivist and individualist cultures with large and small power distances. Hofstede et al. (2010) found a negative correlation between power distance and individualism. The smaller the power distance in a society, the more individualistic the people in the sociey tend to be (generally, this tends to be the case in many western cultures including the United States) and, conversely, the larger the power distance in a society, the less individualistic the people in that society tend to be (Hofstede et al., 2010, p. 103). In other words, where small power distance is valued, there may be more investment and value placed on continuous learning, or learning that produces more learning, while where large power distance is valued, there may be more investment and value placed on the action taken as a result of learning.

In the context of student writing, this tendency toward an individualist or collectivist and/or large or small power distance cultural vantage point might manifest in a student's willingness and ability to receive and apply feedback on their writing. Those students who value large power distance, for instance, may seek very specific directions on what exactly to do or not do in their writing. They may be less focused on the process of writing and what it uncovers while giving much attention to the result, leading to a strong desire for very direct and explicit feedback on specific elements of their writing. They may have less interest in, understanding of, or concern with more general guidance aimed at elements such as clarity, conciseness, and coherence in their writing.

Another important consideration of the cultural dimension of collectivism versus individualism is the extent to which one is comfortable with confrontation and direct communication style. This awareness can impact the effectiveness of guidance and the usefulness of feedback provided on student writing (see the *Providing Useful Feedback* section a little later in this chapter). Hofstede et al. (2010) write that in collectivist cultures "Harmony should always be maintained and direct confrontations avoided" while in individualist cultures, "Speaking one's mind is a characteristic of an honest person" (p. 113). In writing, students from predominantly individualist cultures may tend to employ more direct and linear communication styles while students from predominantly collectivist cultures tend to employ more indirect and less linear communication styles. I will elaborate on this idea through a discussion on monochronic and polychronic time systems and high-context and low-context cultures (Hall, 1976), as well as direct and indirect, understated and elaborate communication styles (Martin and Nakayama, 2018), a little later in this section.

Femininity vs. Masculinity

In the third cultural dimension, Hofstede et al. (2010) address elements of femininity and masculinity in different cultural contexts. In general terms, according to Hofstede et al. (2010), the degree to a certain level of performance is accepted fluctuates between cultures that are considered masculine or feminine. Hofstede et al. (2010) write, "In masculine cultures, students try to make themselves visible in class" and in feminine cultures "assertive behavior and attempts at excelling are easily ridiculed" (p. 160). As mentioned previously, culture is dynamic and different elements of culture may influence others. As such, it is important to note that elements of feminine and masculine cultures may be impacted by other dimensions such as individualism or collectivism. We acknowledge that some readers may not ascribe to the gender binary baked into language like "feminine/masculine" and hence offer this perspective as situationally descriptive rather than universally prescriptive.

Uncertainty Avoidance

The fourth dimension, uncertainty avoidance, may be seen in the classroom in how comfortable students are with classes that are student-driven versus highly structured by the teacher. In discussion-based classes that tend to be more loosely structured, in situations where there may not be one singular right or wrong answer to questions, students from cultures with strong uncertainty avoidance may feel uncomfortable (Hofstede et al., 2010). This discomfort may impact students' communication (written or spoken) when asked to think critically and address a topic based on their own perspective. It may impact professors' perceptions of student behavior as well. On one hand, the quiet that comes from this feeling of discomfort may appear to be model behavior. On the other hand, it may appear to be a lack of knowledge or interest. Neither of these is necessarily true for those from cultures with strong uncertainty avoidance.

Time and Space

When considering cultural contexts that could impact ESL students' writing, it may also be useful to consider Hall's (1976) explanation of how the concept of time and space varies among cultures. In terms of context and meaning, he presents two systems: Monochronic and polychronic. He writes that monochronic systems place importance on "schedules, segmentation, and promptness" while polychronic systems place importance on a variety of simultaneous actions that center on "people and completion of transactions rather than adherence to preset schedules" (p. 17). The adherence to a certain concept of time could manifest in the classroom in a variety of ways.

For example, the students in your class who work within a monochronic time system may methodically plan for the systematic and sequential accomplishment of individual tasks such as a writing assignment. This may result in very neat and organized writing submitted according to the timeline requested. Those who work within a polychronic time system focus on the participation of other people in order to accomplish a variety of tasks simultaneously. This may cause some difficulty with deadlines but could also support a dynamic process of collaboration and depth of thought extending beyond the singular assignment.

The influence of this cultural element of how time and space is viewed may impact a student's approach and execution of written assignments as well as the professor's response to student work. While there are undoubtedly many individual variances within cultures, it can be illuminating to consider the patterns that emerge in terms of geographic regions in general. According to Hall (1976), the United States typically follows the monochronic time system while many countries in Latin America and the Middle East generally follow a polychronic time system. A monochronic system may also align with a direct, linear, and more individually oriented system while a polychronic system might align with a less linear, less direct, and more collectively oriented system. Just as aspects of time and space are impacted by cultural norms, communication style and preferences may also be impacted by one's cultural background.

Communication Style and Preference

Through varying styles of communication ranging from indirect to direct and from understated to elaborate communication styles, culture and communication influence each other (Martin & Nakayama, 2018). Martin and Nakayama (2018) write that in some cultures, "preserving the harmony of relationships has a higher priority than being totally honest" (p. 232), which may lead to prioritizing indirect communication over direct communication. While direct communication is most common in many contexts in the United States, this is not the case in all cultures. Awareness of the cultural context from which you and your students may view and approach the tasks assigned in the classroom can provide invaluable information to all. The insight gained through this awareness can help you to better understand student performance and may allow you to provide more supportive and useful feedback.

Students who communicate most comfortably in an indirect style may have difficulty adapting to the linear, direct style of American English academic writing. Professors who are familiar with and accustomed to the linear and direct style of academic writing in the United States may have difficulty following the train of thought of someone who is implementing an indirect style in this context. This difference in communication style might present itself in the student paper that you read and begin to become frustrated by because the topic is not clear. You may not understand the point of the student's writing until way too late in the paper or maybe it never becomes clear at all. You may provide feedback such as: "Elaborate," or "What is the point of this?" or "What is your thesis?" A student who prioritizes indirect communication may find the convention of stating the thesis or purpose at the beginning of a composition to be abrupt or aggressive and may need additional support and guidance to feel comfortable with this structure.

According to Hall (1976), "one of the functions of culture is to provide a highly selective screen between man and the outside world. In its many forms, culture therefore designates what we pay attention to and what we ignore" (p. 85). The impact of high- and low-context cultures can impact how students write. Hall (1976) describes high-context communication as primarily implicit or indirect and low-context communication as explicit or direct. In Western cultures, which are often low-context cultures, it is the responsibility of the writer or speaker to be extremely explicit and direct to eliminate any confusion on the part of the reader or listener (Gill, 2017). Conversely, in Eastern cultures, which are often high-context cultures, explicit and direct communication can seem superfluous or sometimes aggressive (Gill, 2017). Consider the following of the use of high-context communication style:

> A Japanese man who is invited to a party but cannot go, or does not feel like going, would say yes, but then simply not go; a direct refusal could be seen as more threatening. The receiver of the message is expected to detect contextual clues and appreciate that the man did not directly refuse attendance.
> (Gill, 2017, para. 10)

This example may also be seen in the way a student receives feedback on their writing. If responding with questions or stating outright that they don't understand the feedback you have provided feels confrontational or aggressive, the student may simply say they understand (or avoid a direct response) even if they don't. This is illustrative of the complexity that may exist between interlocuters of high-context and low-context communication styles. Additionally, the desired product of a writing assignment may look quite different depending on the communication style utilized. What is considered well-organized, clear, and succinct writing in English in the United States may sound aggressive and off-putting in some other cultures where a more sensitive, implicit style of writing maybe desired.

In addition to indirect and direct communication styles, elaborate and understated communication styles are also important to consider. An elaborate communication style which "involves the use of rich, expressive language" versus an understated communication style which "values succinct, simple assertions" (Martin & Nakayama, 2018, pp. 232–233) can also impact how students write. According to Gill (2017), in some countries in Europe, the Middle East, Latin America, and Africa, people generally utilize an elaborate communication style. To illustrate, Gill (2017) writes that "in Arab cultures, individuals often feel compelled to over-assert in almost all types of communication because in their culture, simple assertions may be interpreted to mean the opposite" (para. 13). In writing assignments, this may appear in the over-emphasis of information or elaboration on elements that do not align with the student's thesis, thus detracting from the purpose of the paper and diluting the reader's ability to understand. Meaning may also be affected by word choice which may also be impacted by a student's culture.

We can see the impact of word choice both on the student in response to the word choice of the teacher and on the teacher in response to the word choice of a student. For example, in one of my (Becky's) classes, a student from South Asia often used the term "you people" when referring to the audience he was speaking to. It sounded startling, even aggressive at first. After speaking to this student about the tone that resulted from his choice of words and noticing how difficult it was for him to shift this tone, it became exceedingly clear that this phrase does not carry a negative tone in his first language. In terms of the impact of a teacher's choice of words, a student from Ghana in Laura's class shared that in his culture, a comment like "This sentence doesn't make sense" would read as more personally insulting than it does in English/U.S context.

These examples serve as further illustration of how the complexity of cultural context can affect the tendencies and preferences of writers and readers, as well as students and teachers. Open communication and acknowledgement of the variety of cultural norms that both students and teachers bring to the classroom can be enlightening and extremely valuable to all members of the classroom community. Variations in fundamental elements of language must also be considered.

Linguistic Conventions

You may have ESL students in your classroom from a variety of language backgrounds; some who use the Roman alphabet as used in English (e.g., Spanish, French, Portuguese, etc.) and some that use an entirely different written system (e.g., Arabic, Chinese, Farsi, etc.). Different languages and writing systems may vary by multiple characteristics from the symbols that are used to represent the letters and the direction in which the language is written and read (e.g., Arabic is written and read from right to left) to the use of articles, verb tenses, and a variety of other grammatical features. In the book *Learner English: A Teacher's Guide to Interference and Other Problems*, Swan and Smith (2001) address a variety of challenges, including transfer and interference from a person's first language, that may lead to confusion and errors in an ESL student's writing. Transfer occurs when a person applies a common rule (often in terms of grammar and vocabulary) from one language to a different language. When this transfer is not successful, it is considered interference. In the case when language systems are very dissimilar, the student needs to learn and apply an entirely new set of rules. In either case, writing in a second language can pose quite unique challenges.

While grammatical features such as articles (*a*, *an*, and *the*), pronouns (*she*, *he*, *they*, etc.), and prepositions (*in*, *on*, *by*, etc.) are used frequently and with relative ease by native speakers of English, there are languages that use these features quite differently or, in some cases, not at all. Let's first look at a language that may be considered related to English in many ways: Spanish. Spanish and English use the same alphabet system and share cognates that can assist in the use of both languages. However, there are many differences that could also impact the way Spanish speakers write in English. For example, regarding the use of pronouns, Spanish speakers and writers use a variety of verb endings (o, as, a, amos, an) to indicate who is doing the action ("-o" = I, "-as" = you, "-a" = he, she, it; "-amos" = we; "-an" = they). Additionally, adjectives, nouns, and articles all work together to indicate gender (Coe, 2001), which can lead to native speakers of Spanish using a pronoun such as "she" in reference to a noun such as a table. A great video with additional insight into this and other elements similar to this is a TED Talk titled: *How Language Shapes the Way We Think* (Boroditsky, 2017).

Arabic, on the other hand, is a language that has many fewer similarities to English in terms of grammatical structure and orthography and so there exists more opportunities for interference. One example of an important difference between the structure of Arabic and English is the verb *to be* (*is*, *am*, and *are* in English). This very important and commonly used verb in English does not exist in Arabic (Smith, 2001). According to Swan and Smith (2001),

> Since transfer mistakes arise where the systems of two languages are similar but not identical, they are most common (at least as far as grammar and vocabulary

are concerned) in the interlanguage of students who speak languages closely related to English. Speakers of unrelated languages such as Chinese or Arabic have fewer problems with transfer, and correspondingly more which arise from the intrinsic difficulty of the English structures themselves.

(p. xi)

Transfer mistakes may result in written language where it is more difficult to assume what the writer intended to say based on any commonalities in elements such as structure (word or rhetorical) or grammar. As a Francophone, I (Oumarou) have noticed some common transfer mistakes that French speakers might or are likely to make when speaking or writing in English, some of which I briefly discuss in the following.

Word Order

In French, the adjective can usually come after the noun it describes, while in English it comes before the noun. Issues related to word order can lead to errors such as saying, "house red" instead of "red house."

False Friends or "Faux Amis" in French

These refer to some words in English and French that look and sound similar but have different meanings, and there are many of such words. For instance, the French word "actuellement" means "currently," but the English word "actually" means "in fact."

Prepositions

French and English use different prepositions to express similar ideas. For illustration, "I am in the corner of Central Avenue and Main Street" instead of "I am at the corner of Central Avenue and Main Street."

Gender and Pronouns

French has gendered nouns and pronouns, while English does not. For instance, as a French speaker, I often use gendered pronouns or nouns in English, for example "he" or "she" instead of "they," when referring to a group of people.

Verb Forms

French has a more complex system of verb conjugation than English, and French speakers may make mistakes with irregular verbs or verb tenses. For example, they may say "I have went" instead of "I have gone."

Articles

French and English use articles differently, with French speakers often using definite articles where English would use indefinite articles. For example, a French speaker may say "the apple" instead of "an apple." Another example could be "I didn't bring *the* pen. Can I borrow yours?" instead of "I didn't bring *a* pen. Can I borrow yours?"

The common transfer mistakes discussed here are just a few examples, and they can affect the academic writing of ESL students whose first language is French. These common issues tend to have a bigger impact on and are more noticeable in academic writing than in speech, particularly given that academic writing follows a specific convention and style. While these issues may be common, it is also important to note that these transfer mistakes are more likely to affect students or individuals (French speakers) whose English language proficiency may not be solid. In other words, not all French speakers experience the same mistakes.

Before shifting to strategies for instructors in the next section of this chapter, we would like to highlight some factors to consider regarding the languages and cultures you are likely to encounter in your classroom (see Table 5.1). According to the Institute of International Education (2022), the most common countries of origin in higher education institutions in the United States as of 2021–2022 include China (30.6%), India (21%), South Korea (4.3%), Canada (2.8%), Vietnam (2.2%), Taiwan (2.2%), and Saudi Arabia (1.9%). Of these countries, both India and Canada utilize English as a primary language, so they are not included in this table.

Additionally, results of the U.S. Census Bureau American Community Survey in 2019 (Dietrich & Hernandez, 2022) indicate that the most frequently spoken language other than English in homes in the United States is Spanish or Spanish Creole (61.6%). As mentioned earlier in this chapter, Heritage Speakers, or "the children of original immigrants who live in a bilingual/multilingual environment from an early age" (Benmamoun et al., 2013), may also face language-related challenges.

It is important to note that we struggled with this section because we do not wish to reinforce stereotypes. Furthermore, we recognize the rich diversity that occurs within cultures. For example, both the scholarship and our experience tell us that students from Saudi Arabia are accustomed to more gender segregation in education, but individual experiences vary and change over time. Our goal in this section is to provide the reader with broad trends that may be helpful to know when working across language and/or cultural differences. In this table, we have provided only a sampling of interesting factors to consider (this list is in no way comprehensive) that may spark your interest in learning more about the languages and cultures of the students in your classroom.

Table 5.1 Language and Cultural Considerations

Language	Some factors to consider…
Chinese (Mandarin)	• Writing in Chinese tends to be organized less linearly than writing in English; some common elements of English language such as count (singular/plural) and use of pronouns are not used in Chinese language; and the concept of plagiarism as understood in the United States may be unfamiliar to students from China (Flaitz & Eckstein, 2003). • Students from China may be accustomed to a large, formal, teacher-centered classroom where students are expected to listen only unless told otherwise (Flaitz & Eckstein, 2003). • In China, it is a sign of respect and concentration to avoid eye contact with the teacher (Flaitz & Eckstein, 2003). Similarly in Taiwan, direct eye contact is discouraged (Flaitz & Eckstein, 2003).
Korean	• Writing in Korean may be organized to include details, more specific information at the beginning, and broad, more general ideas (including the overall point or thesis) at the end of the essay (Flaitz & Eckstein, 2003). • In Korea, classes are often teacher centered, and students are rarely expected to ask questions or discuss information. Being a student is considered a very serious, professional role (Flaitz & Eckstein, 2003). • Word choice in Korean changes depending on specific characteristics (such as age, status, and relationship) of the people engaged in communication (Flaitz & Eckstein, 2003).
Vietnamese	• Writing in Vietnamese reflects the use of tone through tone markers over each syllable in writing. Six tones (level, high-rising, low, low-falling, high-falling-rising, and low-falling-rising) are used with individual syllables, changing the meaning of words as the tone changes (Flaitz & Eckstein, 2003). • Students in Vietnam may be aware of the traditional Western structure of essay writing (introduction, body, conclusion) due to influences of the French, although the actual writing may not follow these conventions (Flaitz & Eckstein, 2003). • In Vietnam, poetry is an important and common part of everyday life for all people and "Hearing, reading, singing, and writing poetry is considered a natural part of life" (Flaitz & Eckstein, 2003, p. 202). Perhaps this influences the less linear writing style of Vietnamese.

(Continued)

Table 5.1 Continued

Language	Some factors to consider...
Arabic	• Writing in Arabic tends to be more circular in comparison to the linear structure of English. Furthermore, Arabic is written (and read) from right to left and words are spelled phonetically (Flaitz & Eckstein, 2003). • Arabic speakers from Saudi Arabia may be accustomed to classrooms that are separated by gender with male students taught by male teachers and female students taught by female teachers (Flaitz & Eckstein, 2003). • In Saudi Arabia, showing the sole of your shoe is rude and disrespectful (Flaitz & Eckstein, 2003).
Spanish	• Writing in Spanish is generally not organized the same way as in English. Fewer transitions or signal language (e.g., first, next, in conclusion, etc.) are used and tangents are common and acceptable (Flaitz & Eckstein, 2003). • Spanish speakers from Mexico may be more accustomed to being passive learners in a formal and sometimes strict classroom setting, only participating when asked to do so (Flaitz & Eckstein, 2003). • In Mexico, time is less important than in the United States and priority is given to the present moment (versus future or past) (Flaitz & Eckstein, 2003).

Strategies for Instructors

It can be extremely helpful to ESL students—all students really—when professors explicitly state their expectations for a writing assignment. For example, identifying elements such as required page length, purpose, audience, and citation expectations can remove some ambiguity that could otherwise cause confusion about what and how to write. This can impact not only the student's written production, but also the student's confidence in their ability to produce quality work. Providing examples of different genres of work that illustrate those expectations can also be beneficial to the quality of student output. Some useful strategies that college professors can use to support ESL students with academic writing include but are not limited to providing clear guidelines and expectations, providing targeted and useful feedback, providing encouragement, and building confidence and self-efficacy.

Providing Explicit Guidelines—Clear Expectations

In university classrooms in the United States, we typically expect a high level of engagement in the classroom. We expect students to actively listen and respond to questions, discussion prompts, and participate in idea generation. In this sense, students are free to engage in many informal and conversational ways. However, we also expect students to be silent when the professor or others are speaking. We expect students to raise their hand and/or wait their turn in these situations. A lack of knowledge of this cultural norm can lead to feelings of disrespect and offense on the part of those who innately understand this expectation.

In my (Becky's) experience, in some cultures (e.g., Brazilian culture) it is common for students to be very highly engaged in classroom discussions, but much less common for students to be silent when others are speaking, or to wait in order for one person to speak at a time. Conversely, in other cultures (e.g., Japanese culture) it is common for students to be silent while others speak, but not as common to talk freely and engage fully during in classroom discussions. In either case, there is typically no intention to offend or be disrespectful but, if left unaddressed, these different views on how to engage in a classroom setting could lead to frustration on the part of the professor and/or other students that could potentially be avoided. These cultural norms may also present themselves in the way students understand your expectations when it comes to the writing you assign.

Developing an understanding of the cultural norms of your students can help you to avoid confusion and provide them clearer expectations and guidelines, no matter where they are from. Engagement in discussions about cultural similarities and differences can be extremely edifying for faculty and students alike. It can also prevent some perplexing and potentially uncomfortable interactions in the classroom such as addressing concerns related to academic honesty and misconduct.

Issues surrounding plagiarism may need to be explicitly addressed. The prevalence, acceptability, and understanding of plagiarism may vary in different cultures and countries. Based on a variety of conversations with ESL students, I have learned that many students may have some conceptual knowledge of plagiarism but varying views on how to handle plagiarism in their writing. Some of the comments I have heard include: "Most staff and faculty don't really care about plagiarism back in my home country"; "we do not [include] who says what in in-text citation[s]. Just a list of references"; and "the rule is pretty loose. Sometimes people paraphrase an original text and do not give credit, and it is sometimes okay." In order to reach a shared understanding, it is important to set clear expectations when it comes to citations and issues of plagiarism.

Another way to provide explicit guidelines is through comprehensive written assignment descriptions given to students that detail expectations such as purpose, topic, format and length of paper, and citation style. Providing clear directions, and subsequent feedback, that clearly aligns with the stated purpose of the writing assignment is also vital. For example, if the purpose of a writing assignment is for students to increase their facility with technical writing skills in their discipline, it may be necessary to provide feedback that focuses on specific forms (e.g., correcting grammatical inaccuracies even if they do not interfere with meaning). On the other hand, if the purpose of the writing assignment is for students to communicate a broader idea or concept, feedback might be more focused on function while only commenting on form if an error interferes with meaning.

There may be times when the grammatical form is correct, but the meaning is confusing. There may also be times when the grammatical form is incorrect, but the meaning is clear. Bringing clarity, for both you and your students, to what is most important in terms of what you expect from the assignment can make a big difference in the quality of the work provided to you as well as in the effectiveness of the feedback you provide.

In my (Becky's) experience teaching ESL, students often comment that, after spending so much time and effort on a writing assignment, the feedback they receive is often related only to content versus how to revise in order to improve their writing skills. They often request critical, formative feedback that they can apply to the structure of their future writing. In addition, many ESL students, in my experience, greatly appreciate examples of writing that highlight the desired product. Perhaps what the students are craving is feedback that they can engage and interact with in order to ultimately improve their writing (see reference to feedback as a *product* and feedback as a *process* (Price et al., 2011) in Chapter 2). Explicit feedback on their writing along with a solid connection between this feedback and the expectation illustrated through an example can provide a network of support through which the student might be able to make substantive changes.

Providing Useful Feedback

In Dana Ferris' 2003 book, *Response to Student Writing: Implications for Second Language Students*, she highlights multiple studies from the 1990s that indicated that all students, not just ESL students, "valued feedback on all aspects of their writing, that they struggled with vague, cryptic, comments and/or symbols or abbreviations, and that they appreciated both praise and constructive criticism" (p. 17). I (Becky) have also heard from my students that the most helpful feedback they receive from professors includes clear input on what they are doing well and what they need to do differently in order to improve in terms of both the professors' expectations as well as their use of language. Mahfoodh and Pandian (2011), who more recently studied the impact of written feedback on EFL (English as a Foreign Language) students, also found that English Language Learners (ELLs) valued feedback, both positive and negative, and furthermore, that students' ability and/or willingness to accept and apply written feedback is impacted by the way the feedback is written.

While many students desire feedback that highlights both strengths and weaknesses, Ryan and Henderson (2017) found international students to be more sensitive to constructive feedback, viewing these comments as "upsetting, and too critical" (pp. 888–889). They assert that their findings "add weight to the argument that cultural differences are highly relevant to the emotional responses of students, above and beyond issues associated with language experience" (Ryan & Henderson, 2017, p. 889). Even so, it is also believed that while students appreciate accolades in the feedback, constructive feedback may be a more effective support for revision and future writing (Mahfoodh & Pandian, 2011, p. 18). Also worthy of recognition is the fact that commenting on every error in a paper can also become quite overwhelming for the professor. Consider instead identifying a pattern of error. You might acknowledge this pattern and provide a suggestion for improvement that the student can then apply to future occurrences. For longer papers with substantial errors, occasional reminders of the patterns of error as they appear later in the paper may help the student to generalize and apply your feedback throughout.

It is important to be aware of both the quality and quantity of comments offered. Mahfoodh and Pandian (2011) also found that certain practices like writing too many comments, using a red pen, or drawing a big circle around a large chunk of writing may be discouraging to some students and lead to frustration. Ultimately, the way we provide written feedback can impact students' openness and ability to learn from and apply the feedback provided. Attention to individual and culturally focused communication styles, as mentioned previously, can also have a significant impact on the usefulness of feedback provided. For example, indirect comments such as "Can you elaborate on this?" might not prompt the same response for a student as might a more direct comment such as "Please elaborate on this." Therefore, knowledge of students' communication styles can assist with the quality and usefulness of the feedback provided.

Awareness of and attention to the clarity of feedback provided is especially important for ESL students who are writing in a language and/or culture that is different from their home language and/or culture. Mahfoodh and Pandian (2011) highlight that students may react negatively when the feedback provided is unclear to them (e.g., clarity or feedback may be compromised through the use of codes such as "sp" to indicate an error in spelling) and when the student feels that what they meant to write was misunderstood. One participant in their research shared that in some feedback provided, the teacher did not understand what the student meant and so the student rejected the feedback entirely. Audio, video, or student conferences may also be viable options where one can soften the tone and impact of needed, critical, feedback.

In responding to student writing, Ferris (2003) provides suggestions for educators that help them "to prioritize, to treat students as individuals, to be encouraging, to be clear and helpful, and to avoid imposing their own ideas on student writers, leaving final decisions in the hands of the writer" (p. 118). Specific suggestions include: "Use the course grading criteria as a starting point for assessment and feedback" and "Use the specific writing assignment or task to identify possible points for specific feedback" (Ferris, 2003, p. 123). Referring to the grading criteria presented to the students for the course, and the specific assignment description each time you provide feedback, helps the students (and you) to align your feedback to the overarching goal of the course and assignment. In other words, it can help you to avoid getting off track and spending time working on things that are not as important for the specific purpose of the task at hand.

Furthermore, Ferris (2003) suggests that teachers "Get to know the students' abilities as writers as quickly as possible so that you can construct feedback appropriate to their individual needs" (pp. 119–121). Providing personalized feedback can increase a student's investment in the process of revision. It can greatly impact a student's understanding of their personal tendencies as a writer, which can be a motivating force for understanding and using the feedback provided. Ultimately, Ferris (2003) writes, "the instructor needs to see the process of reading the paper, identifying and selecting key feedback points, and constructing comments in a way that communicate clearly and helpfully to the student as a dynamic, creative, cognitively demanding process" (p. 123). Each piece of this process, as it exists for both the student and the professor, is important and necessary in supporting the development of necessary writing skills.

In Chapter 2, Laura addressed the need for faculty to support the attainment of *Student Feedback Literacy* (Carless & Boud, 2018) in order for students to be able to engage productively with the feedback provided. This ability for students to be able to understand, digest, appreciate, and ultimately use the feedback given to them to improve their writing skills is the core purpose of providing the feedback in the first place. Shifting the way students interact with the feedback provided to them can lead to increased autonomy, agency, and confidence.

Building Confidence/Self-Efficacy

In addition to positive feedback on writing, which can encourage increased confidence and self-efficacy (Ferris, 1995; Mahfoodh & Pandian, 2011), there are other pedagogical opportunities to support students' confidence in their writing. Mahn & John-Steiner (2002) emphasize that an important element of the future of education is to support students in becoming lifelong learners. To do this, teachers must help students to use their past experiences in order to "develop the confidence that engenders competence" (Mahn & John-Steiner, 2002, p. 46). This connection between experience, confidence, and competence can be established in the classroom.

In an article titled *The Gift of Confidence*, Mahn and John-Steiner (2002) explore Vygotsky's Zone of Proximal Development (ZPD) in relation to pedagogy.

The ZPD refers to the distance between a student's ability as seen through independent work and their potential ability as seen through supported work. McLeod (2019) writes,

> ZPD is the zone where instruction is the most beneficial as it is when the task is just beyond the individual's capabilities. To learn we must be presented with tasks that are just out of our ability range. Challenging tasks promote the maximum cognitive growth.
>
> (para. 3)

Mahn and John-Steiner (2002) assert that the ZPD "is deepened through an examination of the role of affective factors in learning" (p. 46). They assert that by providing sincere encouragement and support in the classroom, educators can create a space where students feel comfortable taking risks, which can lead to a deeper level of understanding and knowledge. A classroom where students are comfortable taking risks and stretching their comfort zone is important for all students. Writing in a second language may bring an extra layer of fear and uncertainty, which makes this point all the more important for our ESL students.

I (Becky) recently invited a panel of former students, all international, to come to my classroom and, on the basis of their previous experience in the same class, provide the new students with tips and advice to make the most of their time in the class. The majority of the wisdom shared had to do with encouraging the new students to take risks with the language, assuring them that this class is a safe place to do this, and to build a classroom community of support (including providing and receiving constructive feedback). Panelists mentioned the value of the confidence they built as a result of fully engaging in the class. This has motivated me to continue to invest in what Mahn and John-Steiner (2002) call "emotional scaffolding" (p. 52) as part of my teaching practice.

To provide "emotional scaffolding" (Mahn & John-Steiner, 2002, p, 52) is to provide a space where students are free and comfortable to take risks, accept challenges, and seek growth. This collaborative and supportive environment can provide encouragement to students on days that are challenging or when they are struggling with the most difficult of tasks (which of course is relative to each individual student when it comes to expressing your thoughts in writing). I've learned not to underestimate the impact of creating a community that leverages its resources and supports the growth of each individual student.

Embracing a Growth Mindset

In Chapter 1, we discussed the concept of a growth mindset and its relevance to a student's ability to grow and improve their writing. Using the same logic as discussed in Chapter 1, one way to support ESL college students with academic writing can be by encouraging them to embrace a growth mindset. According to Dweck (2016), a growth mindset is the idea that intelligence and abilities can be developed through dedication and hard work, rather than being fixed traits. ESL students generally have high self-determination (Jean-Francois, 2017) characterized by intentional and consistent effort to learn, which professors can use as an asset to foster their growth mindset. College and university professors can use various strategies to encourage ESL students to embrace a growth mindset as they develop their academic writing skills. As someone with ESL background and who identifies with the challenges these students may often face vis-à-vis academic writing in their second or third language, I (Oumarou) found the following strategies helpful based on my personal experiences as an international student in America.

Teaching ESL Students about Growth Mindset

Professors can start their first class by introducing and explaining the concept of growth mindset to ESL students and how it differs from a fixed mindset. For example, in my first semester and year as a new doctoral student, I took a scholarly writing class taught by one of the co-authors of this book. The class was a mixture of domestic and international students. During our first class of the semester, the educator introduced and explained the concept of growth mindset. I (Oumarou) remember she said to us, "Students are at different levels in terms of their ability to write academically but what can often make a difference is their attitude towards a growth versus fixed mindset." She added that "You are not here to compete but to support each other's learning and I am here to support you. Plus, if we know it all," including herself (the educator), "there won't be a need for the scholarly writing class."

That first class disarmed me and created a mental shift in the way I began to think about my academic writing and learning moving forward. I remember some of the students in the class sharing how embracing a growth mindset was a game changer for them. For me and my peers, embracing a growth mindset fostered a supportive classroom culture that values effort, progress, and learning. Such a shared culture can in turn encourage students to support each other and work collaboratively to achieve their goals. It also helps celebrate the diversity and the unique strengths that each student brings to the classroom.

Also, the scholarly writing professor talked about examples of successful individuals or previous ESL students she taught or knows who have embraced a growth mindset and achieved their goals through hard work, perseverance, and intentional and consistent effort. For example, we had a panel on writing where students who previously took the scholarly writing class shared their experiences with academic writing, including their successes and challenges as well as how they overcame those. It was encouraging to hear and learn from the advanced students, particularly those with experiences and backgrounds similar to mine.

Celebrating Effort and Progress

Another way to encourage ESL students to embrace a growth mindset is, instead of only praising them for their grades or final project, to praise ESL students' effort and progress toward their goals. I remember the same scholarly writing class professor consistently reminding us that while we needed the required grades to pass the class, she encouraged us to focus on our learning process and the progress we were making. As such, faculty can encourage ESL students to see their writing issues and challenges as opportunities for growth and learning. Faculty can also provide feedback that focuses on improvement. When faculty provides ESL students with feedback that focuses on how they can improve their writing, rather than just pointing out mistakes, it can encourage these students to reflect on their writing and identify areas for improvement or growth. Also, I personally found it useful when my professors encouraged me to monitor my progress vis-à-vis my writing and praise my achievements along the way.

Modeling a Growth Mindset

Modeling a growth mindset by a professor can help ESL students better put in perspective that everyone, including their teachers, has or has had challenges with academic writing. Professors can model a growth mindset by sharing their own struggles and successes and demonstrating a willingness to learn and improve. They can also share stories of their own writing challenges and journal article rejections and how they used them as opportunities for growth. Two of my professors modeled a growth mindset by either sharing a past or recent rejection of journal article manuscripts. While one of the professors verbally shared about the rejections and often challenging comments from reviewers, the other professor went as far as to project the feedback for us to see during class.

While the modeling of a growth mindset by a faculty may seem like a simple act, it can go a long way to encourage students who are experiencing challenges with their academic writing. The ultimate message could be "*mastering academic skill takes time; you are not alone; we are in this together.*" Even more, for some ESL students who are likely to internalize an inferiority complex related to writing in an unfamiliar language, the modeling of a growth mindset by their professors can help convince them to reframe their thinking about writing as something some people are just "good at" and others "bad at." Reframing can encourage them to think about writing as a skill set and process that requires time, continuous practice, constant effort, and sustained patience and can help reinforce the idea that writing skills are developed, not innate.

Encouraging ESL students to embrace a growth mindset can be a powerful way to promote their academic success and personal growth. By teaching ESL students about growth mindset, praising their effort and progress, providing feedback that focuses on improvement, modeling a growth mindset, and fostering a supportive classroom culture, professors can help ESL students develop the skills and mindset they may need to improve their academic writing.

Using Writing Centers

Writing centers at colleges and universities are critical for supporting ESL college students with their academic writing. They offer individualized support to address unique challenges such as grammar, syntax, cultural differences, and academic conventions. Through one-on-one consultations with trained tutors, ESL students can receive tailored assistance (Moussu, 2013). Writing centers also provide resources, workshops, and sessions that focus on specific writing skills and strategies relevant to ESL students, fostering skill development and revision.

Writing centers can also serve as supportive and inclusive spaces where ESL students can develop their writing skills and habits of revision using organized writing sessions. Organized writing sessions allow students to work on assignments, free write, receive constructive feedback, and revise their work. For effective and helpful writing tutors and ESL students' working relationships, it is important to create a comfortable environment where writing centers' staff normalize asking questions, use inclusive language, avoid assumptions about ESL students' writing abilities, and appreciate the challenges these students face. As a graduate international student, I (Oumaru) have personally benefited from the supportive nature of the writing center at my university, where caring tutors have played a significant role in building my confidence and improving my writing process.

Additionally, colleges and universities should adopt culturally responsive practices to ensure ESL students feel seen and heard at writing centers. Doing so is essential because ESL students come from diverse linguistic and cultural backgrounds. This involves training tutors and leadership to understand cultural perspectives on writing and incorporating diverse perspectives into instruction. With the increasing number of ESL students on campuses, it is crucial to include them as a regular part of tutor training (Moussu, 2013) and to staff writing centers with experienced tutors from various linguistic, cultural, and educational backgrounds. By reflecting the diversity of the student body, writing centers create an environment where ESL students can better relate to tutors and staff, fostering a sense of belonging and support.

Finally, Miller-Cochran et al. (2009) emphasize that writing centers hiring multilingual tutors can provide second language writing students with firsthand strategies and empathy. Miller-Cochran et al.'s point highlights the likelihood of

HELPING SPECIFIC POPULATIONS WITH WRITING

students being heard and supported by tutors who share their background or understand their experiences. A culturally competent and diverse graduate writing center plays a vital role in supporting ESL students by offering individualized support, culturally sensitive practices, resources, workshops, and an inclusive environment. These strategies can empower ESL students to develop their writing skills, build confidence, and achieve academic success.

Spending Class Time on Writing Issues

While a professor can make a case that it is not their job to teach ESL students how to write because they are not a writing instructor, or even recommend that ESL students take a writing course to deal with their writing issues, it is important to note that supporting ESL college students with academic writing requires a combination of collaborative effort, patience, empathy, and understanding of their unique needs. While not the primary focus of the course, it is essential to highlight that a professor, with patience and empathy, may be able to dedicate valuable class time to address writing issues for ESL students. For example, when I (Oumarou) was a first-year master's student, one of my professors took two class sessions to do some writing workshops and refreshers about academic writing conventions, including grammar, syntax, punctuation, and citation styles, to help us understand what is expected. We spent some time together reviewing grammar and syntax rules that are commonly used in academic writing. This proactive approach not only fostered a deeper understanding of English academic writing but also helped identify specific areas requiring improvement.

As previously mentioned, Swan and Smith's (2001) edited book, *Learner English: A Teacher's Guide to Interference and Other Problems*, is a valuable resource for educators working with non-native English speakers and writers. The book provides insights into how students' native languages can affect their English language writing and speaking skills, including pronunciation, grammar, vocabulary, and cultural factors. It offers practical guidance on addressing these challenges in the classroom. For instance, the authors explored the concept of language interference, where the structures and patterns of a learner's native language may affect their acquisition of English, which can translate in writing issues. Educators can use their knowledge of language interference issues to anticipate and help students overcome difficulties, particularly in academic writing. With explanations, examples, and comparisons between the learners' native languages and English, the book equips educators with strategies, exercises, and teaching techniques to support ESL students as they develop their academic writing proficiency in college.

The professor I referenced earlier decided to spend some class time on writing issues when he noticed that we were (his students, majority non-English native speakers) struggling with many writing issues after the first writing assignment. After the writing workshops and refreshers, he had us write a ten-page essay. He gave us extensive feedback on the essays and writing assignments, highlighting areas of strength and areas for improvement. His feedback was constructive and provided specific suggestions for improvement. He subsequently made it a requirement that we use the graduate writing center two or three times before we submit an assignment. While submitting our assignments, we had to submit all drafts from our writing center visits, in addition to the final draft. Such a process allowed us to see our progress from paper 1 to 2 and 3 based on his feedback and that of the writing center tutors. We all appreciated the professor for his proactiveness, patience, and empathy. While building some time for a writing workshop during class may be challenging, the example I share here demonstrates its possibility and one way (out of many) to go about it, even though it may look different for different professors and students.

Additional ways professors can use in their classes to support ESL with academic writing can include providing writing prompts that are interesting and relevant to ESL students to help them generate or brainstorm ideas. Interesting and relevant writing prompts can be helpful especially for those who struggle to come up with ideas for writing. For example, allowing students to choose their own topics for writing assignments that are relevant to their experiences and interests can encourage them to use their strengths and personal interests to engage in meaningful writing tasks. Writing prompts can also be related or relevant to the class materials to help students practice writing and develop their writing skills while also strengthening their understanding of the course content. Also, it can be helpful to provide and encourage some peer review opportunities within class assignments. When carefully planned, a peer review can be a helpful tool for ESL students to work together in a supportive environment to review each other's writing and provide/receive constructive criticism/feedback from their peers. Alternatively, students can be encouraged to create or join peer support or writing groups as a collaborative and a supportive environment to practice writing.

Additionally, encouraging ESL students to carefully use technology as a helpful tool to improve their writing skills may be helpful. With technology, students can access a vast range of relevant resources, including writing guides, writing tools, and language learning platforms. Introduce and encourage them to explore and use tools like Grammarly to check their grammar and syntax or Zotero to help with references. They can also watch YouTube videos about writing and resources to support their writing. However, excessive reliance on these tools may discourage some students from developing their own critical thinking and writing skills. Thus, many students may need guidance to ensure they maintain authenticity, integrity, and ethical writing practices when utilizing technology to enhance their academic writing. To maximize the benefits and mitigate the costs, educators should provide guidance and instruction on effective and responsible use of technology for writing. It is important to strike a balance, leveraging technology's advantages while nurturing students' independent writing abilities and critical thinking skills.

Furthermore, providing extra time for ESL students to complete writing assignments is a helpful practice. Additionally, faculty can model exemplary writing by sharing examples/samples of well-written academic papers and essays or class assignments by students with similar backgrounds in a previous class. Writing samples can serve as a reference to help students understand the characteristics of solid academic writing and to identify ways to improve their own writing. Finally, it is important for faculty working with ESL students to be patient, supportive, encouraging, and empathetic vis-à-vis these students. Writing or learning to write in one's second or third language can be a challenging and frustrating process for many of these students.

Spending class time on writing issues that ESL students may face can be an effective way to support and help them develop the skills and confidence they need to succeed in academic writing. With consistent support, patience, empathy, and focused feedback, ESL students can improve their writing skills and feel more confident in their ability to express their ideas orally and on paper.

Using Appreciative Advising Practices as a Strength-based Approach

By way of background, the Appreciative Advising (AA) framework (Bloom et al., 2008) is grounded in positive psychology (Seligman, 2002; Seligman & Csikszentmihalyi, 2014) and Appreciative Inquiry (Cooperrider & Srivastva, 1987) theories. As a strength-based approach and collaborative learning practice, AA is a social-constructivist philosophy and approach to education that provides a theory-to-practice framework for educators and higher education leaders to optimize their interactions and relationships with students (Bloom et al., 2013). AA has been adapted to enrich international students' educational experience in the United States, including advising (Elliot, 2012; Palmer, 2009; Zhang, 2016) and new international student orientation activities (Abdoulaye Balarabe, 2022). Using AA to help ESL students with academic writing from a strength-based perspective means focusing on these students' strengths and abilities rather than just identifying and trying to fix their weaknesses. Using a strength-based approach means identifying and building on the strengths and positive qualities of ESL students.

As outlined in the following, AA offers many possibilities that college and university professors can use to help ESL students with academic writing from a strength-based perspective.

Identify Students' Strengths as Writers

Faculty can start by identifying the strengths of ESL students as writers. They can identify a student's strengths through conversations with the student or by reviewing their past writing assignments. ESL students' strengths can include their unique perspectives and experiences, their ability to speak multiple languages, and their creativity. Encourage these students to draw on some of their strengths when writing. Once areas where a student excels are identified, the professor can work collaboratively with the student to develop strategies that leverage their existing skills and support their growth as writers.

Build Confidence by Providing Positive Feedback

Building confidence through positive feedback requires using appreciative language to build ESL students' confidence and encourage them to see themselves as capable writers. It is also important to employ positive reinforcement to acknowledge these students' progress and successes and celebrate their achievements. Finally, provide ESL students with positive feedback that focuses on their strengths and the progress they have made by emphasizing and recognizing the strengths they bring to their writing.

Encourage Reflection/Self-reflection

Professors can encourage ESL students to reflect on their writing and identify the areas where they feel most confident and successful. Then, support them to focus on building on these strengths rather than just trying to fix their weaknesses. Alternately, ESL students can be encouraged to reflect on their writing process and identify areas for growth. Through feedback giving, faculty can help the student to recognize patterns in their writing and to develop strategies to address challenges they may be facing.

To conclude, helping ESL students with academic writing from a strength-based perspective means focusing on their strengths and building on their abilities. Professors can adapt the appreciative advising approach to help ESL students see themselves as capable and potentially skilled writers. By focusing on strengths, using positive reinforcement, encouraging self-reflection, using student-centered teaching approaches, and leveraging existing skills, ESL students can be supported to develop the confidence and skills they need to succeed in academic writing.

CONCLUSION

In this chapter, we explored the unique experiences of ESL students with academic writing. For consistency and clarity, we used ESL to refer to college students for whom English is not a first language. However, it is important to note that this category of ESL students is large and diverse and can include refugees, heritage speakers, naturalized, native-born citizens, international students on student visas, and permanent residents in the United States, Canada, the United Kingdom, Australia, and so on. These students come from diverse cultural, linguistic, and educational backgrounds and arrive at their host institutions with a wealth of assets, including self-determination, different learning and communication styles, and linguistic diversity.

Because of the differences in writing conventions and styles that may exist between ESL students' home countries and their study abroad host countries, many of these students may face some challenges with academic writing. With an understanding and appreciation of the complex experiences and diverse backgrounds of ESL students, there are many practical strategies and resources that faculty can use to help some of these students who may have potential academic writing issues. These resources and strategies include but are not limited to: Providing clear expectations and guidelines; using appreciative approaches, encouraging self-reflection, and building confidence; providing effective, specific, and constructive feedback on writing assignments; and utilizing available resources such as culturally competent writing centers. Writing or learning to write in a different language takes time and can often be a frustrating process for many ESL students. It is here that professors can play a major role by being patient, encouraging, and empathetic toward ESL students in their classes. Doing so can help create a conducive, welcoming, inclusive, and supportive learning environment for these students as they navigate their academic writing journeys.

REFERENCES

Abdoulaye Balarabe, O. (2022). Enhancing international student orientation at U.S. colleges and universities using appreciative advising practices. *Journal of Appreciative Education*, 9, 3–14. https://libjournal.uncg.edu/jae/article/view/2203/1657

Andrade, M. S. (2008). International graduate students: Adjusting to study in the United States. In K. A. Tokuno (Ed.), *Graduate students in transition: Assisting students through the first year* (Monograph No. 50, pp. 71–88). National Resource Center for The First-Year Experience and Students in Transition. https://styluspub.presswarehouse.com/browse/book/9781889271613/Graduate-Students-in-Transition

Baklashova, T. A., & Kazakov, A. V. (2016). Challenges of international students' adjustment to a higher education institution. *International Journal of Environmental & Science Education*, 11(8), 1821–1832. https://doi.org/10.12973/ijese.2016.557a

Benmamoun, E., Montrul, S., & Polinsky, M. (2013). Heritage languages and their speakers: Opportunities and challenges for linguistics. *Theoretical Linguistics*, 39(3–4), 129–181. https://doi.org/10.1515/tl-2013-0009

Bloom, J. L., Hutson, B. L., & He, Y. (2008). *The appreciative advising revolution*. Stipes Publishing Co. https://stipes.com/catalog/academic-advising-student-success/appreciative-advising-revolution/202

Bloom, J. L., Hutson, B. L., He, Y., & Konkle, E. (2013). Appreciative education. *New Directions for Student Services*, *2013*(143), 5–18. https://doi.org/10.1002/ss.20055

Boroditsky, L. (2017). *How language shapes the way we think* [Video]. TED Conferences. https://www.ted.com/talks/lera_boroditsky_how_language_shapes_the_way_we_think

Carless, D., & Boud, D. (2018). The development of student feedback literacy: enabling uptake of feedback. *Assessment & Evaluation in Higher Education*, *43*(8), 1315–1325. https://doi.org/10.1080/02602938.2018.1463354

Cheng, M.C., Chang, J., Chen, Y., & Liao, Y. (2010). "Do they want the same thing?" Learner perspectives on two content-based course designs in the context of English as a Foreign Language. *Asian EFL Journal*, *12*(4), 67–84. http://asian-efl-journal.com/PDF/Volume-12-Issue-4-Cheng.pdf

Coe, N. (2001). Speakers of Spanish and Catalan. In M. Swan & B. Smith (Eds.), *Learner English: A teachers guide to interference and other problems* (pp. 90–112). Cambridge University Press. https://doi.org/10.1017/cbo9780511667121.008

Cooperrider, D. L., & Srivastva, S. (1987). Appreciative inquiry in organizational life. In R. W. Woodman, & W. A. Pasmore (Eds.), *Research in organizational change and development* (pp. 129–170). JAI Press. https://www.researchgate.net/publication/265225217_Appreciative_Inquiry_in_Organizational_Life

Deardorff, D. K. (2015). A 21st century imperative: Integrating intercultural competence in Tuning. *Tuning Journal for Higher Education*, *3*(1), 137–147. https://doi.org/10.18543/tjhe-3(1)-2015pp137-147

Dietrich, S. & Hernandez, E. (2022, August). *Language use in the United States: 2019*. United States Census Bureau. https://www.census.gov/content/dam/Census/library/publications/2022/acs/acs-50.pdf

Duff, P. (2001). Language, literacy, content, and (pop) culture: Challenges for ESL students in mainstream courses [Abstract]. *The Canadian Modern Language Review*, *58*(1), 103–132. https://doi.org/10.3138/cmlr.58.1.103

Dweck, C. S. (2016). *Mindset: The new psychology of success*. Ballantine Books. https://www.penguinrandomhouse.com/books/44330/mindset-by-carol-s-dweck-phd/

Elliot, M. J. (2012). International students and the appreciate advising way. *Journal of Appreciative Education*, *1*(1), 35–40. http://libjournal.uncg.edu/jae/article/view/592

Ferris, D. R. (1995). Student reactions to teacher response in multiple-draft composition classrooms. *TESOL Quarterly*, *29*(1), 33–53. https://doi.org/10.2307/3587804

Ferris, D. R. (2003). *Response to student writing. Implications for second language students*. Routledge. https://doi.org/10.4324/9781410607201

Flaitz, J., & Eckstein, L. K. (2003). *Understanding your international students: An educational, cultural, and linguistic guide*. University of Michigan Press ELT.

Gill, C. (2017, April 25). *Intercultural communication and considering a different perspective*. OUPblog. https://blog.oup.com/2017/04/intercultural-communication-styles/

Hall, E. T. (1976). *Beyond culture*. Anchor Books. https://www.penguinrandomhouse.com/books/73813/beyond-culture-by-edward-t-hall/

Hofstede, G., Hofstede, G. J., & Minkov, M. (2010). *Cultures and organizations: Software of the mind: Intercultural cooperation and its importance for survival*. (3rd ed.). McGraw-Hill Education. https://www.mhprofessional.com/cultures-and-organizations-software-of-the-mind-third-edition-9780071664189-usa

Institute of International Education. (2021). International student enrollment trends, 1948/49-2020/21. *Open Doors Report on International Educational Exchange*. https://opendoorsdata.org/data/international-students/enrollment-trends/

Institute of International Education. (2022). Leading places of origin of international students, 2000/01-2021/22. *Open Doors Report on International Educational Exchange*. https://opendoorsdata.org/data/international-students/leading-places-of-origin/

Jean-Francois, E. (2017). Exploring the perceptions of campus climate and integration strategies used by international students in a US university campus. *Studies in Higher Education, 44*(6), 1069–1085. https://doi.org/10.1080/03075079.2017.1416461

Le, E. (1999). The use of paragraphs in French and English academic writing: Towards a grammar of paragraphs. *Text & Talk, 19*(3), 307–344. https://doi.org/10.1515/text.1.1999.19.3.307

Mahfoodh, O. H. A., & Pandian, A. (2011). A qualitative case study of EFL students' affective reactions to and perceptions of their teachers' written feedback. *English Language Teaching, 4*(3), 14–25. https://doi.org/10.5539/elt.v4n3p14

Mahn, H., & John-Steiner, V. (2002). The gift of confidence: A Vygotskian view of emotions. In G. Wells & G. Claxton (Eds.), *Learning for life in the 21st century: Sociocultural perspectives on the future of education* (pp. 46–58). Blackwell Publishing Ltd. https://doi.org/10.1002/9780470753545

Martin, J. N., & Nakayama, T. K. (2018). *Intercultural communication in contexts* (7th ed.). McGraw-Hill Education. https://www.mheducation.com/highered/product/intercultural-communication-contexts-martin-nakayama/M9781260837452.html

McLeod, S. (2019). Zone of proximal development and scaffolding. *Simply Psychology*. Retrieved January 30, 2022 from https://www.simplypsychology.org/Zone-of-Proximal-Development.html

Miller-Cochran, S., Hooper-Ortmeier, C., Cox, M., Dadak, A., DePew, K. E., Crusan, D. J., Hoang, H., Jordan, J., Matsudu, P. K., Moore, J., Scott, G., & Simpson, S. (2009). CCCC Statement of Second Language Writing and Writers. https://corescholar.libraries.wright.edu/english/246

Moussu, L. (2013). Let's talk! ESL students' needs and writing centre philosophy. *TESL Canada Journal*, *30*(2), 55–68. https://doi.org/10.18806/tesl.v30i2.1142

Palmer, E. (2009). Using appreciative advising with international students. *The Mentor*. https://doi.org/10.26209/MJ1161523

Price, M., Handley, K., & Millar, J. (2011). Feedback: Focusing attention on engagement. *Studies in Higher Education*, *36*(8), 879–896. https://doi.org/10.1080/03075079.2010.483513

Ryan, T., & Henderson, M. (2017). Felling feedback: Students' emotional responses to educator feedback. *Assessment & Evaluation in Higher Education*, *43*(6), 880–892. https://doi.org/10.1080/02602938.2017.1416456

Seligman, M. E., & Csikszentmihalyi, M. (2014). Positive psychology: An introduction. In *Flow and the foundations of positive psychology* (pp. 279–298). Springer. https://link.springer.com/chapter/10.1007/978-94-017-9088-8_18

Seligman, M. E. P. (2002). *Authentic happiness: Understanding the new positive psychology to realize your potential for lasting fulfillment*. Atria. https://psycnet.apa.org/record/2002-18216-000

Siepmann, D. (2006). Academic writing and culture: An overview of differences between English, French and German. *Meta*, *51*(1), 131–150. https://doi.org/10.7202/012998ar

Silva, P. J. (2007). *How to write a lot: A practical guide to productive academic writing*. American Psychological Association. https://psycnet.apa.org/record/2006-23317-000

Smith, B. (2001). Arabic speakers. In M. Swan & B. Smith (Eds.), *Learner English: A teachers guide to interference and other problems* (pp. 195–213). Cambridge University Press. https://doi.org/10.1017/cbo9780511667121.014

Swan, M., & Smith, B. (Eds.). (2001). *Learner English: A teacher's guide to interference and other problems*. Cambridge University Press. https://doi.org/10.1017/cbo9780511667121

Zhang, Y. (2016). Appreciative advising with international students in American community colleges. In R. L. Raby, & E. J. Valeau (Eds.), *International education at community colleges* (pp. 93–109). Palgrave Macmillan. https://link.springer.com/book/10.1057/978-1-137-53336-4?page=2

Chapter 6
Accessible Writing Pedagogy

INTRODUCTION—WHAT WE KNOW

According to the National Collaborating Centre for Determinants of Health (2023), marginalized populations are defined as "groups and communities that experience discrimination and exclusion (social, political, and economic) because of unequal power relationships across economic, political, social and cultural dimensions" (para 1). Students with disabilities can be categorized as one such group and are sometimes the students that faculty may feel least prepared to teach, exacerbating the potential to further marginalize them. Gilson and Dymond (2011) assert that many faculty members have never been adequately trained to teach, or even exposed to, students with disabilities, making them unaware of how to develop curriculum that meets the needs of this population of students. Additionally, many university faculty may be unaware of how many people have disabilities, which can lead to the creation of curriculum that does not take into consideration the needs of a large population of learners.

In this chapter, we will provide a statistical overview as well as general factors to consider when teaching students with some of the more commonly reported disabilities. We will also share our individual perspectives, including where we have been and where we are now in our own educational and professional journeys. We believe that with practice, a change in mindset, and a willingness to try new pedagogical strategies, writing can be made more accessible for all students. We will also discuss three main areas of study that could support your teaching effectiveness with students with disabilities in higher education classrooms: Universal Design, strengths-based approaches to teaching and learning, and differentiated instruction. We will also provide recommendations for including these practices in your classrooms with tangible examples of accessible writing pedagogy. Know that each of these areas of focus may require a change in mindset.

Statistics and Other Factors to Consider

According to the United States Census Bureau (2021), 13% of people (an estimated 42,485,034 of the total 326,912,547 surveyed) who responded reported having a disability, approximately 8% (5,584,573 people) of who were between 18 and 34 years of age. Of those, respondents reported having the following impairments: Hearing = 1%; vision = 1.5%; cognitive = 5%; ambulatory = 1%; self-care = 1%; and independent living = 3%. This means that more than 55,000 people between the ages of 18–34 in the United States reported having a hearing or ambulatory disability; more than 83,000 people reported a visual disability; and nearly 280,000 people reported a cognitive disability.

We now turn to the higher education context more specifically. According to the National Center for Education Statistics (2018), 19% of undergraduate students and 12% of postbaccalaureate students in the United States have a disability. In their 2015–2016 data set on postsecondary students with disabilities, the National Center for Education Statistics (n.d.) found that undergraduate and postbaccalaureate students reported having at least one of the following:

> Blindness or visual impairment that cannot be corrected by wearing glasses; hearing impairment (e.g., deaf or hard of hearing); orthopedic or mobility impairment; speech or language impairment; learning, mental, emotional, or psychiatric condition (e.g., serious learning disability, depression, ADD, or ADHD); or other health impairment or problem.
>
> (para 5)

The percentage of students with disabilities enrolled in higher education has steadily increased over the past decade. For example, the number of higher education institutions (both public and private) that enroll 10 percent or more of students with disabilities has risen from 2.4% of institutions in 2010–2011 to 11.8% of institutions in 2021–2022 (National Center for Education Statistics, 2023). This data can offer context to the number of students faculty may encounter with disabilities in today's college classroom versus ten years ago. Identified disabilities range anywhere from mild to severe and from visible to invisible (also referred to as seen to unseen and apparent to less apparent). According to Statistica (2022), 15% of more than 33,000 respondents (all of which are college students in the U.S.) reported having attention deficit and hyperactivity disorder (ADHD), 4.5% reported having a learning disability, 3.5% blind or low vision, 2.9% autism spectrum disorders, 2.1% deafness or hearing loss, and 1.5% mobility or dexterity disabilities (Statistica, 2022). See Table 6.1 for a snapshot of some of the disabilities that students in your classroom may have and some factors to consider when creating assignments and lessons that address their needs.

HELPING SPECIFIC POPULATIONS WITH WRITING

Table 6.1 Factors to Consider When Planning

Disability Type	Factors to Consider
ADHD	Students with ADHD may benefit from clear, succinct, and consistent communication in the form of deadlines (including a schedule and reminders for upcoming assignments/assessments), written and oral assignment descriptions (including examples), assignments broken down into specific, individual steps when possible, and plentiful opportunities for individual consultation with the professor (Tyrone, 2020).
Learning Disabilities	Students with learning disabilities may benefit greatly from clear, detailed, and consistent guidelines and expectations as well as study guides and alternative options for completing evaluations (e.g., handwritten versus typed or vice-versa) and assignments (e.g., in-class activities that may be completed outside of class) (Chang et al., 1996).
Visual Impairments	Students with visual impairments may benefit from seating near the front of the room, adapted printed materials (large text, digital, braille), and/or detailed oral descriptions (e.g., say aloud what is written on the board) (Chang et al., 1996).
Autism Spectrum Disorders	Students with autism may benefit from support with understanding the instructions and the overall goal of writing assignments (with particular attention to any changes to assignments) as well as reminders and support centered around the organization of thoughts in writing, incorporating their viewpoint as the writer, and staying on topic (Wolf et al., 2009).
Hearing Impairments	Students with hearing impairments may rely on lip reading or sign language to communicate fully. Seating arrangements and positioning (as well as sufficient lighting) that allows for a clear view of a speaker's face is important and they may benefit from important information (important points, deadlines, changes to goals or schedules, etc.) being written on the board or printed on handouts as well as the use of visuals (charts and graphs) and captions on videos (Chang et al., 1996).
Physical Disabilities	Accessibility may be one of the biggest issues for college students with physical disabilities. This may require moving/arranging desks and furniture and other physical modifications including relocating the class to a more accessible location before or during the term (Chang et al., 1996).
Anxiety Disorders	This disability may impact students' willingness to ask questions during class or via messaging systems. This type of disorder can also impact the student's successful performance on certain kinds of assessments or assignments (University of Washington, 2012).

Individual Perspectives

Erin

When I was being trained as a middle and high school English teacher in the United States during my undergraduate program, a majority of the course curriculum outside of my English classes was centered on pedagogy, learning outcomes development, and teaching methods. At first, these topics were complex and difficult to understand because they seemed both philosophically high level and simultaneously weedy in practice. However, slowly my mind began to consider the vital importance and application of these concepts more easily once I saw the return on investment in classroom preparation and planning. It wasn't until much later during my higher education career that I realized how few administrators and faculty had the same opportunities I had to learn these concepts early on and come to think about them almost innately when establishing their programs, lectures, and assignments.

I will never forget a mandatory learning outcomes training session I attended as an early student affairs administrator at my university. I was immediately annoyed by this half-day requirement since I spent half a decade learning the ins, outs, and importance of learning outcomes, curriculum development, and methods when creating any type of educational program as an undergraduate. I was already developing these things intuitively in my work with college students and was frustrated that I had to go to training I believed would not add to my skill set. However, what I quickly learned is how vital my understanding of these concepts was in aiding my colleagues as they were tediously working through the nuances of the training. When I would see their eyes squint and looks of annoyance spread across their faces, I started to recall the feelings of frustration I initially felt when going through those first few years of my undergraduate teacher education program learning these critical educational practices.

An important aspect of holistic K-12 teacher education training programs in the United States is the amount of time spent on how to create modifications and accommodations for students who have disabilities in your classroom. Unfortunately, once students enter postsecondary institutions, the responsibility of tracking their disability accommodations is placed on them and is no longer advocated for by the school system the way it was before they entered college. We will get into this issue later in this chapter. Elementary, middle, and high school teachers across the United States come into their first year of teaching already knowing there is a high likelihood they will need to adapt their curriculum every year for specific students. These adaptations may be due to students' Individualized Education Plans (IEPs), modifications of complex learning activities for children with physical and cognitive disabilities, and implementation of differentiated instruction throughout an academic term depending on the subject matter (e.g., reading interventions). I will never forget the countless scholarly papers and Ohio Learning Standards unit and lesson plans I developed over four years of my undergraduate teaching training (Ohio Department of Education, 2023). After writing hundreds of pages on how I would adapt my methods based on the needs of individual students with a vast array of learning and physical disabilities, I felt confident in creating appropriate activities and lessons for students with a range of disabilities.

However, my training represents an outlier experience compared to the type of training the vast majority of higher education faculty receive when completing their terminal degrees before moving into the collegiate classroom. While K-12 teacher preparation programs are spending sizable amounts of time educating new teachers on how to modify and adapt their curriculum for students with disabilities before they enter the classroom, higher education takes a less stringent approach to teaching preparation. A graduate degree in the content area (as opposed to pedagogical training) is considered the official credential for teaching at the college level (Robinson & Hope, 2013; Jensen, 2011). There are also varying degrees of experience required, depending on the graduate program and subject matter, to be the primary instructor of record before acquiring an advanced or terminal degree. If funding is available, some graduate students will obtain teaching assistantships with minimal required training before teaching courses. However, if an academic department does not offer such assistantships, many graduate students will have to take it upon themselves to gain much needed teaching experiences through non-paid means (e.g., volunteering with faculty, classroom observations, etc.).

There is little consistency across the United States for graduate teaching preparation, which can specifically affect the way new faculty come to understand how to adapt their instruction for students with disabilities. From a legal perspective, state and federal court decisions during the 1980s and 1990s found that the standards for postsecondary faculty were not mandated through the Rehabilitation Act of 1973 and ADA of 1990 to be trained on adapting curriculum for students with disabilities (Polk, 2021). This is an area of growth in many institutions, and in this chapter we will discuss some opportunities for how to fill those gaps through simple adjustments to faculty mindset, implement course design elements, and seek support for students with disabilities in classes where writing skills play an important role in the instruction and assessment—especially if training and affordable professional development for faculty are lacking on their campus.

Becky

As an undergraduate student, I studied special education. I was fortunate to gain a variety of experiences as a student teacher in both a high school English

Literature class for students with learning disabilities and an elementary school Basic Life Skills class for students with severe and profound disabilities. Just out of school, my first job was teaching in a supplemental kindergarten (not specific to children with disabilities), followed by a short time as an assistant in a classroom for middle school–age students in a multiple disabilities support classroom. From there, I took on an administrative role as the Disabilities Specialist for a Head Start Program. In this role, I worked with children ages three to five and their teachers to coordinate classroom support for children with existing and suspected disabilities in addition to connecting the teachers, students, and families to the needed and/or desired evaluations and/or support services.

It was in this role that I became aware of both the similarities and differences between the needs of students with speech and language delays and students who speak English as a second language. For example, students with speech and language disabilities may need specific interventions including the support of a speech and language therapist while students who are learning the English language may need time and language instruction. I became acutely aware of the fact that a student may both be an English language learner and have a disability, but that this is not necessarily the case. I also became aware that it may be very difficult to determine the difference between a language difference and a language delay in some cases.

As I noticed referrals for speech evaluations for students who had just recently arrived in the United States, I began to ask questions. I began to talk to people and read about others' experiences related to the overlap between speech and language disorders and second language acquisition. I had the most wonderfully supportive supervisor who encouraged me to go back to school for a master's degree in Teaching English to Speakers of Other Language (TESOL) degree and who hired an English as a Second Language (ESL) teacher to work with me to develop a system and resources for teachers to respond to the full range of students identified as ESL, students with disabilities, and students with disabilities also identified as ESL in their classrooms.

The next step in my professional career was to begin teaching English language in a higher education setting; first in China, then in the United States where I have been teaching for the past 14 years. I was again so fortunate to have yet another wonderfully supportive supervisor who encouraged me to pursue a PhD. In my Higher Education and Student Affairs Ph.D. program and in my career, I can incorporate all of these experiences into an eclectic approach to teaching.

Nearly 25 years after those first experiences as a student teacher in special education, I still carry many of the lessons I learned with me, which became part of my mindset. They drive the way I view the classroom, my role in the classroom, the student's role in the classroom, the potential within me and within the students. Incorporating this range of experiences into my teaching practice prompted me to shift my early teacher mindset that focused mostly on my ability to deliver the curriculum broadly to the class into a more flexible approach that allows me to structure the class in a way that maximizes students' ability to learn the content.

Working with students of different ages, abilities, and cultural backgrounds has significantly shaped my mindset, perspective, and approaches to teaching today. One simple example of this is that I choose not to assign or require specific seating arrangements in my classrooms (except for specifically designed activities). By allowing students to self-select their seats, students who need to sit in the front of the classroom to see, or to hear, or to focus better, can do so without drawing unnecessary attention. I have found this is one simple, basic form of collaboration within the classroom that can lead to a curriculum that is adaptable to individual student needs.

Additionally, I allow and encourage flexibility within some of the traditional norms of the classroom. For example, I tell my students, if you are feeling tired or having trouble focusing at any point during class, feel free to stand, sit on the floor, or move your seat. I tell students what is important is that they can engage with the material and activities, not that they are quiet and still. I recognize that I teach a skill, English language, and so this might be easier in my context. However, the element that has been most important in my experience is to build a community in the classroom where students feel comfortable sharing their needs and helping each other create a functional learning environment for all.

This shift in mindset from a focus on how I deliver information to how individual students receive this information has transformed the way I view and approach my role as an educator. Because in postsecondary settings, unlike K-12 school systems, students with disabilities do not necessarily come to class with IEPs, it is essential for faculty to build awareness and shift their mindset to support all students in achieving their educational goals. Building a safe and collaborative community in the classroom where the teacher and the students are proactively addressing the unique needs students bring to the classroom can be the first step in working effectively with students with disabilities.

A UNIVERSAL DESIGN (UD) MINDSET

Some U.S. higher education institutions have incorporated principles of UD throughout their campus services, operations, and curriculum with success. In this section, I (Erin) will talk through what UD is and then work through how you can conceptualize it in the classroom and adjust your instructional mindset to support students with disabilities. This will be an important starting point as you consider what you already know about working with students with disabilities, how you create and prepare your course curriculum each term, and how you have adjusted and accommodated students with disabilities in your teaching practice before.

In education, we often find ourselves in a place where new terms, methods, and concepts are being developed faster than we can learn about and implement them, let alone test them to see if they work for us or our students. As both an environmental and educational concept that was introduced in the late 1990s, it is not a surprise that many people have not heard of UD because it is still in the early stages of development and implementation across multiple sectors. Historically speaking, UD came out of an era of global civil rights social movements and federal laws in the late 1970s to early 1990s that emphasized the need for Americans with disabilities to have equal access to services, physical spaces, and resources to succeed in society (e.g., Section 504 of the Federal Rehabilitation Act of 1973, Fair Housing Amendments Act of 1988, Americans with Disabilities Act of 1990). So, what is this concept and how can it benefit you to know how it fits into your work as an educator?

As a term, UD was first coined by Ronald L. Mace, an architect and educator who held the belief that all designs should start with the idea that the final product be usable by anyone. Initially in higher education, UD was implemented to create safe physical environments when new layouts for classrooms, academic buildings, walkways, and common spaces were being designed in the 1990s with the "barrier free" UD concept (The R.L. Mace Universal Design Institute, 2019). Since the concept of UD has been adopted and implemented over the last 30 years, its principles have been extended to approaches in higher education around instruction, web design, technology, student services and more. One comprehensive resource for how UD can be utilized in dozens of areas of educational design can be found on The Center for Universal Design in Education website through the University of Washington, which has been funded by the U.S. Department of Education and the National Science Foundation. Another long-standing and trustworthy resource for expanding your understanding and application of universal design for learning (UDL) concepts is the Center for Applied Special Technology (CAST).

Though UD has gone from an inclusive concept to physical manifestations in design (e.g., accessible buildings, campus services), its extension to student learning is where UD's proverbial rubber meets the road for faculty. UDL can be a challenge and change in mindset at first for many faculty (Strange & Banning, 2015). However, once your mindset shifts to this way of developing curriculum, you will find yourself proactively accommodating students before they enter your classroom and feeling more confident in your ability to adjust to students with disabilities in the future— regardless of the subject matter.

Three Principles of Universal Design for Learning (UDL)

What if you always felt confident about your teaching methods and how you designed your curriculum each semester? What if you were always prepared to work with students of any ability? What successes would you see that you don't see now? These are questions you can address proactively and easily by implementing three simple principles of UDL when making updates to old curriculum or creating a new course or assignments. I (Erin) will also offer some examples of how to use these principles when specifically assigning a new writing assessment or updating an old one you have been using for years.

Building on the overarching concept of UD, the three principles of UDL were created for the context of classroom learning and how educators can promote inclusion and accessibility through their curriculum. The three principles can be read as both provisions educators can take and the type of learning that occurs when these provisions are incorporated (Strange & Banning, 2015):

1. Provide multiple means of representation (i.e., the what of learning)
2. Provide multiple means of action and expression (i.e., the how of learning)
3. Provide multiple means of engagement (i.e., the why of learning)

The first principle, *provide multiple means of representation*, acknowledges that all students comprehend information presented to them differently, whether due to "sensory or learning disabilities, cultural differences, or differential preference for visual or auditory resources over printed text" (Strange & Banning, 2015, p. 169). Starting with the idea of how students with differing abilities learn allows you to pre-emptively consider the types of examples used to model concepts or the terminology you use in the classroom to discuss a topic.

Consider the following example of two students listening to the directions for an upcoming writing assignment. One student has disclosed to you via the accessibility office that they have ADHD and may need additional time to complete writing assignments or require additional meetings to review course deadlines and requirements. Another student in your class has not disclosed their disability but has struggled with anxiety in high school and is trying to make it through college without requesting aid or advocacy from the accessibility office. Both disabilities could benefit from multiple means of representation to aid the students in feeling well-informed about this assignment and examples of how to complete the assignment to your standards. To best accommodate the students who disclose, as well as those who choose not to disclose their learning needs or accommodation, you can provide both written and verbal explanations of the assignment and offer multiple examples and rubrics that outline your expectations. Something I have implemented is simply recording videos of myself going through an assignment's requirements and examples during class and then posting that same video on my learning management system site for them to review anytime. By incorporating multiple means of representation, you can not only help those students who have indicated their needed accommodations, but those who have not disclosed disabilities as well.

The second principle, *provide multiple means of action and expression*, incorporates "development of curriculum and instruction that includes multiple options for physical action, expression and communication, and executive functions" (Burgstahler, 2020, p. 42). Looking back at Table 6.1, consider how you might adjust for a student who has disclosed their autism diagnosis at the start of the term and has expressed difficulty with understanding the instructions and overall goal of the final writing assignment that is not due until the final week of class. For you, this may seem frustrating because class has just begun, and you plan to go over the final writing assignment closer to the midpoint in the term. However, for this student, waiting that long to know what the expectations are for the assignment could be detrimental to their success. This second principle encourages you to plan for students with these concerns, whether due to a diagnosed disability or not. Offering examples for all writing assignments, giving instructions on the syllabus with details, and multiple options for writing formats for completing a final assignment can relieve the tension a student may have as they begin your class. These UDL approaches will also ultimately give you time to review the assignment early and often to avoid last-minute concerns or frustrations that students face where final graded projects are concerned.

With the third principle, *provide multiple means of engagement*, motivation for learning becomes center stage and focuses on the way students are motivated to engage or sustain their engagement in the learning process. For instance, engaging in course content and assignments in groups may benefit and motivate some students to stay focused and on task with peer support. For others, working in groups may be frightening or anxiety inducing, especially for students with social anxiety disorders. On countless occasions, I (Erin) have heard faculty tell me how students need to know how to work in groups or on teams if they want to be successful in the real world, so they assign groupwork or collaboration in all their courses and assignments. This makes me cringe a bit when I think about the principles of UDL and know what I do about different learning preferences and disabilities. This third principle encourages faculty to consider multiple means of engagement and options students can choose from to experience success in a course without being attacked or feel they have deficient skill sets. This is not to say you should completely rule out group work when we know it is a beneficial skill for students to learn. It is just to emphasize that it shouldn't be the only thing you do for larger class assignments or every project you require in class. Variety is important, and you can easily incorporate this principle into writing assignments by allowing students to choose to work in small groups, pairs, or alone and request peer critiques on smaller writing assessments to help students build upon their abilities and improve their writing.

To offer a clear view of how the UDL principles can be incorporated into a college-level writing assignment or assessment, explore Table 6.2. Information in this table was compiled from *Applying the Principles of Universal Design for Learning (UDL) in the College Classroom* by Boothe et al., 2018.

Table 6.2 Adjusting College-level Writing Assignments with UDL

Principles of Universal Design for Learning (UDL)	Adjustments to college-level writing assignments with UDL
Principle 1: Multiple Means of Representation	Provide both written instructions and verbal explanations (maybe a video that can be rewatched) of the assignment. This small adjustment can aid in accommodating different learning preferences. Be sure to include visual aids (e.g., screenshots or videos) and examples to support student understanding. Incorporate multimedia elements such as tables, charts, or infographics to enhance comprehension of the assignment (e.g., a YouTube video link on the writing topic with subtitles). Provide options and university resources for students to use and/or request available assistive technologies, such as text-to-speech software or screen readers, to access any course written materials (e.g., articles or e-books).
Principle 2: Multiple Means of Action and Expression	Offer "good student" writing examples and resources, like graphic organizers or outlines, to help students organize their thoughts and structure their writing. Allow students to choose from different writing formats (e.g., essays, research papers, blog posts, presentations) to accommodate diverse learning preferences and strengths. Divide assignments into multiple parts for students to feel less overwhelmed and more in control of their actions and expression. Provide clear guidelines and rubrics outlining expectations and assessment criteria for all assignments at the beginning of the term to allow students time to process and ask questions about the assignments. Offer multiple options for students to demonstrate their understanding of the course content (e.g., recorded presentations, audio recordings, or visual/photo essays). Create both an ideal and flexible timeline for some or all assignments. For instance, instead of hard deadlines, incorporate date ranges for multiple assignments. Offer choice and autonomy in selecting subject-related topics or research questions to increase student motivation and engagement.
Principle 3: Multiple Means of Engagement	Integrate real-world or authentic writing tasks that connect to students' interests and experiences. For instance, create a list of questions for reflection that students should address in their writing assignments to help them connect to the material personally and deepen their critical thinking.

(Continued)

Table 6.2 Continued

Principles of Universal Design for Learning (UDL)	Adjustments to college-level writing assignments with UDL
	Provide opportunities for reflection and self-assessment throughout the process of a writing assignment that students can turn in during class or submit as mini assignments. This will allow students to evaluate their own progress and set goals that you can offer feedback on as part of the overall writing process.
	Provide options for students to collaborate on writing assignments in groups or as individuals. Incorporate both peer and faculty feedback/critique incrementally as part of every writing assignment.
	Provide ongoing feedback and support on smaller assignments in a timely fashion, including individualized guidance and questions to help students improve their writing skills throughout the term.

As a faculty member, you may already offer these options in your classroom and learning management systems (e.g., Blackboard, Canvas). However, taking time to elevate your pre-existing curriculum to proactively prepare for the needs of students with disabilities can relieve stress and feelings of overwhelm when challenges do arise during the academic term. I (Erin) have found that when I have incorporated these principles in my classes, I have significantly fewer questions from my students about my expectations of their scholarly work and writing assignments. As Dr. Sheryl Burgstahler (2020) so pointedly states in her book *Creating Inclusive Learning Opportunities in Higher Education*,

> Think small. Universally design something in a course, at your worksite, in your home, or in your community, or share the idea with someone who will! If you just look for them, you will see UD opportunities everywhere. Take incremental steps toward the ideal.
>
> (p. 209)

You can simply begin by looking at what you already do and use the principles of UDL to make small changes that are growth minded, manageable, and help students feel they can be successful regardless of their disclosed or undisclosed disability.

TOWARD A STRENGTHS-BASED APPROACH

We now turn to the strengths-based approach to teaching and learning when specifically working with students with disabilities. Felton and Lambert (2020) write that every student should have the opportunity to build human connections, networks, with people all over campus (teachers, administrators, staff, etc.) that help them "explore the big questions of their lives" (p. 7). These "big questions" prompt students to contemplate what defines them as humans, what is motivating to them, and what brings meaning and purpose to their lives. Sometimes, it seems as though the benefit of this depth of thought is overlooked for students with disabilities because their goals are often decided by their diagnosis versus their own voice. However, all college students are faced with big decisions regarding their field of study and future. The conscientious effort to help all students work through "big questions" not only helps them navigate their college experience on a personal level but also will help faculty identify strengths and needed accommodations early on and avoid placing inappropriate expectations on them.

Using a strengths-based approach does not mean ignoring a student's disability. On the contrary, having a strengths-based mindset means beginning with what you know about a student's disability and recognizing that the accommodations they require will positively benefit everyone in the long run. For instance, consider that a student's disability is related to an anxiety disorder and the university's accessibility office has requested that you accommodate them by offering longer time to complete written assignments. Instead of viewing an adjustment of a due date from a deficit perspective, consider how offering more time for this student to complete an assignment allows them to more fully meet your expectations. In this case, we are not looking at this student's disability as a deficit, ignoring their needs, or lumping them into the general student population, but simply accommodating them with simple supports to allow them to learn at their own pace and meet your expectations of the class. Supporting students enhances their confidence and well-being, enabling them to focus on their abilities rather than limitations, which is the essence of a strengths-based approach to education.

Knowing our own strengths is also important; this knowledge gives us essential information for feeling satisfied and achieving goals. Imagine a time when someone (a friend, a family member, a teacher, a stranger, anyone) gave you feedback that made you aware of one of your own strengths. How did this impact you? Did it reinforce your existing knowledge? Did it open a whole new door of possibility for you? The ability to identify strengths in others can add tremendous value and awareness to the person's experience and abilities and help retain college students. Linley (2008) highlights the importance of "day-to-day strength spotting" where we identify strengths in ourselves and others by noticing things such as the level of engagement in certain tasks, speed of mastery or understanding, completion of and strong performance in certain tasks, and prioritization of certain tasks, just to name a few (p. 74). "Strengths can come to the fore at any time, from anyone – even from possibly unlikely people and unlikely places" (Linley, 2008, p. 76). For example, an educator's strengths can surface when successfully handling a challenge they didn't anticipate for a student in a class in which they are struggling. We all have strengths that can be uncovered unexpectedly through shared experiences both in and outside the classroom. Helping students find their strengths while navigating both the specific course content and writing skills that are vital to their success in your classroom can be a fulfilling and worthy pursuit and make them feel they are supported and can be successful in college.

You might be thinking, "I already have so many students in my classes and have so much to grade already. How could I possibly find extra time to engage in strengthspotting or other strengths-based approaches in my already busy faculty life?" We know how you feel, and as co-authors we are all too familiar with the "do more with less"' conundrum of higher education. However, we will map out some simple and easy steps that can quickly become part of your teaching toolbox without feeling like more time will be taken away from your already packed schedules.

Strengths-Based Approaches in Writing Assignments

When students can develop greater self-efficacy through strengths-based discussions with university faculty and staff, they are more likely to continue their studies and be retained from year to year (Soria & Stubblefield, 2015). Additionally, viewing students from a strengths perspective and growth mindset allows students with disabilities to overcome feelings of deficiency and increase their confidence over time (Gutshall, 2013). In essence, adjusting expectations for student writing using strengths-based approaches can help them improve and make your life easier in the long run.

It is important to look at things from a growth mindset when considering ways to easily implement a strengths-based approach to written assignments. Instead of moving from one or two definitive writing assignments that could make or break a student's grade in a class, consider dividing things into smaller and more easily digestible assignments. This way, you can see student growth over time and offer feedback and help along the way. Engaging in this type of adjustment to writing assignments can also preemptively aid students with disabilities who require time adjustment accommodations per requests from the accessibility office on campus.

Other ways to adjust writing assignments from a strengths-based approach is to create opportunities for students to build upon their strengths from the

HELPING SPECIFIC POPULATIONS WITH WRITING

beginning through the help of positive modeling, strengths-focused feedback, and peer supports that will not take time away from your already crammed schedule each term. Consider the example in Table 6.3 of a typical final high-stakes writing assignment for a college level course and how you might adjust it using strengths-based approaches to learning (Kahn & Holody, 2009). In this case, Kahn and Holody (2009) defined high stakes as a graded writing assignment that involves significant research and requires "higher-ordered academic skills" (p. 90).

Table 6.3 Adjusting High Stakes Assignments

High Stakes Writing Assignment Example	Strengths-Based Adjustments
Choose one of the theories that were discussed in our class this term. Your paper should describe the (1) historical background of the theory; (2) cite at least 5–7 scholarly sources (e.g., journal articles, not websites) related to the theory you are discussing (beyond the course textbook); (3) describe how you could apply this theory to our field outside of the classroom; and (4) discuss the success and shortcomings of the theory if applied in today's context. Minimum word count with reference page should be between 5K and 7K.	Model positive writing examples at the start of the term and regularly discuss these examples in class. Share examples of strong writing in different styles and format. Showcase how different strengths contribute to excellent writing and encourage students to learn from these examples. When giving feedback on writing assignments, be specific about the strengths you see in their work. Instead of only focusing on errors, highlight areas where writing strengths shine and provide tips on how they can further develop those aspects. Encourage students to work in pairs or groups during or outside of class throughout the term. Have them bring in their outlines and drafts regularly for this assignment so they can learn from each other's strengths and offer constructive feedback. This fosters a positive learning environment where strengths are celebrated. Share success stories of other students who have improved their writing over time with a similar assignment. This can inspire and motivate your students to believe in their abilities and potential for growth.

Think about the last time you celebrated the work of your students, whether aloud in class or in a one-on-one email or meeting. How does it make you feel to spend time on something positive and uplifting, if only for a few minutes? What if you did a little bit more of that every day? Incorporating strengths-based approaches into your teaching and how you engage students in the writing process can boost their confidence while making the educational setting more enjoyable. Whether you require one or two large-scale, high-stakes writing assignments in your course or are seeking ways to be better prepared to engage with students with disabilities each term, strengths-based approaches can be an easy concept to implement and incorporate into your daily practices as an educator.

INCORPORATING DIFFERENTIATED INSTRUCTION

As was mentioned earlier in this chapter, disabilities, both diagnosed and undiagnosed, are handled quite differently in higher education than in school-age settings. According to the Child Find principle of IDEA (2017), it is incumbent upon each state to ensure that all children "who are in need of special education and related services are identified, located, and evaluated" (para 1). Conversely, according to the United States Department of Education Office for Civil Rights (2017), and in accordance with Section 504 of the Rehabilitation Act and the Americans with Disabilities Act (ADA) for post-secondary accommodations, "A postsecondary student with a disability who is in need of auxiliary aids is obligated to provide notice of the nature of the disabling condition to the college and to assist it in identifying the need for an auxiliary aid" (para 7). In college it is the responsibility of the student to disclose any relevant information (diagnosis, need for evaluation or accommodation) and access the university's available support services.

Some students may find college to be a good time to experiment with and examine their ability to succeed without seeking accommodation (e.g., a student with autism who is very detail focused and a strong researcher may wish to explore that skill without accessing on-campus accommodations). Ultimately, students may request an evaluation for a suspected disability and/or share an existing diagnosis (this is not required). It is entirely up to the student to share (or not share) this information as they see fit for their education. Therefore, being proactive and meeting each student where they are, regardless of disability status, and utilizing approaches such as differentiated instruction, is a beneficial practice.

I (Becky) first learned about the concept of differentiated instruction as an undergraduate student studying special education. Widely known for her work on differentiated instruction, Carol Tomlinson (1995) defined the fundamental nature of differentiated instruction as the "shaking up" of "what goes on in the classroom so that students have multiple options for taking in information, making sense of ideas, and expressing what they learn" (p. 3). Differentiated instruction acknowledges the individual needs of students within the context of the larger classroom (Tomlinson, 1995). Differentiated instruction is often referenced in relation to primary and secondary education settings but it can be argued that differentiated instruction belongs in every classroom.

In their study on the use of differentiation in an introductory course for graduate students, Santangelo and Tomlinson (2009) found that this approach allowed all students to access the activities and content in the classroom. This finding is encouraging since students come to us, especially in introductory courses, with varying levels of background knowledge, experience, interest, and skills. The need for differentiated instruction may be even more apparent now, as we address the varying academic needs of students who likely experienced interruptions to their high school education due to the COVID-19 pandemic. The United States Department of Education Office for Civil Rights (2021) found that for school-age students with disabilities, "COVID-19 has significantly disrupted the education and related aids and services needed to support their academic progress and prevent regression" (p. 25). This interruption in support provided for students with disabilities in high school can impact their ability to pursue their goals and succeed in a higher education setting.

As mentioned in the introduction to this chapter, 19% of undergraduate students and 12% of postbaccalaureate students in the United States have a disability (National Center for Education Statistics, 2018). According to the United States Department of Education Office for Civil Rights (2021), "students with disabilities on college campuses faced significant hardships and other barriers due to COVID-19, which threatened their access to both education and basic necessities" (p. 49). Some of the challenges identified for students with disabilities that were amplified by the pandemic include a reduced sense of support and belonging, increased financial and safety concerns, and mental health concerns such as depression.

The impact of the COVID-19 pandemic on the mental health of students is significant. "The COVID-19 health crisis spawned what has been described by some as a mental health pandemic for America's college students – one that took a particularly harsh toll on students from historically marginalized, underserved communities" (United States Department of Education Office for Civil Rights, 2021, p. 43). These individual needs, whether they be physical or mental, seen (apparent, visible) or unseen (less apparent, invisible), continuing or exacerbated by the pandemic are needs that deserve attention in the college classroom. Attention to and appreciation for the uniqueness of each student lies at the heart of differentiated instruction.

When addressing what constitutes a differentiated classroom, Tomlinson (1999) asserts that awareness and acknowledgement of the individuality that each student brings to the classroom is vital. Being cognizant and responsive to students as individuals leads teachers to "accept and act on the premise that teachers must be ready to engage students in instruction through different learning modalities, by appealing to different interests, and by using varied rates of instruction along with varied degrees of complexity" (Tomlinson, 1999, p. 2). Teachers who prioritize being flexible, creative, and engaging, and partnering with students to reach the established objectives and outcomes, can create this dynamic learning environment.

In their study on the use of differentiated instruction in a higher education setting, Santangelo and Tomlinson (2009) found that "Incorporating a wide variety of materials and activities, using flexible grouping strategies, providing options for expression, supporting text comprehension, offering choices, and being flexible with timelines were some of the strategies that proved to be most beneficial" (p. 319). One way to incorporate flexibility, creativity, and to partner with students in a collaborative effort is through a flexible timeline (see also UDL Principle 2: *Multiple Means of Action and Expression* in Table 6.2). For example, instead of requiring students to submit their paper by 11:59 on Tuesday, consider offering a submission opening and closing day/time by opening a submission period from 6 pm on Tuesday to 11 pm on Sunday. As you create the assignment, set it up so students can submit at any time during the submission window. Allowing a five-day span for submission allows flexibility for students who need extra time, regardless of their circumstance. This may help empower students to manage their time as well as eliminate a possible fear that their early submission may communicate a lack of seriousness or effort by not using every minute afforded.

You can also establish parameters around the flexibility provided while encouraging collaboration with students by asking them to sign up for a submission day (e.g., five submission slots each day during the five-day window). This demonstrates your attention to and respect for students' individual needs while encouraging them to honor their own strengths, weaknesses, and tendencies, and use their unique knowledge of themselves to guide their selected submission day. For example, someone who is self-aware of their tendency to procrastinate might choose an earlier submission date to avoid unnecessarily drawing out the stress of the assignment. Or perhaps a student who is self-aware of their strengths in writing might also choose an earlier submission day while students who are self-aware of their challenges in writing might choose a later date in the window to allow them more time to consult and gain feedback from their peers and/or professor. Discretely allowing those with known disabilities to be the first to access the sign-up might also be appropriate.

This method may also provide some flexibility for the professor in terms of spacing out the grading into more manageable chunks. We've all tried to grade all 25 compositions in one short weekend, haven't we? Additionally, in a situation where a student would benefit from a later submission but wasn't able to sign up for their preferred day, an adjustment could be arranged based on individual need without much disruption to the assignment deadline or future

HELPING SPECIFIC POPULATIONS WITH WRITING

assignments. Ideally, a flexible timeline should be presented in the syllabus, creating a collaborative culture in the classroom from the start of the semester. See Table 6.4 for an example of how a flexible timeline might be presented, as well as multiple writing assignment options for students in the syllabus.

In addition to providing options with the timeline, alternatives within specific assignments may also be beneficial for students. Having multiple assignment options to reach the same course objectives could be provided. For example, maybe a traditional paper is not the only way a student could demonstrate their understanding of a specific concept in the class. Perhaps they could write a blog, create a mock informational website, or write a script and record an informational video presentation of the information. Allowing students to have a voice in the way they demonstrate their understanding of course content may give instructors a more accurate view of their proficiency.

Offering flexibility in how feedback is provided during the planning period for writing and using rubrics that allow for individualization are also forms of differentiation. Does the class structure allow for time during class to outline a paper or to explore alternative assignment options? Do students access office hours for planning and/or revision purposes? Could you pair consultation options at various stages of the planning and completion of writing assignments?

Table 6.4 Assignment Description and Submission Timeline for Syllabus

Assignment Description	Submission Timeline
Assignment #1: Personal Narrative Demonstrate your understanding of XXX by writing about your personal experience with this topic. Please choose 1 of the following: • Traditional Composition/Essay Structure—This paper should be 2–3 pages, 1-inch margins, double spaced, 12-pt Times New Roman font and should include an Introduction, Body, and Conclusion. • Blog Post—This post should be approximately 1,200–1,500 words long. Feel free to include images, photos, audio, drawings, etc. to support your ideas (be sure to cite anything that is not your original work). *This work does not need to be published or made publicly available. • Script/Video—This video should be 5–7 minutes long and should be accompanied by a detailed script. Clear organization of content must be apparent.	September 20–24 *Slots are limited to 5 submissions/day during this timeframe.* **Please sign up for a submission day no later than August 15th.** *If no slots are available on your preferred day, please schedule an appointment to meet with me.*

(Continued)

Table 6.4 Continued

Assignment Description	Submission Timeline
Assignment #2: Compare and Contrast Demonstrate your understanding of XXX and XXX by comparing these two concepts. **Please choose 1 of the following:** • Traditional Composition/Essay Structure — This paper should be 3–5 pages, 1-inch margins, double spaced, 12-pt. Times New Roman font and should include an Introduction, Body, and Conclusion as well as a formal reference page and in-text citations using APA 7. • Blog Post — This post should be approximately 1,500–2,000 words long. Please include images, photos, audio, drawings, etc. to support your ideas (be sure to cite anything that is not your original work). *This work does not need to be published or made publicly available. • Script/Video — This video should be 7–10 minutes long and should be accompanied by a detailed script. Clear organization of content must be apparent. Be sure to include oral citations in the video as well as written citations in the script.	October 25–29 *Slots are limited to 5 submissions/day during this timeframe.* **Please sign up for a submission day no later than October 20th.** *If no slots are available on your preferred day, please schedule an appointment to meet with me.*
Assignment #3: Synthesis Demonstrate your understanding of the readings by synthesizing information from a minimum of 5 sources from this course. **Please choose 1 of the following:** • Traditional Composition/Essay Structure — This paper should be 5–7 pages, 1-inch margins, double spaced, 12-pt. Times New Roman font and should include an Introduction, Body (including summary and response to the 5 sources selected), and Conclusion as well as a formal reference page and in-text citations using APA 7. • Blog Post — This post should be approximately 2,000–3,000 words long. Please include images, photos, audio, drawings, etc. to support your ideas (be sure to cite anything that is not your original work including the 5 sources selected). *This work does not need to be published or made publicly available. • Script/Video — This video should be 10–15 minutes long and should be accompanied by a detailed script. Clear organization of content must be apparent (including summary and response to at least 5 clearly identified sources). Be sure to include oral citations in the video as well as written citations in the script.	December 6–10 *Slots are limited to 5 submissions/day during this timeframe.* **Please sign up for a submission day no later than December 1st.** *If no slots are available on your preferred day, please schedule an appointment to meet with me.*

Is there potential for establishing writing groups within the class? Individual input during class or office hours as well as peer support and feedback may provide a range of support and input for a variety of writers' needs. In addition, differentiated rubrics may be a useful tool. Consider designating one category in the grading rubric, maybe worth 10 points out of 100 total, that provides flexibility for the prioritization of individual students' needs.

Ultimately, differentiated instruction is "a way of thinking about teaching and learning that advocates beginning where individuals are rather than with a prescribed plan of action, which ignores student readiness, interest, and learning profile" (Tomlinson, 1999, p. 108). Students may not be accustomed to this style of teaching in college classrooms. Having discussions with students regarding the instructional strategies used and clearly identifying roles and expectations in the syllabus as well as in the classroom throughout the semester is very important for this style of teaching to be effective (Santangelo & Tomlinson, 2009).

With the use of differentiated instruction, faculty can "move away from seeing themselves as keepers and dispensers of knowledge and move toward seeing themselves as *organizers of learning opportunities*" (Tomlinson, 2001, p. 16). In their study on differentiated instruction specifically in higher education classrooms, Dosch and Zidon (2014) found that "differentiation could be the difference between academic success and failure for many students" (p. 352). Their participants commented that the classes that implemented differentiated instruction highlighted "the relaxed environment, engaging instruction, interesting material, and a caring teacher as beneficial to their learning" (p. 352). They also found evidence through evaluations that a deeper level of understanding of material was achieved in sections of a class that used differentiated instruction versus sections that did not (Dosch & Zidon, 2014). This evidence illustrates the authenticity of a classroom that implements differentiation as well as the potential impact of this strategy.

Differentiated instruction involves so much more than teaching. Teachers also function as architects, collaborators, and coaches or mentors in the classroom to best support each student's needs. Rutter and Mintz (2016) argue that it is not enough to simply share expertise with students as one large entity (see Chapter 4 for more on the "generic student"), but instead, college professors must be "designers of educational experiences" (para. 9). I (Becky) believe that this is an accurate description of the art of teaching as it addresses the reality of the beautifully complex nature of teaching and learning.

CONCLUSION

With a rising number of students with disabilities enrolling in higher education and new challenges stemming from the nature and disruption of the recent global pandemic, providing careful and deliberate support for students with disabilities, both seen and unseen, is essential to provide an effective learning environment (NCES, 2023; United States Department of Education Office of Civil Rights, 2021). In this chapter, we discussed the shift in mindset that may be necessary in order to address students' individual abilities, strengths, interests, and priorities. With the help of the concepts discussed in this chapter, we hope you understand how you can easily adjust your own mindset as you adapt your teaching practice, especially regarding writing assignments for students with disabilities. Incorporating Universal Design, strengths-based approaches to teaching and learning, and differentiated instruction can help college educators create accessible classroom communities.

REFERENCES

Boothe, K. A., Lohmann, M. J., Donnell, K. A., & Hall, D. D. (2018). Applying the principles of Universal Design for Learning (UDL) in the college classroom. *Journal of Special Education Apprenticeship*, 7(3), 1–14. https://files.eric.ed.gov/fulltext/EJ1201588.pdf

Burgstahler, S. E. (2020). *Creating inclusive learning opportunities in higher education: A universal design toolkit*. Harvard Education Press.

Chang, M. K., Richards, J. S., & Jackson, A. (1996). *Accommodating students with disabilities: A practical guide for the faculty*. U.S. Department of Education, National Institute on Disability and Rehabilitation Research. https://files.eric.ed.gov/fulltext/ED404827.pdf

Child find – Individuals with Disabilities Education Act (2017). § 300.111. Retrieved January 2, 2024, from https://sites.ed.gov/idea/regs/b/b/300.111

Dosch, M., & Zidon, M. (2014). "The course fit us": Differentiated instruction in the college classroom. *International Journal of Teaching and Learning in Higher Education*, 26(3), 343–357. https://files.eric.ed.gov/fulltext/EJ1060829.pdf

Felton, P., & Lambert, P. F. (2020). *Relationship-rich education: How human connections drive success in college*. Johns Hopkins University Press. https://www.press.jhu.edu/books/title/12146/relationship-rich-education

Gilson, C., & Dymond, S. (2011). Constructions of disability at a university in Hong Kong: Perspectives of disabled students, staff members, and instructors. *Disability Studies Quarterly*, 31(2). https://doi.org/10.18061/dsq.v31i2.1589

Gutshall, C. A. (2013). Teachers' mindsets for students with and without disabilities. *Psychology in the Schools*, 50(10), 1073–1083.

Jensen, J. L. (2011). Higher education faculty versus high school teacher: Does pedagogical preparation make a difference? *Bioscene*, 37(2), 30–36. https://files.eric.ed.gov/fulltext/EJ972012.pdf

Kahn, J. M., & Holody, R. (2009). WAC: A strengths-based approach to student learning. *The Journal of Baccalaureate Social Work*, 14(1), 83–94. https://doi.org/10.18084/basw.14.1.a704430454532w32

Linley, A. (2008). *Average to A+: Realising strengths in yourself and others.* CAPP Press.

National Center for Education Statistics. (2018). *Digest of education statistics.* U.S. Department of Education. Retrieved June 4, 2023, from https://nces.ed.gov/programs/digest/d18/tables/dt18_311.10.asp

National Center for Education Statistics. (2023). *Digest of education statistics.* U.S. Department of Education. Retrieved May 29, 2023, from https://nces.ed.gov/programs/digest/d22/tables/dt22_312.80.asp?current=yes

National Center for Education Statistics. (n.d.). *Fast facts: Students with disabilities.* U.S. Department of Education. Retrieved May 21, 2023, from https://nces.ed.gov/fastfacts/display.asp?id=60

National Collaborating Centre for Determinants of Health. (2023). *Glossary of essential health equity terms.* https://nccdh.ca/glossary/entry/marginalized-populations#:~:text=Marginalized%20populations%20are%20groups%20and,political%2C%20social%20and%20cultural%20dimensions

Ohio Department of Education (2023). *Ohio's learning standards.* https://education.ohio.gov/Topics/Learning-in-Ohio/OLS-Graphic-Sections/Learning-Standards

Polk, D. (2021). *College faculty preparation and comfort teaching students with disabilities.* Publication No. 2894. [Doctoral Dissertation, Seton Hall University Dissertations and Theses]. https://scholarship.shu.edu/dissertations/2894

Robinson, T. E., & Hope, W. C. (2013). Teaching in higher education: Is there a need for training in pedagogy in graduate degree programs? *Research in Higher Education Journal, 21,* 1–11. https://files.eric.ed.gov/fulltext/EJ1064657.pdf

Rutter, M. P., & Mintz, S. (2016, May 4). *Differentiated instruction in the college classroom: Multiple forms of learning in the same classroom.* Inside higher ed. https://www.insidehighered.com/blogs/higher-ed-gamma/differentiated-instruction-college-classroom

Santangelo, T., & Tomlinson, C.A. (2009). The application of differentiated instruction in postsecondary environments: benefits, challenges, and future directions. *International Journal of Teaching and Learning in Higher Education, 20*(3), 307–323. https://www.isetl.org/ijtlhe/pdf/ijtlhe366.pdf

Soria, K. M., & Stubblefield, R. (2015). Knowing me, knowing you: Building strengths awareness, belonging, and persistence in higher education. *Journal of College Student Retention: Research, Theory and Practice, 17*(3), 351–372. https://doi.org/10.1177/1521025115575914

Statistica. (2022, February). *Percentage of U.S. college students that reported select disabilities or health conditions as of fall 2022.* https://www.statista.com/statistics/827023/disabilities-among-us-college-students/

Strange, C. C., & Banning, J. H. (2015). *Designing for learning: Creating campus environments for student success* (2nd ed.). Jossey-Bass.

The R.L. Mace Universal Design Institute (2019). "Design for human diversity." https://www.udinstitute.org/

Tomlinson, C. A. (1995). *How to differentiate instruction in mixed-ability classrooms.* Association for Supervision and Curriculum Development.

Tomlinson, C. A. (1999). *The differentiated classroom: Responding to the needs of all learners.* Association for Supervision and Curriculum Development.

Tomlinson, C. A. (2001). *How to differentiate instruction in mixed-ability classrooms* (2nd ed.). Association for Supervision and Curriculum Development.

Tyrone, B. (2020, September 11). *How to support your students with ADHD.* Duke Learning Innovation. https://learninginnovation.duke.edu/blog/2020/09/how-to-support-your-students-with-adhd/

United States Census Bureau. (2021). *Disability characteristics, 2021 American community survey 1-year estimates.* Retrieved from https://data.census.gov/table?q=S1810:+DISABILITY+CHARACTERISTICS&g=010XX00US&tid=ACSST1Y2021.S1810&moe=false

United States Department of Education Office for Civil Rights. (2017). *Auxiliary aids and services for postsecondary students with disabilities: Higher education's obligations under Section 504 and Title II of the ADA.* Retrieved from https://www2.ed.gov/about/offices/list/ocr/docs/auxaids.html

United States Department of Education Office for Civil Rights. (2021). *Education in a pandemic: The disparate impacts of COVID-19 on America's students.* Retrieved from https://www2.ed.gov/about/offices/list/ocr/docs/20210608-impacts-of-covid19.pdf

University of Washington. (2012). *Invisible disabilities and postsecondary education.* Disabilities, Opportunities, Internetworking, and Technology. https://www.washington.edu/doit/invisible-disabilities-and-postsecondary-education

Wolf, L. E., Brown, J. T., & Bork, R. K. (2009). *Students with Asperger syndrome: A guide for college personnel.* Autism Asperger Publishing Co. https://collegeautismspectrum.com/students-with-asperger-syndrome/

Chapter 7

Professional Writing Matters

INTRODUCTION

According to the National Association of Colleges and Employers, written communication remains at the top of the list for desired skills by employers across industries (NACE, 2023). As we have discussed throughout this book, writing is a fundamental assessment tool for most college courses regardless of the subject. We also know that "with burgeoning numbers of students and increased faculty workload, much career direction has been outsourced to professional career advising staff" at most institutions (McKinney et al., 2021, para. 6). However, even though faculty sometimes consider themselves unable to provide career advice due to time constraints and other responsibilities, they are more likely to "influence students than will professionally trained career counselors" (para. 7). Therein lies the rub. How can faculty provide more time for skill development, especially regarding professional writing, with limited time in their already busy lives?

According to McKinney et al. (2021), faculty feel that lack of time in career preparation with students is their largest barrier, but that they also enjoy being able to help students on their career journeys when possible (para. 25). I (Erin) always want my students to succeed in my class, and I often celebrate that growth with them when it shows up weeks later in the semester. But it is a different level of celebration when you have a student that seeks your guidance on their career journey, gets their first job and comes into your office to personally thank you for your support through one of the most challenging moments of their lives. The satisfaction and gratitude that can flood your psyche in those moments make that extra time you offered them worth every minute you may have gotten behind in a deadline or administrative task.

In this chapter, we will provide helpful tips, tricks and easy-to-implement strategies for incorporating writing exercises for professional communication into your teaching and advising practices. I will also offer ways to engage in one-on-one discussions with your students to help them learn the nuances and appropriate tone for professional written communication versus scholarly writing. My co-author, Oumarou, will also offer tips for working on professional and grant writing with students from diverse backgrounds a little later in this chapter. All these suggestions will provide additional support to your students as they embark on their professional internship/job searches and grant writing endeavors without adding to your own time in advising and consultation with them.

PRACTICING PROFESSIONAL WRITING IN THE CLASSROOM

Higher education faculty are important authorities in their field, but their knowledge differs from practical experience in some contexts. For example, teaching counseling is different from providing therapy. Professors may be helpful in mentoring students who want to take on academic positions but may be somewhat disconnected from the job market when it comes to practitioner roles. According to a 2022 article from *Inside Higher Ed*, the author (a faculty member) stated, "I have not applied for a job in 15 years; for many of my colleagues it's been even longer, and some of them have never worked outside academe" (Toor, 2022, para. 10). This may be true for many faculty in higher education, but it doesn't mean they can't guide students through career exploration and professional written communication activities. On the contrary, their years of experience communicating with diverse colleagues, leaders in their institutions and connections they have maintained with folks in industries around the world are extremely relevant and relatable. If your time is already constrained beyond your classroom instruction time, let's start with some activities you can do in class that can offer your students time to reflect and practice professional writing that will benefit them in their individual career journeys.

College students have anxiety about the job search early on in their college experience, which can lead to significant mental health concerns and employment issues after graduation (Kim et al., 2022). Faculty can have a positive impact on the experiences of college students when this type of job seeking anxiety sets in by offering time in and outside of their classrooms to work through this process with their students. One of the easiest ways to incorporate career exploration and practice professional writing is through exercises in the classroom. In my years teaching both undergraduate and graduate students, I (Erin) often had my students engage in warm up activities to help them (and me) get in the right state of mind to learn (and teach). I call these activities "grounding exercises" and offer specific examples later in this section. I determined that the grounding exercises I wanted to conduct in class needed to be a moment of reflection; a time when my students could leave what happened outside of the classroom at the door and refocus their attention on the work we would be doing in class. I tested these grounding exercises over several years throughout different courses, and I learned quickly that they were working.

As with much of my own professional development as an instructor, I went through a lot of trial and error with my use of many in-class activities and exercises. Halfway through my college teaching experiences, I began to incorporate midterm course evaluations with my students to see what they thought was working and gain direct feedback from them before diving into the second half of the semester. I came to learn that I could also improve my teaching practices by incorporating this system of feedback (Murray, 1997), which I longed to do as I grew in my love of higher education instruction. This professional exercise in conducting regular course evaluations offered me significant insight into the strengths and weaknesses of my curriculum and instruction.

I learned quite a bit about how these grounding exercises were affecting my students' states of mind in each of my classes; in part due to what they often wrote in my midterm evaluation open-ended questions format. For instance, I regularly saw statements like, "please keep doing the grounding exercises" and "the grounding exercises make me look forward to coming to class" and "I feel so much better after our warm-up exercises" (Morgenstern, personal communication, 2017–2020). With the help of these mid-term evaluations, I also discovered early on that regardless of the topic I was planning to cover on any given day, I could incorporate any number of grounding exercises with my students whether it related to what we were going to discuss or not. This was an epiphany for me as an instructor because I felt for over a decade that I needed to have the perfect and most connected warm-up activities for my classes each day, which sometimes took hours to create, test, and rework.

In the latter part of my teaching career, I was instructing graduate students who were also graduate assistants doing significant job searches throughout their second year in the program. Though they were always looking for feedback on assignments and course content, I spent a significant amount of time before and after class with a line of students waiting to speak to me about their job search. Most of these chats revolved around their anxiety about their job search, how to send emails to future employers, and what to incorporate into their interview presentations. Because of these regular concerns, I started to offer time in class for students to grapple with these issues together instead of waiting patiently, sometimes for 20 minutes, to have a turn talking to me one on one. As a related aside, over the years my colleagues and I often discussed the number of students that would not come to our office hours but prefer to talk right before or after class. I am sure if you are reading this, you may have faced similar circumstances with your students.

Grounding Exercises for Professional Writing and Reflection

In my pursuit to incorporate grounding exercises that enhanced students' professional writing, I wanted to make sure the students had takeaways from this reflective time. I knew that much of their concerns were communication related (e.g., how to talk about their professional values and beliefs in an interview or the right terminology to use in their resumes and cover letters). Over time, I collected these grounding exercises and have listed them in what follows. They can be adapted to your own style and the time you have in your classes to incorporate them. As a reminder, none of these exercises were necessarily directed toward daily course topics. Some were used virtually and others in person; I never used more than ten minutes in class to facilitate them.

Professional Values Reflection

Write or type between three to ten values. These are things you are not willing to compromise on and are part of what makes you who you are. Under each word give examples of how this value plays a role in your life and why it matters for you to be successful.

Example for the professional value of innovation:

> I am most successful in a place or a relationship where I can be innovative, I am valued for my ideas and people trust me to make thorough decisions that are executed for the purpose of making something better. At the core of this value is my belief that you should ALWAYS leave something better than how you found it. If I don't have INNOVATION, I feel stifled, sad, and worthless.

Communicating Expertise

Everyone here has expertise. It doesn't mean there aren't other people with the same or even more expertise than you, but you do have some. So, what are those things?

Using a piece of paper or your laptop, list at least five things you have an expertise in.

Example of personal expertise:

> I am an expert in creating online curriculum. I have a strong knowledge of career development theory and practice. I am able to easily communicate with professionals in all education spheres (local, state, and national). My expertise comes from my years in higher education and countless hours learning about technology.

If you need a way to get started, use the words at the start of the example.

HELPING SPECIFIC POPULATIONS WITH WRITING

Communicating Your Needs in a Work Environment

A big part of interviewing and determining if a job is right for you is thinking about what you need in a work environment to be successful. This will make it easier to discuss when you are sitting across from your potential employer and telling them what you need to be successful should they decide to hire you. Remember, half of the interview is telling an employer what you have to offer. The second half is making sure they have what is right for you, too. Think through the following questions and write down your answers. It's okay if you don't know everything you want but take the next five minutes to jot down a few ideas. We will spend five minutes debriefing this exercise as a group.

> What qualities do I value in a work environment?
> What kind of external community do I need outside of my job to feel successful?

Overcoming Interview Anxiety

Take two minutes to write down up to three questions that you are the most nervous to answer in a job interview.

Now, in pairs, conduct a mini mock interview with your partner and ask them at least one of the questions you wrote down. Give them at least three minutes to answer the question. Then, switch and allow them to ask their question. We will debrief after all pairs have completed the activity.

What Your Online Presence Says about You

Let's Google ourselves. Following are several ground rules for conducting this exercise:

1. Go beyond the first page of links, or scroll down through at least 30 links on a single page (depending on your Google browser layout)
2. Do this same search on Google Images
3. Make note of things you are seeing, what content you can control, and if you want to take time to make amends to these posts (request removal, make updates to links, etc.)

Successful Presentation Experience

For three minutes, reflect on and write about a time you have successfully presented information to a group of people. Use the following questions to guide your reflection:

> What was the presentation?
> What were the circumstances?

Who was there/the audience?
How did you know it was successful?

In pairs, take turns telling your partner about that experience (1 minute per person).

Sharing Professional Success (Online Course Exercise)

For one minute, think of a five-word phrase to describe a success from your professional life this week. Once you have your words/phrase, share in our class chat.

Questions to ask the group for discussion (5–8 minutes):
What are your first impressions of these shared phrases?
How can these words or phrases be reframed or used in an interview or on a resume?

If you decide to incorporate any of these exercises into your teaching practice, be sure to allot time to debrief. Know that debriefing can be in a larger group or simply asking students to share with one another what they wrote in pairs or small groups. I found over the years that it isn't always necessary to ask them to share what they discussed or force volunteers to report out. When it comes to professional communication-based grounding exercises, they are meant to allow that reflective time for students to consider the way they think about their personal strengths, values, ideas, and strategy for their professional career. This is a very individualistic and ongoing process, so do not be afraid to leave space and time for them to sit with what they wrote and talk to one another about their discoveries. Something accidental that can also emerge from these collective moments in class during grounding exercises is a sense of belonging. During the 2–3 minutes of group debriefing or pair and share, students can talk to one another about their nervousness, anxiety or fears instead of feeling alone in their pursuits. Even better, you may start to notice they will come to your office hours more intentionally and with more directed questions that will be easier for you to address and advise.

ADVISING PROFESSIONAL WRITTEN COMMUNICATION

For many of us, interacting with students in groups is where we thrive. This may mean that incorporating some of the previously listed grounding exercises makes the most sense for you and your teaching practice. For those whose strengths lie in individual work with students, meeting students for advising appointments one on one is your preferred method of engaging in career-based conversations and practicing professional writing skill development. In this section, I (Erin) will discuss some ways you can prepare your students for advising sessions related to career development and professional written communication.

Setting Standards for Writing Professional Emails

It is amazing to think back on the number of conversations I (Erin) have had with faculty each term that start like this, "Listen to the way this student emailed me" or "It's like they have no idea how to send an email" or "They write like they are texting me!" If you want more examples of this faculty frustration, feel free to read through the dozens of posts on the sub-Reddit r/Professors page that focuses on poor student email communication. I found myself often replying to these statements with a simple, "You're not wrong." However, what we need to remind ourselves of is that digital communication and the etiquette of how to send professional emails is not something that is taught to most people today.

Students and faculty alike believe that professional writing is an important skill, yet faculty do not see the classroom as a place where it should be prioritized (Island, 2016). Students rated career preparation and employability skills as not simply a course expectation, but as an important component of their college experience whereas "faculty underestimated the importance of career and employment preparation" (Island, 2016, p. 2481). This is a case of *yes, and*. If we know that email communication is poor among our college students, and they do want to be prepared for the world of work before they leave college, it behooves us to share what we know and start with applying simple expectations through role play and direct instruction.

For a few years, I created some informative text in my syllabus and through role modeling appropriate email communication in all my classes. I have since adjusted my expectations to simply spending time in class the first few weeks going over ways to write and respond to emails with my students. Following is an example of the wording I used in my syllabus and an email I sent to students the first week of class as an example of how to communicate appropriately with me. I must also note that I discovered this technique from several online university writing centers' resources. The one I have listed here was adapted from the writing centers of Purdue University and George Mason University. If you work in an institution with a writing center for students, you may find that they also have similar wording they offer as a guide for college students on their websites.

How to Email Me (Wording for Syllabus)

Emailing me as your instructor may seem intimidating, but I assure you that I am going to help you get over that quickly and help you feel more confident in emailing other faculty and staff across campus. Following are a few guiding rules that can help you start off on the right foot to write your emails professionally and correctly.

1. Always start out your email with a polite "Dear" or "Hello" followed by your professor's name/title (e.g., Hello Dr. Erin Morgenstern). If you're not sure what their proper title is, using "Professor" followed by their last name is almost always a safe bet, and folks will correct you if they prefer you call them something less formal.

Tip: If you want to know any university personnel's proper title, just look them up in the university directory.

2. Even if your instructor knows who you are, it can't hurt to give a brief introduction. Simply give your preferred name, year, major, and the course you're enrolled in for context.
3. An email is more formal than a text or DM on social media, so be sure this is reflected in your writing (no abbreviations/acronyms—I only learned what GOAT meant a few weeks ago). Be sure to use spelling/grammar check and proofread the email. You can even ask a friend or roommate to give it one final read-through before you send it.
4. Conclude your email with a closing, such as "Kind regards," "Sincerely," or "Thank you" followed by your name. Simply ending an email can feel like it was sent as a text and not to be taken as seriously or for you to be taken as seriously.

As you start to write your emails to me or any other faculty/staff on campus this year, consider using this example template and make it work for your purposes.

Dear Dr. Morgenstern,

My name is John Smith, and I am a second year in your Campus Environments Class that meets on Wednesdays. I am writing because in class yesterday you mentioned knowing some faculty across campus that are hiring students to conduct research. I would like to learn more and possibly talk to you about introducing me to these faculty. Is there a time in the coming weeks that we could meet outside of your office hours since I have class during those times of the week? I am also happy to meet on Zoom if that works better for you.

Thank you for your time and I look forward to hearing from you soon!
Sincerely,
John

While some of the points in this section might seem very small picture, students benefit from examples that make abstract points like "be professional" more concrete. Providing students with opportunities to practice professional writing in class can reduce anxiety and conserve some of the time college educators may be approached to spend outside of class for this kind of advice. These ideas are particularly helpful for students unfamiliar with the U.S. employment context, a point addressed in the next section.

CULTURAL CONSIDERATIONS IN PROFESSIONAL WRITING

In addition to academic writing, college and university students also must master professional writing, which is distinct from the academic writing they do for their class assignments, thesis, peer review articles, and dissertation, to mention just a few. As Erin mentioned in earlier sections of this chapter, professional writing can include, but is not limited to, cover letters, curriculum vitae/resume, grant writing, and so on. While faculty may not have the time teach their students professional writing, they can serve as resources to these students based on their personal experiences with professional writing and/or refer them to other online resources or professionals who might be able to help them. Next I (Oumarou) will discuss ways you can support students from diverse cultural backgrounds with professional writing. Like academic writing, professional writing also follows certain conventions, and these conventions often vary from one culture to another as discussed in Chapter 5.

For illustration, Hou (2014) examined the cross-cultural similarities and divergences of linguistic structures in 80 internship cover letters written by college students from Taiwan and Canada. The outcomes of the study showed that Canadian students leaned toward writing longer letters. They also demonstrated a wider spectrum of word choices and sentence structures, along with a preference for more professional terminology compared to their Taiwanese counterparts. The findings of this research imply that the divergence in communication style is rooted in cultural differences and the writers' knowledge and understanding of the genre's rhetorical and lexical complexities. Additionally, Blitvich and Fortanet-Gomez (2008) analyzed resumes in two languages and two cultures—Peninsular Spanish and American English. They found varying cultural expectations when it comes to the kind and amount of personal information observed on examined resumes. For example, while Spanish resumes did not include a picture, most of them included the candidate's date of birth, marital status, place of birth, national identification card or passport number, and hobbies. However, for resumes in the United States, the only personal information included are the candidates' name and contact information.

As an international student from a French-speaking country, when I (Oumarou) went to my university career and leadership development center, they helped me rework my curriculum vitae (CV), and I learned there are some differences between the American and Francophone ways of writing a CV/resume. If I am applying for jobs in America, it is important that my CV reflects the professional style and cultural etiquette and expectations in the country. As such, it is also important for students who come from a different culture to understand the professional writing style of their host culture. We also know that different cultures have distinct communication styles, structures, and expectations when it comes to professional writing, including CV/resume and cover letters. In the following I share my experience with professional writing as an international graduate student in the United States.

Cultural Nuances of Professional Application Documents

Toward the end of my master's degree at Ohio University, I (Oumarou) decided to start preparing myself for the job market. I knew at the very least, I had to craft a compelling CV or resume and cover letter tailored for the American job market. Coming from a French-speaking country where the expectations and norms of professional documents such as resume and cover letter may differ from those in the United States, I felt both excited and nervous about seeking guidance from my university's career center, the Career and Leadership Development Center (CLDC). With a sense of anxiety and excitement, as well as encouragement from faculty and fellow students, I mustered the courage to make my way to the CLDC, a center that offers guidance and support for students navigating the intricate pathways of career exploration and leadership development, at least during the time I sought help. The process of seeking help for these unfamiliar professional documents highlighted the vulnerability many international students may experience when faced with the challenges of adapting to a new cultural and professional context.

It was the spring of 2017 when I walked into the CLDC, carrying my crafted CV and cover letter from my home country. I met with a cordial CLDC staff member. As she welcomed me into the center's suite with a warm smile, her approachable demeanor put me at ease, dissipating my initial nervousness. The staff walked me to her office, where the bulk of our interaction took place. After introducing myself as Oumarou from Benin, a French-speaking country in West Africa, I explained my purpose for seeking assistance. With genuine interest, she patiently listened as I shared my background and aspirations. Attentive listening, often an underappreciated art, lays the foundation for fostering meaningful connections and offering effective guidance. I handed her my CV and cover letter, hoping for constructive feedback about my documents. She explained the cultural nuances of a professional document like a CV in the United States and potential challenges that an international student like me might encounter as well as how to adapt my CV to the American standard.

The CLDC staff took a few minutes to review and scan through my CV/resume.

"Oumarou," the CLDC staff started, with an eagerness to help, "your credentials are remarkable, and you have some great experiences. However, there are a few nuances between the documents you have brought and the expectations of American employers that we should address." After her quick scan of my document and a brief compliment, she provided insights into the formatting, organization, and content. This moment of recognition not only reinforced my confidence but also emphasized the value of my past experiences. I felt validated and encouraged as we worked together to refine my application materials. She pointed out that in the American context, brevity and specificity were vital. She suggested that I focus on quantifiable achievements and tailor the documents to the specific job I was applying for. She also recommended that I utilize action verbs to describe my key accomplishments under each major professional experience. In contrast, my original CV from Benin was more comprehensive, emphasizing a broader range of responsibilities without delving deeply into my specific key achievements.

In my (Oumarou) country (Benin) and most Francophone countries, the CV is typically a detailed document with several pages, outlining personal information, education, work experience, skills, and often includes a photograph, following a chronological format. However, in English-speaking countries such as the United States, resumes and CVs are generally shorter, around one to two pages, emphasizing key skills, achievements, and relevant work experiences. Personal information such as age, marital status, and photographs are typically omitted. One noticeable contrast in my CV, similar to the varying cultural expectations in resumes noted previously, was the inclusion of personal details, like date of birth, nationality, marital status, and a concluding statement translated from French to English, aiming to certify the accuracy of the information. The concluding statement reads like, "*I certify with confidence that all the information given above genuinely introduces my situation, qualification and experiences.*" The CLDC staff pointed out that such information and certifications are not common in U.S. resumes, providing clarity on the differences in formatting and content expectations between French-speaking and English-speaking contexts.

After the resume, our conversation moved on to focus on my cover letter. The conversation around the cover letter was also interesting. The CLDC staff emphasized the importance of storytelling, using it to communicate not just skills, but also personality, passion, and match with the values of the companies one aspires to join. I had drafted a formal cover letter that was heavy on formality but lacked personal flair. While writing my cover letter, I wrote it with a Francophone mindset with all the formalities, style, and convention translated.

After her quick review of my letter, she explained and offered guidance through rewriting my cover letter to emphasize my professional experience journey, accomplishments, motivations, and how they fit with the prospective employer's needs and values as well as the prospective employment requirements.

We then dove into the cultural differences between American and French-speaking countries cover letters (particularly my letter). I realized that in my original documents, the tone leaned more toward humility and formality. However, she stressed the importance of confidence in American applications while maintaining professionalism. The aim is to strike a balance between presenting oneself as capable and self-assured, while also maintaining a respectful and polished demeanor in the application process. For me, our conversation highlighted the need to balance cultural authenticity with adapting to the expectations of the target job market. The staff shared that international students often faced this challenge, but through guidance they were able to craft compelling documents that showcased their unique strengths while complying to American standards without losing their cultural authenticity. However, it is important to note that these differences can vary depending on the industry, country, and individual preferences. Thus, when assisting students with their professional writing, it is helpful to consider the specific requirements and cultural expectations of the target audience.

Technically, in Francophone countries, cover letters (*lettres de motivation* as they are referred to in French) tend to be longer and more formal in tone, using precise and elaborate language. The letter often follows a structured format, including an introduction, body paragraphs that highlight relevant skills and experiences, and a conclusion expressing interest and availability for an interview. Based on our discussion and my experience in the United States with the passing of time, I notice that cover letters in America and most English-speaking countries are commonly shorter and focus on the key points that make the candidate a strong fit for a position. The letter often starts with a greeting formula, followed by an introduction, body paragraphs that highlight relevant skills and accomplishments, and a closing paragraph expressing interest and availability. Also, in U.S. culture, both resumes and cover letters tend to be more concise, direct, and use active language. Achievements and impact are often emphasized. It is vital to explain these cultural and contextual differences to students who might not be familiar with these customs. Understanding these differences can help students write more effective and targeted professional application documents that align with the preferences and cultural norms of their intended audience, increasing their chances of success in the application process.

The CLDC also gave me access to online and hard copies of resources, including a book that has a list of action verbs, sample CVs, resumes, and cover letters using different styles and formats. The resources have been a very helpful reference as I work on various drafts of my resume, CV, and cover letters.

HELPING SPECIFIC POPULATIONS WITH WRITING

My experiences at and with the CLDC have several implications and valuable lessons for both students and people who might be called to support them to develop their professional writing and grow professionally. For foreign students, my experience and story at the CLDC underscored the significance of understanding and embracing cultural differences when it comes to professional communication and writing, such as CV/resume, cover letters, and interviews. It is important to highlight that students sometimes miss out on job opportunities not due to lack of qualifications, but rather because of issues related to communication, cultural understanding, and interview preparation. Students can benefit greatly from mentorship and resources that help them navigate the intricacies of the job application process, particularly in diverse cultural contexts. In other words, with the right support, students can enhance their chances of securing employment opportunities.

Mock Interviews as a Professional Communication Strategy

As discussed previously in this book, oral and written communication are linked. Expressing one's thoughts verbally assists in the writing process and, conversely, students are expected to be able to speak intelligently about their written materials. Hence helping students make connections between their verbal and written self-presentation is a vital part of mentoring them through their education and into future employment.

During my various visits to the CLDC, I (Oumarou) scheduled mock interviews with a staff member. The staff and I conducted the mock interviews, and those experiences simulated the pressures of real-world interactions, offering me valuable insights into my communication style, body language, and ability to effectively articulate my experiences, strengths, and qualifications. The interview practice sessions like the ones I went through can help students to refine their storytelling skills, empowering them to talk and write about their background, experiences, and journey with an authenticity that can resonate across cultures. The mock interviews put me in simulated real-life interviews and helped me to anticipate and prepare for a variety of questions that I may encounter in a real-world interview. The staff gave me constructive feedback that helped me identify my strengths and areas for improvement. This feedback ultimately helped me refine my interview skills. Because my mock interview sessions helped improve my interview techniques, I became more comfortable with the interview process. Also, I was very nervous during my first mock interview, but I became better with several more rounds of practice. Practicing in a controlled environment increased my confidence, and it helped me become less nervous and anxious during real interviews. In the summer of 2017, I went through several rounds of job interviews and secured a summer paid practicum in Washington, DC, and New York, a testament to the help I received from the CLDC.

Other Support Strategies

For educators and faculty who champion the growth of their students and other staff at colleges and universities' career and leadership development centers, following are concrete ways in which they could provide essential support to help their students with professional writing.

Workshops and Resources

One way to help college students with professional writing is through workshops and sharing relevant resources as initiative collaborative efforts. For example, staff at colleges and university career centers can collaborate with student organization leaders to host workshops dedicated to the CV/resume, and cover letter writing sessions could help students understand the basics and develop these documents effectively. During these sessions, facilitators could provide templates and guidelines tailored to the diverse cultural backgrounds of the student population. Also, to promote sessions effectively and aggressively like these, flyers and digital ads can be created to help get the word out in the library, various colleges, and departments. Faculty can, in turn, encourage their students to attend these sessions. Alternatively, students can seek guidance and support from career development professionals at their college or university.

Peer Engagement and Support

Oftentimes, students constitute their first resource. With a good working relationship, a cohort of students can support each other while going through a similar experience like working on professional documents for prospective employment. I (Oumarou) had a pleasant experience in some classes where faculty provide peer review opportunities for writing assignments. In the same vein, it can be helpful for faculty to encourage peer review of CVs, cover letters, and interview strategies to foster a culture of collaborative learning. Peer support can also be a form of peer mentorship where senior or more experienced students guide and support new or junior students. Experienced mentors can provide real-world insights and guide their mentees through the nuances of professional writing based on their needs. Students from diverse cultural backgrounds could provide unique insights into the cultural relevance and impact of each other's materials as they learn and grow together.

Feedback from Faculty

Educators can also play a crucial role in preparing students for the professional world. Another way to support students with professional writing is by giving them feedback on written materials. Since faculty have gone through writing professional documents such as CV, resumes, and cover letters, they can review their students' documents and give them both verbal and written feedback (see Chapter 2 of this book for how to prepare students for feedback). We have extensively discussed ways to prepare students to be receptive of constructive, supportive, and interactive feedback on their written assignments. Fundamentally, giving students constructive feedback on written documents can help them grow, improve, and become effective communicators and writers. When done effectively, feedback empowers students to refine their writing skills, tailor their content efficiently, and produce documents that resonate with their intended audience. Whether in educational, personal, or professional contexts, giving students solid feedback is a foundation of solid writing and can help them build confidence and competence in their ability to write.

HELPING STUDENTS WITH GRANT WRITING

According to Karsh and Fox (2019),

> A grant is an award of money that allows you to do very specific things, usually according to very specific guidelines that are spelled out in painstaking detail and to which you must respond very clearly in your grant proposal.
>
> (p. 33)

As such, obtaining grants can provide needed financial support and recognition for students' work. Grant writing is a valued skill in the academic job market because grants are important for funding research and academic initiatives. Also, due to reduced public funding, the ability to effectively write and secure grants is vital for academic institutions and researchers to support their work. With strong grant writing skills, students can better position themselves to secure jobs and funding for their research and creative activities projects. However, grant writing can be a complex and nuanced process, and students may need guidance and support to develop and refine such a crucial skill. Before offering some tips for successful grant writing, it is important to discuss some key and common components of a grant proposal. See Table 7.1 for an example of grant proposal structure.

We provide this proposal structure to offer the reader a broad template. As noted previously, it is important to check and comply with the specific requirements and guidelines of the grant or fellowship you are applying to. This is because each grant or fellowship may require something different in terms of structure and content. However, the elements we discussed tend to be common components of many grant proposal requirements. Now that we have discussed

Table 7.1

Example Structure of a Grant Proposal

While every grant may have different requirements and guidelines in terms of structure and content, the following elements seem to be common in most grant proposals

Introduction	**Framing the proposed research topic in the broader literature**
	The purpose of the introduction is to provide context and background information related to the proposed research by demonstrating how it fits into the existing body of knowledge. Generally, this section briefly synthesizes the current state of research in the field, emphasizing the primary areas of focus. Also, the section highlights the gaps or deficiencies in the literature. Thus, it is critical to identify and fill a clear gap in knowledge and explain how the proposed research will fill the identified gap. For example,
	Yet, while the current literature focuses on ABC, there is a lack of research addressing DEF. My research will fill this gap by focusing on XYZ.
	Research Question(s)
	Research questions are central to every research project. Thus, strong research clearly states the main research question(s) the proposed research will answer by posing specific and focused research question(s) related to the identified gap in the literature. Additionally, it is common for grant applicants to specify that they are applying for a fellowship or grant (X) to support their research on (Y). For instance,
	I am applying to X fellowship/grant to support my research on Y.

(Continued)

Table 7.1 Continued

Example Structure of a Grant Proposal
While every grant may have different requirements and guidelines in terms of structure and content, the following elements seem to be common in most grant proposals

Proposal Narrative: What, who, when, where, and how of your research	The proposal narrative section should focus on the specifics of the proposed research. As such, it provides a detailed enough overview of the key aspects of the research, including what will be studied, who the participants will be, when and where the research will take place, and how you plan to conduct the research. The proposal narrative is a clear and comprehensive picture of the scope and objectives of the research project.
	Methodology
	What are the specific research methods and techniques (qualitative, quantitative, or mixed methods) you plan to use to answer your research question(s)? After addressing the research methods, be straightforward and explain the rationale behind your choice of methods. That is why the selected methods are appropriate for your research, considering the scope and nature of the proposed study. The methodology section also includes information on the specific data collection, data analysis, and any other relevant procedures.
	Literature Review
	In the literature review section of the proposal, the applicant provides a review of the relevant literature, focusing on seminal studies, theories, and findings that inform the proposed research. The objective is to demonstrate a mastery of the existing research in the field, emphasizing its strengths and limitations. Ultimately, you should clearly point out how your proposed research builds upon and contributes to the existing knowledge and evidence base.
	Budget
	If required, follow the guidelines of the funder, and provide a budget that outlines the costs associated with your research project. The budget comprises all the necessary expenses fundable through the grant. These expenses can include equipment, materials, travel, participant compensation, and any other relevant expenditures. Most importantly, each budget item should be justified and aligned with the scope and objectives of your proposed research as well as the funder's requirement(s).
Conclusion	Most grant proposals end with a conclusion. The objective is to end the proposal with a concise and strong recap by making a compelling case for why the research project, if funded, will be impactful. To do this, the applicant should conclude the proposal by summarizing the key points and re-emphasizing the significance of your research. Further, the conclusion can restate the importance of addressing the identified gap in the literature and highlight the significance and potential impact of the proposed research. For example,
	My research demonstrates ABC. I expect this research to contribute to discourse on XYZ.

some ideas about the potential structure and contents of a grant proposal, let's shift to some key strategies and tips that can be used to help students enhance their grant writing skill and process.

Key Strategies for a Successful Grant Writing

As a graduate student, I (Oumarou) have secured many funding opportunities, including research and professional conference presentation travel grants. Through my years of experience with grant writing, I have learned some pearls of wisdom from both my successes and rejections. I am sharing those pearls of wisdom in the form of key strategies for successful grant writing. These suggestions are not intended to be an exhaustive list, so they include but are not limited to: Stay informed and organized, understand the funder's priorities, engage actively in the application process, reach out for clarifications and insights, leverage the experience of others, allow sufficient time for writing and review, collaborate effectively with recommenders, prepare for multiple application cycles, and show gratitude and persistence.

Stay Informed and Organized

At various colleges and universities, students can take advantage of internal grant opportunities. Internal grants often can come from the Graduate College, Student Senate, and specific departments as well as academic colleges on campus. To stay updated on grant opportunities and deadlines across the university, I make sure I regularly check and pay special attention to my email communications, especially from the Graduate College and related research offices on campus. Checking those emails frequently will make students aware of the internal award opportunities available at their institution. Most importantly, faculty mentors can encourage their students to effectively use digital tools like calendars to track application deadlines, set reminders, and apply on time. Using digital tools to track application deadlines is a helpful strategy to stay up to date and prepared for opportunities.

Understand the Funder's Priorities

Whether you are encouraging your students to apply for internal or external grants, instruct students to find out and carefully review the funder's priorities, goals, and eligibility requirements before they start writing. These can often be found online. Careful review will allow applicants to strategically tailor their grant proposal to align with the funder's mission. Also, understanding a funder's priorities, objectives, and eligibility requirements will help the grant writer provide specific examples of how their project aligns with the funder's priorities to demonstrate a clear connection. In my case, that has always been my starting point. When I do not understand a grant's goals and eligibility requirements, I try to reach out to the grant administrators to seek clarification. This is worth mentioning because students don't often know they are allowed, and it is a good practice to reach out to funders to learn more about funding priorities and requirements.

Engage Actively in the Application Process

One important strategy is to attend information sessions organized by grant funders, grant officers, or administrators. For every grant that I have applied for, I have regularly attended several information sessions whenever the opportunity is available or offered. I have found those sessions helpful because they constituted an opportunity to network and hear what the grant is about from the horse's mouth. I also consider information sessions as vital occasions to seek further clarifications for questions I may have developed from my initial perusal of the available information about a grant prior to the session. After every session, I make note of the speaker's contact information and follow up with a thank-you email expressing my appreciation for the insights gained during the session. Sending a thank-you email can help prospective applicants build a professional rapport with grant officers, and it shows their genuine interest in the opportunity.

Reach out for Clarifications and Insights

Sometimes you may not have questions to ask or there may not be enough time for everyone to ask questions during an information session. Also, questions may arise sometime after the session or during your proposal writing. In this case, students should be encouraged to email program officers or administrators if they have questions or need further explanation about the application process. The guidance of program officers or people in charge of administering a grant can provide valuable insights and enhance an applicant's proposal quality. A few times, I requested meetings with grant program officers to discuss my research project and seek their potential input. Whenever suitable and possible, faculty should encourage students to request short meetings with program officers to discuss their project. These personal interactions can help potential grant applicants better understand the funder's expectations and priorities.

Leverage the Experience of Others

Learning from the experience of others is another strategy that I have used while preparing to apply for grants. For example, when I was preparing my applications for the Society for Research on Educational Effectiveness fellowship and the National Academy of Education and Spencer dissertation fellowship, I reached out to successful fellowship awardees listed on these funding agencies' websites. I was able to connect with former grant or fellowship awardees, and they shared their experiences with me as well as their application materials. This is a helpful outreach strategy to seek advice, sample applications, and feedback from former grant awardees. In some cases, when I get to the interview level, I reach out again to hear about their interview experiences and seek further guidance on potential interview sample questions, answers, and strategies. Based on my experience, leveraging the experiences of former successful grant awardees can provide prospective applicants with diverse perspectives into what makes a compelling and winning proposal. Following is an example of an outreach email:

Hello...,

I hope my email finds you well and thriving. My name is X, and I am a student at X institution.

I saw you are a 2022 X grant awardee. Congratulations on such a remarkable achievement! I really enjoyed reading and learning about your research on X subject. I am sure your findings will be engaging and consequential, particularly for X, Y, and Z audiences.

I just finished working on my 2023 X grant application due on October 6th at 5 PM. I was wondering if you could please spare some time to help look at my documents and give me some feedback. Also, please feel free to share any practical advice/tips that you may have for me. I am also available for an online meeting at your convenience.

Thank you so much in advance! I look forward to hearing from you.
Sincerely,
Your name

Allow Sufficient Time for Writing and Review

Once you know the deadlines and have gathered sufficient information about the grants you are interested in applying for, I have found it helpful to start the writing process well in advance to avoid last-minute rush and stress. Starting early is crucial because it will give you sufficient time to ensure careful planning and thoughtful writing as well as review process. I always make sure my proposal goes through as many rounds of revision as possible. Simply put, I plan ahead and give myself ample time. Faculty can teach students to effectively manage the grant writing process by emphasizing the importance of early planning and ample time for drafting and revisions. Also, they can encourage students to connect with older, successful peers, mentors, and other experienced faculty advisors who can provide valuable insights and guidance throughout the writing process. Promoting a culture of seeking feedback from multiple perspectives, including peers and mentors, can help students hone their grant proposals and enhance their writing skills.

Collaborate Effectively with Recommenders

Most competitive grants or fellowships require applicants to submit at least one recommendation letter. As such, recommendation letters are a significant aspect of grant application. Because of the prominence of these letters, it is important for prospective applicants to approach their potential recommenders early and provide them with their CV/resume, key information on the grant or fellowship, proposal draft, and potential talking points. I always make sure I give my recommenders ample information and time so they can write strong letters on my behalf. Also, students should be encouraged to discuss the significance of their research project and the aspects they would like their recommenders to emphasize. Giving your recommenders clear information and sufficient time helps them write solid letters of recommendation. Following is an example of an email to ask for a recommendation:

Dear ...,

I hope my email finds you well.

I am writing to bring to your attention that I am interested in pursuing X fellowship/grant opportunity. I will need your endorsement and a letter of support from you as my department chair. I have attached the 2023–2024 X fellowship/grant brochure for your reference. Please see below the summary of eligibility criteria and nomination process. Also, attached is a copy of my CV for your perusal.

Thank you so much for your support and time beforehand!
Sincerely,
Your name

PROFESSIONAL WRITING MATTERS

Prepare for Multiple Application Cycles

Planning has made it possible for me to prepare for multiple cycles of application be it for internal or external grants opportunities. Particularly for some external grants and fellowships, I was able to start my applications earlier in my academic journey. I gave myself multiple chances to reapply in case my initial attempt happened to be unsuccessful. In navigating the challenges of grant applications and rejections, it is crucial to teach students to persevere. For instance, I consistently embraced impediments as opportunities for growth and improvement. By embracing a resilient mindset, I actively sought feedback and utilized it as a tool for improvement. A persistent approach not only allowed me to enhance my grant proposals but also enabled me to reap the fruits of sustained effort. My experience with the Student Enhancement Award at Ohio University demonstrates this commitment, as I utilized feedback from the previous application to strengthen my proposal and ultimately secured the grant in the subsequent year. Such an experience serves as a reminder that perseverance and a willingness to learn from rejections can pave the way for eventual success. Following, we share an example of an outreach email to show gratitude and request feedback after a rejection:

Dear ...,

I hope my email finds you well.

Thank you very much for getting back to me with the decision regarding my X grant application. Thank you for taking the time to review my application and I truly appreciate the opportunity to apply for X grant. Most importantly, I have learned a lot throughout this process. Thank you again for your time and consideration. I am excited and I look forward to receiving and reading the committee's comments about my application.

Warm regards,
Your name

Show Gratitude and Persistence

Behind every successful grant writer lies a litany of rejections. National and international grants and fellowships are extremely competitive. Thousands of people apply for those opportunities. Do like I do. Regardless of the outcome, I endeavor to express gratitude for the opportunity to apply. I know it is not easy but, in my experience, showing gratitude has generally helped me better deal with rejections. Also, whenever possible, make it a point to ask for feedback even if you are not selected. Why? Because the feedback you get, if you are lucky to get it, can help guide your improvements for future opportunities.

I encourage you to embrace and maintain a persistent and positive mindset throughout your grant writing and application experience. It is fine to feel bad about a rejection. After all, if you have gone through the strategies I have been discussing, you would have invested a lot of your time, emotion, and energy in the process. Be mad! Be angry! Cry and complain! In fact, anytime I received a rejection, I felt bad, angry, and sad, and I allowed myself to go through these emotions for some time. However, I have always made a conscious choice to express gratitude and move on to the next opportunity. I understand it is a process and grants and fellowships can be competitive, but perseverance is key to eventual success. Following is an example of an email to express gratitude:

Dear Dr...,

I hope my email finds you well!

Thank you for sharing the news about the selection process for the 2023–2024 X Fellowship. I appreciate your kind words and the recognition of my department's nomination. It is an honor to be considered among a group of quality nominees, and I am grateful for the opportunity to have been nominated.

I will continue to work hard and strive for excellence in my field of study, as I am committed to advancing my knowledge and skills in order to make meaningful contributions to my profession. While this news is not what I had hoped for, I am optimistic about my future and look forward to exploring other opportunities to support my academic pursuits.

Once again, thank you for your message and consideration. Please extend my sincere gratefulness to the selection committee for their time and commitment.

Sincerely,
Your name

Additionally, it is helpful to encourage students to explore online resources. Exploring online resources is important because the majority of grant and fellowship websites and grant writing books (Karsh & Fox, 2019; Rustick, 2019) have valuable resources and templates. These resources generally include samples of previously funded proposals, guidelines, tips for writing winning proposals, and frequently asked questions. Studying these materials has helped me better understand efficient application tactics. Moreover, to develop their professional grant writing skill, students can attend grant writing workshops and/or take a class. I have taken advantage of free online grant writing workshops or sessions conducted in-person at Ohio University. I attend these workshops because they often provide prospective applicants with practical insights and practices for refining their writing skills. Otherwise, if offered on campus, students who have an interest in grants can take a class on grant writing.

Alternatively, students can advocate for grant writing opportunities and resources. That is, if you happen to be at an institution that does not offer grant writing workshops, you should not shy away from proposing the idea to your Graduate College or department. They might be able to do something about it if students ask and show interest. Chances are there might be some opportunity to learn from professors who have been successful with grants within your department or college. Those professors may have had positive experiences with some of the grants you are considering. As such, the profiles and experiences of those professors can serve as models for your own grant writing efforts.

For additional tips and strategies for a winning grant proposal and mindset, consult Sathian et al. (2016) and Liu et al. (2016), where you can dive into their valuable discussion on ten tips for successful grant writing and key components of a well-written grant proposal based on their experience of obtaining grants. Also, by implementing the tips and strategies I (Oumarou) have discussed here and using resources available to you, you can improve your grant writing skills and augment your chances of securing funding for your research, creative activities, and academic endeavors. It is necessary to be cognizant and remind students that grant writing is both a skill and an ongoing learning process that requires a continuous practice to polish one's approach based on feedback and experiences. Remember, the more grants you write and apply for, the more success you will see. Encourage your students to keep practicing and honing their grant writing skill set.

CONCLUSION

As faculty members, it is our job to both offer expertise in our disciplines and successfully replace ourselves with our own students for our fields of study to remain relevant, valued, and critically researched. It is imperative that we offer intentional resources and strong systems of support that are manageable for our own practices that can aid our students in walking across the graduation stage, as well as move into the workforce successfully. In this chapter, we (Erin and Oumarou) offered supportive elements needed by many students working their way through the nuances of professional writing and written communication beyond the classroom. We offered our personal experiences, examples, and strategies for helping your students engage in professional writing to help build their confidence in professional writing skill set. As faculty, we find ourselves in a unique position to have the biggest positive impact on our students and their ability to be successful during and beyond our classrooms. We are also busy folks with a lot on our plates. Finding easy strategies to add value and writing skill development to our students' experiences in and out of the classroom are important and can have a big impact on their future success.

REFERENCES

Blitvich, P. G.-C., & Fortanet-Gomez, I. (2008). The presentation of self in résumés: An intercultural approach. *ESP Across Cultures, 5*, 69–90. https://www.academia.edu/8190801/The_presentation_of_self_in_résumés_an_intercultural_approach

Hou, H.-I. (2014). "Please consider my request for an interview": A cross-cultural genre analysis of cover letters written by Canadian and Taiwanese college students. *TESL Canada Journal, 30*(7), 45. https://doi.org/10.18806/tesl.v30i7.1151

Island, H. D. (2016). "OMG! You Said What in Class? TMI!" College student and professor perceptions of professional etiquette violations. *Universal Journal of Educational Research, 4*(10), 2477–2482. https://doi.org/10.13189/ujer.2016.041027

Karsh, E. & Fox, A. S. (2019). *The only grant-writing book you'll ever need*. Basic Books. https://www.hachettebookgroup.com/titles/ellen-karsh/the-only-grant-writing-book-youll-ever-need/9781541617810/?lens=basic-books

Kim, J., Oh, J., & Rajaguru, V. (2022). Job-seeking anxiety and job preparation behavior of undergraduate students. *Healthcare (Basel, Switzerland), 10*(2), 288. https://doi.org/10.3390/healthcare10020288

Liu, J. C., Pynnonen, M.A., St John M., Rosenthal, E. L., Couch, M. E. & Schmalbach, C. E. (2016). Grant-writing pearls and pitfalls: Maximizing funding opportunities. *Otolaryngology–Head and Neck Surgery, 154*(2), 226–232. https://doi.org/10.1177/0194599815620174

McKinney, L., Sinley, R., Ansburg, P., Daughtrey, C., Rajan, R., Meyer, J., Lopez, J., & Eaker, R. (2021, May). *NACE Journal*. Faculty are our allies in teaching career preparation and readiness skills. https://www.naceweb.org/career-readiness/best-practices/faculty-are-our-allies-in-teaching-career-preparation-and-readiness-skills/

Murray, H. G. (1997). Does evaluation of teaching lead to improvement of teaching? *International Journal for Academic Development, 2*(1). 8–23. https://doi.org/10.1080/1360144970020102

NACE (2023). *The job market for the class of 2023: Key skills/competencies employers are seeking and the impact of career center use.* https://www.naceweb.org/about-us/press/5bcffa5b-6fa6-4091-860e-c5ae5b103949

Rustick, H. (2019). *The beginner's guide to grant writing: Tips, tools, & templates to write winning grants.* Rustick Productions. https://grantwritingandfunding.com/books/

Sathian, B., Simkhada, P., Van Teijlingen, E., Roy, B. & Banerjee, I. (2016). Grant writing for innovative medical research: Time to rethink. *Medical Science, 4*(3), 332–333. http://eprints.bournemouth.ac.uk/30623/1/Writing%20grants%202016%20Med%20Sci.pdf

Toor, R. (2022, January). Faculty should do more to help students prepare for careers (opinion). *Inside Higher Ed.* https://www.insidehighered.com/views/2022/01/18/faculty-should-do-more-help-students-prepare-careers-opinion

Conclusion

We opened this work with an overview of writing challenges faced by college students generally, then moved into the specific topics of effective feedback practices, troubleshooting strategies, and writing course development with an eye toward new majority students. The authors who wrote Part 2 of the book focused on best practices for helping students write professionally and special considerations when working with international students and students with disabilities. We offer this conclusion as a culmination of the broad themes and takeaways we aim to provide the reader.

Speaking of the reader, you probably noticed that we wrote much of this book in the second person tense. This is a bit unusual, but we made this choice because we wanted to communicate as friendly colleagues in the spirit of comradery. We strove to share knowledge and strategies, but also rapport and uplift. Our goal was to model both the vulnerability and encouragement that can come from working in community. I know my (Laura's) experience of writing this book was deeply enriched by having three talented colleagues to offer insights and motivation throughout this process.

COMMUNITY

I always tell my students that Hollywood portrays writing as a solitary activity involving a lone writer toiling away cordoned off from others. This is sometimes true; I wrote this conclusion at a retreat site where I could concentrate without distractions. But much of this book came from conversations, written notes, and other manifestations of synergy among all of us as collaborative authors. Writing can be delightfully social and those relationships can stretch us in ways we might not be able to accomplish on our own. I know Becky, Erin, and Oumar made me both smarter and happier as I persevered through challenges and celebrated successes along the way. Given the anxiety and loneliness crises prevalent among today's college students, we hope our readers will create opportunities for students to experience the reassurance and connection that comes from collaborative learning. Hence the underappreciated role community can play in helping students write is the first takeaway we hope our readers picked up as a theme in this book.

BALANCE

The second unifying idea we wish to reemphasize here is the importance of balance. We consistently acknowledged that faculty schedules are so packed that any additional suggestions can read like impossible demands. Our goal was always to offer ideas that might require some investment upfront, but that recover time and energy later when students understand expectations, have resources, and work in collaboration so that performance is improved and the need for remediation is mitigated. That said, we understand that portions of the book may have raised the reader's anxiety about how much more we could all be doing. We want to reiterate the old adage about not letting the perfect be the enemy of the good. If we made a suggestion that would not work in your life, save it for later or skip it entirely. The goal was to offer all the tools so the reader could pick and choose what works for them.

FACULTY DEVELOPMENT

We stated so often that faculty are not trained to teach that part of the revision process was correcting for this repetitive point. Still, there is a reason we felt so compelled to make this statement. There has been a movement toward more pedagogical training, and centers for teaching and learning have proliferated in recent years. We applaud this development and encourage readers to advocate for further expansion of investment in teaching. This is particularly important when considering the need to shift from the college-ready to the student-ready mindset in light of the prevalence of new majority students, international students, and students with disabilities. In all but the most elite higher education institutions, we can neither assume nor demand college readiness. Consequently, faculty need more opportunities to dive deeply into what a truly diverse student population needs. This time and bandwidth have to come from somewhere given that most faculty are stretched thin as it is. We hope readers will push back on the nonsensical meetings and administrative demands—many of which could be outsourced and/or automated—in the name of reclaiming that energy to uphold the academic mission of the university.

CONCLUSION

STRENGTHS

Higher education can be exhausting these days with budget cuts, enrollment pressures, anti–DEI politics, and student mental health issues just to name a few. And yet human flourishing occurs every day on college campuses. I experienced a small example of this recently as I was swimming in our university pool and watching a class of undergraduates in a beginning swimming course. I thought about how much courage these young adults showed in admitting they didn't have a skill many people learn as children and deciding to do something about it. I feel the same way about my students who leave their homelands—whether that's thousands of miles away on another continent or right in our Appalachian backyard of Southeast Ohio—to choose to develop their talents. At the end of the day, helping students write is about convincing them that they have something to say and teaching them how they might say it. It's sacred work in a sense; a student lets you inside their mind and sometimes even their heart in hopes that you will help them get it out into the world. Teaching writing epitomizes Martin Buber's I/Thou relationship (1970) because language is how we cross the border between self and others. Communion is baked into the very notion of language, which is defined by sharing. Helping students to do so with civility and coherence is possibly the best use of our time and talent as educators.

REFERENCE

Buber, M., & Kaufmann, W. (1970). *I and Thou*. Charles Scribner's Sons.

Index

Pages in **bold** refer to tables.

anxiety 6–7, 27, 61, 83, 136–137, 153–154, 156–157, 160, 179
assets *see* strengths
assignments 4, 14–15, 32–33, 62–67, 77–80, 111–113; accessible assignments 136–139, 141–143, 145–**147**
attention 4, 8–14
Aull, L. 76, 80–81

bad writing *see* dislike of writing
balance 19–22, 63, 78, 121, 163, 179

Carless, D. & Boud, D. 27, 115
case for significance 17–18, **28**, 33, 41, 77, 80, 82
cheating 5, 59; *see also* plagiarism
clarity of writing 16–17, 20–21, **28–29**, 81–82, **167**–170
clear expectations 78–79, 88, **111**–113, 124
civility and coherence 80–81; *see also* Aull, L.
citation *see* reference
coaching 50, 83, 85–87; *see also* dissertation chairing
comments *see* stock comments
community 89, 106, 116, 134, 178–179; *see also* peer review

concentration *see* attention, focus
confidence *see* self efficacy
convention 76–77, 82–83, 98–101, 105, 109–**110**, 120, 124; *see also* linguistically diverse conventions
course planning 73, 77–79, 90; students with disabilities, factors to consider **130**
critical thinking 61, 81–82, 101, 121–122, **138**; *see also* Paul, R. & Elder, L.
criticism *see* judgement
Csikszentmihaly, C. 34–35
cultural context 101–107; professional writing 160–164; *see also* Hall, E.; Hofstede, G. et al.

Deep Work 11–12; *see also* Newport, C.
differentiated instruction 128, 131, 143–149
digital 8–9, 13–14, 83, 158, 169
disability *see* assignments, course planning
dislike of writing 57–58
dissertation chairing 87–90
distraction *see* attention, concentration, focus
diverse *see* new majority
draft 10, 19, 20, 23, 121, 172
Dweck, C. 6

INDEX

editing *see* revising
ESL defined 96
expert blind spot 4–6, 15–16, 23, 51
extrinsic motivation *see* motivation

faculty development 179; *see also* clear expectations
feedback: constructive feedback 36–37; defined 30–32; for ESL students 113–115; formative feedback 32–34; reflective feedback 123; student feedback literacy 26–27; *see also* Carless, D. & Boud, D.
Flow 20, 34–35, 61, 98; *see also* Csikszentmihaly, C.
focus 8–14, 134; *see also* attention
free writing 55–57

generative AI 22, 59–61
good writing *see* Aull, L.
grading rubric 28–29, 32, 148; *see also* feedback
grant writing 153, 160, 166–175
grounding exercises 153–157

Hall, E.T. 103–104
helping *see* coaching
heritage speakers 95, 97, 100, 109, 123
Hofstede, G. et al. 101–104

imposter phenomenon 51, 65–68, 70
intrinsic motivation *see* motivation

judgement 5, 7, 36, 62, 89

Kuhlthau, C. 82–83

learning outcomes 77–79, 131
linguistically diverse conventions 101, 107–**111**

mental health *see* anxiety

Mindset 6–7, 116–119, 141; *see also* Dweck, C.
motivation 29, 45–47, 58–63, 69–70, 137–**138**, 163

Newport, C. 11–12; *see also* concentration
new majority 70, 73–75, 86–87, 90, 178–179

organization *see* structure and organization
outcomes *see* learning outcomes
outline 15–16, 18, 21, 57, 98, **138**, 142

paper *see* assignments
paragraph 19, 36, 38, 98–99, 163
Paul, R. & Elder, L. 81–82
peer review 44–46, 72, 121, 160, 165
perfectionism *see* imposter phenomenon
plagiarism 22, 59, **110**, 112; *see also* cheating
planning *see* outline
Pomodoro Method 9, 59; *see also* time management
positive *see* strengths
problem solving *see* troubleshooting
procrastination 10, 15, 22, 33, 45, 75
professional email communication 158–160
publishing *see* research
purpose *see* case for significance

quality *see* standards

reading: critical 14; strategic 12–14, 24
reference 13, 16, 112, 121–122, **142**, 147
relationship *see* community
research 16, 80–84, 87; literature review 84, **167**–**168**
revising 3, 14, 19, 22–24, 36, 83–85, 90; revision sheet 42–44; *see also* Thomson, P.
rubric *see* grading rubric
rules *see* convention

INDEX

scholarship *see* research
search process 82–83; *see also* Kuhlthau, C.
self-efficacy 29–30, 44, 111, 115–116, 141
sentences 5, **28**, 33, 38, 99, 160
significance *see* case for significance
standards 27, 56, 77–78, 81–82, 136, 158; *see also* Aull, L.
stock comments 37–42, 60
strengths 23, 34–37, 122–123, 140–143, 180
structure and organization 18–21; cultural and linguistic differences in writing structure 98–101
study *see* research
style 62–63, 95, 109, **110**, 124, 162–164; communication style 104–106, 114, 160–161
support for professional writing 164–166

teaching *see* course planning
thesis 17, 79, 81–82, 105–106

thinking *see* Deep Work
Thomson, P. 84–85
time management 4, 72, 79, 82
transfer 75–76, 90, 99, 107–109
transitions 18–19, 21, **28**, 98, 111
troubleshooting 50–51, 57–58, 67–68

underrepresented *see* new majority
using sources 21–22
Universal Design 128, 134–137, **138–139**, 149

voice 20, **29**, 51–52, 54, 56, 63–65

warm-up *see* grounding exercises
Wiggins, G. & McTighe, J. 4, 79
word choice 64, 106, **110**
writer's block 3, 6, 34, 52–54, 57, 65
writing centers 22, 119–121, 158
writing process *see* draft